Laboratories of Learning

Laboratories of Learning

Social Movements, Education and
Knowledge-Making in the Global South

Mario Novelli, Birgül Kutan, Patrick Kane,
Adnan Çelik, Tejendra Pherali and Saranel Benjamin

First published 2024 by Pluto Press
New Wing, Somerset House, Strand, London WC2R 1LA
and Pluto Press, Inc.
1930 Village Center Circle, 3-834, Las Vegas, NV 89134

www.plutobooks.com

British Library Cataloguing in Publication Data
A catalogue record for this book is available from the British Library

ISBN   978 0 7453 4892 6   Paperback
ISBN   978 0 7453 4894 0   PDF
ISBN   978 0 7453 4893 3   EPUB

This book is printed on paper suitable for recycling and made from fully managed
and sustained forest sources. Logging, pulping and manufacturing processes are
expected to conform to the environmental standards of the country of origin.

Typeset by Stanford DTP Services, Northampton, England

Simultaneously printed in the United Kingdom and United States of America

This book is dedicated to Aziz Choudry (1966–2021) comrade, freedom fighter, international solidarity activist, prolific author, reluctant academic, teacher, popular educator and friend.

Rest in Power Comrade Aziz

If there is no struggle there is no progress. Those who profess to favor freedom and yet deprecate agitation are men who want crops without plowing up the ground; they want rain without thunder and lightning. They want the ocean without the awful roar of its many waters.

—Frederick Douglass (1857)

Education doesn't change the world, it changes the people who change the world.

—Paolo Freire, 1921–1997

Contents

Acknowledgements

We began working on this project back in early 2016 when we invited a number of social movement leaders to Sussex University for a public seminar, and as we finalise this book we are in 2023. Over these seven years, we have many people to thank, people who have invested their time, shared advice, offered support and resources and encouragement, and participated in the different events that we have organised across four continents. First, we would like to thank War on Want, our partner in this project since its inception. Particularly we would like to thank Asad Rehman, Ruth Ogier and Liz McKean for their encouragement and support throughout the period. Similarly, we would like to thank all of the members and activists of HDK, Turkey; NEMAF, Nepal; NOMADESC and the Universidad Intercultural de los Pueblos, Colombia; and the Housing Assembly, South Africa for giving up their time to attend workshops, share documentation, be interviewed and provide feedback on research findings. In particular, we would like to thank Dr Tula Shah, NEMAF; Berence Celeyta, NOMADESC; Faeza Meyer, Housing Assembly; and Onur Hamzaoulou, Gulistan Kilic Kocyigit, Ertugrul Kurkcu, Fatma Gok, HDK, for their leadership and guidance in the respective movement research processes, and for accompanying us on many of the research visits. We would also like to thank several anonymous reviewers and Dr Becky Tarlau, Penn State University, USA, and Dr Laila Kadiwal, Institute of Education, UCL, UK, for their helpful comments and feedback on an earlier draft of this text. All of the aforementioned have contributed to the richness of the research, whilst we alone are responsible for any weaknesses, omissions, errors and mistakes.

Prologue

Back in 2005, Francia Marquez, a young, poor, Afro-Colombian, single mother, walked into the headquarters of NOMADESC, Cali – a Colombian Human Rights NGO led by Berenice Celeyta, a long-time social leader and activist. Francia had enrolled on the Diploma in Human Rights as a delegate of the Process of Black Communities (PCN). The Diploma programme, on a weekly basis, brought together social leaders from the southwest of Colombia, ranging from indigenous, black, trade unionist, feminist, student and community organisations. It was a popular education programme that explored issues of human rights in Colombia, their history, their contemporary reality, the mechanisms for their defence and for their strengthening. It was initially financed through funds secured by War on Want, a British-based NGO that emerged out of the UK labour movement in the 1950s and works with solidarity and social movements around the world.

At the time of the Diploma's creation, I was living and working in Cali, Colombia. I had travelled there as a teacher, and later began to work in the Human Rights Department of SINTRAEMCALI, a powerful public service trade union that had led an unprecedented and successful struggle against the privatisation of water, electricity and telecommunications in Colombia's second city of Cali. During those years of struggle, SINTRAEMCALI was demonised by the state, targeted by shadowy state and para-state security forces, and lost multiple leaders and activists to assassination. It also lost many more activists to exile, both internally and externally, and operated in a context of fear and repression. Despite this, SINTRAEMCALI managed to build a mass movement in defence of public utilities, and constructed a city-wide trade union and community alliance that proved too powerful for the repressive forces of the Colombian state. Through mass political action, occupations and grassroots mobilisations, the trade union successfully fought off a series of attempts by foreign multinationals to buy off Colombia's natural resources and public services.

Out of the critical self-reflection of many of the leaders and activists engaged in that movement, there was an analysis and recognition of the need to improve the human rights protection of Colombian social movements and to strengthen knowledge of, and solidarity between, the wide variety of resisting subjects and organisations that co-existed in the southwest of Colombia. The Human Rights Diploma was one product of that self-analysis, and the evolution of that programme continues today under the name of the 'Intercultural University of the Peoples', an institution and a movement that constitutes one of the key partners in the production of this research, and this book.

I learnt so much during those Cali years about popular education, social movement struggle and the power and possibility of grassroots movements and international solidarity, and I have continued working with comrades in Colombia for the last two decades. I went on to write a PhD thesis on SINTRAEMCALI's struggles and the learning and education processes that underpinned it, and I have since worked as an academic, reading, writing and teaching about these and related issues. Yet, despite all the reading and writing, I look back on those days embroiled and engaged in the social struggles in Colombia as being my most formative. It was there that I learnt about the power of organising against all odds, the imagination of the movements and activists, and the impressive ways that ordinary people struggling together can do the most amazing things. It also taught me about knowledge and knowledge-making, and that new and imaginative ways of knowing and being are emerging not just out of universities, but also out of social movements, and that the Global South – as a metaphor for all those left out of the benefits of the global capitalist system – was a rich source of new ideas and strategies to make the world a better place. It was there that I learnt that social movements are a rich source of education, learning and knowledge-making: a grounded, contextualised and rooted type of knowledge that emerges out of the analysis and the struggles of the everyday. These issues constitute the central focus of this book and provide its key focus: How do social movements learn and make knowledge? What do they learn, and what knowledge do they make? What is the effect of this learning and knowledge-making on their movements and their social conditions?

Project forward to the summer of 2022, and Francia Marquez, that young, Afro-Colombian, single mother, who had entered the Diploma in Human Rights in Cali two decades earlier, had just been elected as the first black vice-president of Colombia. Francia, now a leader of the Process of Black Communities (PCN), was a part of the 'Pacto Historico' (Historic Pact), an electoral coalition, that brought together movements and supporters of a wide range of social movements and progressive political organisations across Colombia. This victory was a huge milestone, and constituted the first time in the history of Colombia that the political left had won a general election. What was amazing was not just that Francia Marquez had been elected to one of the highest offices of the state, but that she was there as a representative of the PCN – a grassroots movement of Afro-Colombians that had emerged out of the struggles of Afro-Colombian communities in the 1990s, and one of the most marginalised and exploited sectors of the population. In that post-election period, I contacted my friend Berenice Celeyta, to congratulate her on the success, and she responded that they were now having to shift their thinking 'desde la resistencia, hasta el poder' (from resistance to power). That struggle, from resistance to social transformation, is also part of the focus of this book, to think through how social movements, learning through struggle, build power from below and then exercise this power to change the world, a dream that all of the authors of this book, coming from very different parts of the world, hold close to their hearts. This book then is also a collective message of hope in difficult times. A message of hope underpinned through detailed evidence that social movements are powerful agents of social change, learning and knowledge-making, and need and deserve to be taken seriously.

One person that embodied this belief that social movements matter, that they need to be taken seriously, and that researching how movements learn and make knowledge was an important intellectual endeavour, was Professor Aziz Choudry. He was a key figure in this whole project, a leading member of our advisory board, and a close friend. Sadly, Aziz passed away suddenly in 2021 and left a gaping hole in all of our hearts. Aziz's work had been pathbreaking, and his legacy remains as a beacon guiding new researchers interested in this area. This book is dedicated to him. We miss you comrade Aziz.

Mario Novelli, March 2023, Brighton, UK

Introduction

In an era of increasing global inequality, conflict, crisis, pandemics and rising authoritarianism (Streeck, 2014; Piketty, 2014; Scahill, 2013; Rogers, 2016), social movements often represent a first line of defence for some of the most marginalised communities on the planet, seeking to defend and extend the conditions for a basic and dignified human existence. That is to say, 'social movements matter', and they matter in a myriad of different ways (Cox, 2018; SC, IDS and UNESCO, 2016; Giugni et al., 1999). Yet they often operate, organise and advocate in conditions of state and para-state repression, threats and insecurity; conditions which can serve to undermine movement cohesion, solidarity and effectiveness (Earl, 2013). This is particularly the case in countries affected by or emerging out of armed conflicts, where violence and intimidation are often part of everyday life.

Despite these challenges, and as we shall see – maybe because of them, social movements are often incredibly productive 'laboratories of learning', producing radical new insights and ways of understanding how the world works, the tools to change it, and the visions for alternative ways of being and living. Whilst mainstream society, and the academy, often underestimate both the political and intellectual contribution of social movements (Cox, 2018), we beg to differ, and this book seeks to evidence the exciting new ways of learning and knowing that emerge out of social movements' attempts to change the world.

This research locates itself firmly within the project of the 'epistemologies of the South' articulated by Boaventura de Sousa Santos (2014), with the 'Global South' serving as a metaphor for all those left out of the benefits of our contemporary colonial, capitalist and patriarchal world, regardless of their geographical location. Within this project, there is a strong recognition that there can be 'no global

1

social justice without global cognitive justice' (Santos, 2014: 127). That is to say that ideas, learning and knowledge matter in the struggle for a better, more just and equal world. Central to Santos's worldview is the idea that the most innovative ideas and practices are coming from both outside the 'Global North' and outside universities, and that it is there that critical academics should be looking for new ideas and insights with which to reinvigorate social theory.

This book explores the learning and knowledge-making processes of four very different social movement institutions that are part of broader movements for social change, located in four distinct countries and continents, as they advocate for peace with social justice in contexts of violent conflict, authoritarianism and/or its aftermath. The institutions, which were core partners in the research, are: NOMADESC, a radical human rights NGO based in Colombia that through popular education programmes and human rights support and accompaniment has brought together a range of diverse social movements in southwest Colombia; the Housing Assembly, a grassroots organisation from Cape Town that fights for decent housing in post-apartheid South Africa; the HDK (Peoples' Democratic Congress), an umbrella organisation that brings together diverse social movements from across Turkey with a vision for a pluri-ethnic and democratic state; and the Madhes Foundation, Nepal, an organisation that works with and for the excluded Madhes community of the Tarai plains of southern Nepal. Each organisation, in different ways, advocates with and for marginalised communities seeking to defend and extend their basic rights to education, health, housing, life, dignity, democracy and equal treatment before the law. Each organisation, to different degrees, has also been the victim of state and para-state repression, violence against its members and activists, and sustained surveillance and persecution.

The three-year research project that laid the foundations for this book began in 2018, and combined detailed case studies of the learning and knowledge-making processes of each social movement institution, and incorporated within that a dynamic process of inter-movement learning and knowledge exchange, facilitated through a series of workshops and field visits to the respective country contexts, with the objective of building collective knowledge and inter-movement solidarity. For all of us in the team, this research process was as important as the research product, and was itself an act and space of solidarity and learning, where loyalties were forged, friendships made, and dreams shared.

The research process, the inter-movement solidarity, and the social movements themselves were all affected by the COVID-19 pandemic that arrived in late 2019 and continued deep into 2021. The pandemic shifted priorities, reduced interaction, prevented air travel and diverted attention towards other more pressing activities, which slowed down the data analysis and writing up phases of this work. However, that did not diminish its importance. The pandemic highlighted our global interconnectivities, amplified and placed a spotlight on inequalities both intersectional and geographic; and its economic and social costs are likely to be with us for a generation. More than ever, we need strong and imaginative social movements fighting for social and ecological justice, peace, democracy and equality, and to ensure that the price of COVID-19 globally is not paid by the most marginalised and oppressed in the years ahead.

This book brings together cross-case insights produced from the case study research that was ably carried out by a committed group of researchers in collaboration with the movements themselves, their leaders and activists, in a dynamic process of research co-production. The overall research project was led by Mario Novelli, University of Sussex. Research in Colombia was led by Patrick Kane, University of Sussex, with support from the NOMADESC team. Research in Turkey was led by Birgül Kutan, University of Sussex, UK, and Adnan Çelik, Institute for Advanced Studies in the Humanities (KWI), Germany, with support from the HDK team. In Nepal, the research was led by Tejendra Pherali, UCL, UK, with support from Tula Narayan Shah, NEMAF Director, Kusumlata Tiwari, research assistant, and the NEMAF team. Finally, in South Africa the research was led by Saranel Benjamin, Independent Researcher, and the Housing Assembly Team. We also partnered and worked in collaboration with War on Want, a UK-based NGO that works on issues of international development and solidarity, has strong links with trade union and social movements in the UK and internationally, and a long history of engaging with anti-imperialist struggles in the Global South. War on Want has played a vital role in linking the research to broader social movement debates, enhancing the project's impact through enabling access to its international and UK networks, and facilitating inter-movement exchange and dialogue (https://waronwant.org/). The project was generously funded by the UK's Economic and Research Council grant ES/R00403X/1.*

This book will proceed as follows. In the rest of this introductory chapter, we lay out the research objectives and questions and then explain how we approached the overall research process, the methodology, data collection and writing up. In Chapter 1, we reflect upon the theoretical background of the research, and explore some of the key thinking that underpins it. In Chapter 2, we provide some brief contextual background to each of the social movement institutions. In Chapter 3, we then go on to explore *how* these social movements learn and make knowledge. In Chapter 4, we explore *what* social movements learn and the types of knowledge they make. In Chapter 5, we then explore the *effects* of this learning and knowledge on both the movements and the society. Finally, in the Conclusion we *reflect* on the overall findings of the study, and we draw together some final critical reflections.

This book is not a synopsis of the individual case study reports, but instead seeks to explore cross-case issues and theoretical insights that emerge from the individual reports. We encourage the reader to read those rich individual reports, available free online, to gain a much clearer, contextualised understanding of the respective movements and the education and knowledge-making processes therein.**

We hope that you enjoy this book, that it is thought-provoking and useful, and that it helps to move the discussion forward. On behalf of the authors, we can attest to the extremely inspiring

---

* The full project description is available here: https://gtr.ukri.org/project/F8840D88-3340-4AF0-9E23-F6240A333FDD. Last accessed 4 April 2023.
** All of the case studies and other project materials are available at: https://knowledge4struggle.org/. Last accessed 4 April 2023.

and transformative process that we have been through during this project. We wish to thank all the amazing activists and leaders from the movements that we have had the privilege to engage with, for sharing their thoughts, their passions and their stories. Their struggles have become our struggles in rich, unpredictable and inspiring ways, and these will continue beyond the lifecycle of this research and long into the future.

BACKGROUND TO THE RESEARCH, OBJECTIVES, QUESTIONS AND METHODOLOGY

How research is conducted, the relationship between the researchers and the researched, and the way the data is collected and processed, are often seen as less important than the research findings. Whilst of course findings matter, how research is conducted also matters. Research can be quite an extractive industry and serve to reproduce social and geographical inequalities, and we were keenly aware that in this project we needed to pay careful attention to these issues, even if they are sometimes difficult to resolve. In this section, we explore these issues and more, and try to provide the reader with a sense of the what, why and how of this research project. Below we provide a little background on how this research came about. We then move on to explore the fundamentals of the research: what we set out to do, our key objectives, the main questions and the methodological approach we deployed in conducting the research and analysing the data. Finally, we explore the ethics of the project and provide a brief conclusion.

Background to the research

Research on social movements, particularly participatory research, often relies on the trust and relationships between the researchers and the researched. In contexts of conflict, violence and authoritarianism, these trusting relationships become all the more important. The idea for this project emerged out of an event held at the University of Sussex, UK, back in October 2016, but has its roots in long and sustained relationships between the respective social movements and the researchers involved. The event, 'Social Movement Learning and the Struggle for Social Justice: Radical Voices from the Global South', brought together social movement leaders from Colombia, South Africa, Turkey and Nepal and was sponsored by the University of Sussex, War on Want, The Transnational Institute (TNI) and the UK-based left-wing magazine, *Red Pepper*.

Prior to the public event, a small group of researchers and the invited social movement leaders spent a day together in meetings exploring ideas for potential projects that would be useful for both the movements and the researchers involved. What emerged out of both the closed and public events was a vibrant discussion around education, knowledge-making and learning in social movements, with four very different types of social movement, but all with a strong interest in exploring the theme more deeply and of continuing the dialogue. The respective movements were diverse, both in terms of their geographical context, nature and context of conflict, the challenges they faced, the type of social movement institution they were, and their primary focus. Despite their differences, the leaders and the researchers felt that working together over a sustained period of time, researching their respective movements and sharing findings, would be a useful process, and potentially a valuable contribution to both knowledge and the social movement struggle. The project was later funded by the UK's Economic and Research Council and began in January 2018.

Objectives

The overarching aim of the study was to identify and critically analyse the knowledge-making and learning processes of the four social movement institutions that constitute our research focus. This was facilitated through developing four empirically grounded, co-produced case studies of the respective social movement institutions, combined with inter-movement engagement, drawing on 'popular education' techniques and ethnographic research methods, and a final cross-case synthesis report, which drew together comparative insights from the case studies, and upon which this book is based. This project was rooted in an ethos of co-production and dialogue: processes of intra- and inter-movement reflections – gathered through interviews, workshops, meetings and focus groups – that explored these knowledge and learning processes. The process provided spaces for activist and movement self-reflection with a view to improving their effectiveness, strengthening the respective movements, and supporting the promotion of peace with social justice. This was combined with regular researcher engagement within and between the case study teams to support critical reflection, peer mentoring, theory building and comparative insights – a process which continues to date.

The specific objectives were to:

1. Critically examine the learning and knowledge-making processes of four social movement institutions in conflict-affected contexts
2. Strengthen the social movements' learning and knowledge-making processes, their reflexivity and strategic development
3. Promote South–South and South–North dialogue and relationships to foster improved practice and international solidarity
4. Enhance national and global understanding of social movement learning and the role of social movements in promoting sustainable peacebuilding (peace with social justice)
5. Co-produce four detailed social movement case studies and a critical cross-case synthesis.

Research questions and methodology

At the heart of the case study research were three basic but important questions:

1) *How do social movements learn and produce knowledge in complex conflict-affected situations?*
2) *What types of knowledge have the social movements produced and what have they learnt?*

3) *What have been the effects of these learning and knowledge-making processes on the promotion and realisation of peace with social justice within each country's context?*

Finally, and as a conclusion to the research, we then asked the following question:

4) *What emerges from the four case studies about learning and knowledge-making within social movements that can assist in supporting the possibilities for strengthening social movements' roles in building peace with social justice in complex, conflict-affected contexts?*

This book is an attempt to bring that final question together and offer some initial, tentative responses. These responses will form part of the ongoing dialogue with the respective social movements and others around the world as we seek to disseminate the research findings.

COMPARING LEARNING AND KNOWLEDGE-MAKING IN SOCIAL MOVEMENTS

This research falls broadly into the tradition of Comparative Education, but one that seeks to speak back to its colonial and elitist history (Sriprakash et al., 2020). Speaking back, both in the sense that our subject matter of learning and knowledge-making in social movements is not even on the radar of most comparative educationists, and second that ours is actively anti-imperialist, anti-capitalist and revolutionary in aspiration. Yet, it owes a legacy to the idea, enunciated by Noah Sobe (2018: 339), that rather than rejecting comparison: 'the challenge before us is to develop an ethical mode of comparison, perhaps even a politically progressive comparison, a comparison that respectfully engages with (as opposed to injures) epistemic and ontological diversity across the globe'. In this, we draw upon Sobe's (2018: 325) development of a 'criss-crossing comparison' that puts:

relationality at the center, sees research as an active process of criss-crossing, and aims to surface the entangled complexity of sometimes disparate educational actors, devices, discourses, and practices ... It emphasises reflexivity, relationality, and the active role played by the researcher in recognising the translations and alchemical transformations that are sometimes involved in comparative activities.

Central to this is not to conceive of comparison as something that occurs at the end of a research project, but rather as something that happens from its inception to completion, and that everyone can be involved in this comparison, from researchers to participants. A process that 'weaves multiple perspectives together at all stages of the inquiry process' (2018: 336). From our initial deliberations in 2016, through inception to completion of the project, we have engaged with this notion of criss-crossing comparison, raising issues from one context, and asking questions in another to enable dialogic spaces for learning and critical reflections. Inter-team visits, online meetings and workshops, team retreats, collective writing and editing – have all facilitated this process of criss-crossing comparison, to help us collectively frame issues, define challenges, and understand difference. This influence can be felt not only in this book, but across the case study research.

RESEARCHING LEARNING AND KNOWLEDGE-MAKING IN SOCIAL MOVEMENTS: THE SYSTEMATISATION OF EXPERIENCES

The research was inspired by the belief that rich knowledge exists inside social movements, so our challenge from the beginning was about how to unlock that knowledge, create the conditions and develop the strategies, to allow it to emerge out of the minds and the words of the social movement activists and leaders, and from accessing insights into their work in newspapers, movement archives, pamphlets and texts.

In this process, we are following Santos' call for the search for 'rearguard theory' (Santos, 2014: 44), based on and emergent from the experiences of activists and communities left out of the benefits of contemporary capitalist globalisation, with the explicit aim of strengthening theirs and others' resistance.

This 'rearguard theory' follows and shares the practices of the social movements very closely, raising questions, establishing synchronic and diachronic comparisons, symbolically enlarging such practices by means of articulations, translations and possible alliances with other movements, providing contexts, clarifying or dismantling normative injunctions, facilitating interaction with those who walk more slowly, and bringing in complexity when actions seem rushed and unreflective and simplicity when action seems self-paralyzed by reflection. The grounding ideas of a rearguard theory are craftsmanship rather than architecture, committed testimony rather than clairvoyant leadership, and intercultural approximation to what is new for some and very old for others.

We do this not out of naivety (though some will no doubt disagree), but out of a genuine conviction that it is at the margins, the edges, at the points where theory meets practice, where new ideas can emerge to challenge a status quo that has not been transformed by classical social science theory (which Santos terms 'vanguard theory'), whether in its orthodox or critical form. This strategy of 'listening to the South' seeks both social science and societal renewal, does not reject other knowledges, but recognises that the contemporary orthodox and critical knowledge reservoirs are not even close to encompassing the vast array of knowledges that exist around the world and need to be opened up to new tributaries and sources. Ours is thus a call for an 'ecology of knowledges', where movement knowledges can be put into dialogue with other knowledges, particularly critical theory knowledges, to enrich and explore new ideas and possibilities. That is the aspiration underpinning this work.

In thinking about suitable methodologies to do justice to these commitments, we were drawn towards the rich history of research strategies that have emerged out of 'popular education'. Popular Education, initially proposed by the Brazilian educator Paolo Freire, has captured the imagination of many social movements seeking to challenge elite structures of domination. For Freire (2000), true education was not monological but dialogical. Leaders cannot merely tell activists what to do, and if this occurs, then even a victory is a hollow achievement. Nor can education ever be understood as 'neutral', quite the opposite. Education is a process riven with power differentials and placed at the service of competing political projects. 'Popular Education' is thus seen as one of the vehicles through which the process of challenging unequal structures can be strengthened (Kane, 2001). At its core lies a fundamental commitment to social change in the interests of the oppressed. Furthermore, there is a direct relationship between this type of education and the institutions and organisations that have historically emerged to defend the interests of the poor and the marginalised, such as trade unions and social movements, whereby popular education seeks explicitly to strengthen these movements (Jara, 1989 cited in Kane, 2001: 9). This organic relationship means that the 'organisation' or the movement itself becomes the 'school' in which popular education takes place, and their 'struggles and actions, their forms of organisation, their "culture", in the broadest sense, constitute the starting point of popular education and its on-going field of enquiry' (Kane, 2001: 13).

As popular education has evolved, there has been a parallel interest in research strategies which are able to somehow capture the collective learning and knowledge-making processes that take place within social movements (Torres Carrillo, 1999, 2010). This has led to an overlap between popular education and participatory research, with participatory research methods and strategies being developed for popular education contexts (ibid.). These attempts are rooted in recognition of the important knowledge and insights into social reality that grassroots communities and ordinary people hold. The most prominent example here is the work of the Colombian sociologist Orlando Fals Borda, whose technique of 'participatory action research' (PAR) has been influential and is widely recognised as one of the most commonly used research techniques in popular education, especially in Latin America (Torres Carrillo, 2010; Fals Borda, 1979–1984, 1987).*

During the 1990s, a participatory popular education research method that builds on PAR, known as the 'systematisation of experiences', gained prominence within the field of Latin American popular education. This was based on the recognition that unique, valuable knowledge can be produced through popular education processes. The 'systematisation of experiences' is a collective research process which seeks to deepen understanding and improve practice through collective reflection and analysis of experience (Jara, 1989, 2006, 2010; Kane, 2012; Torres Carrillo, 2010). According to Kane (2012: 78), systematisation 'enables organisations and educators to learn from each other's experiences, successes, problems and failures; it helps educators analyse and evaluate their own work; it is part of the educative process itself, in which encouraging people to interpret developments helps them reach new levels of understanding'.

A range of different systematisation methodologies exists, but broadly it can be understood as an intentional, collective process of knowledge-making which tries to 'recover and interpret the meanings that manifest themselves in social practices, with the purpose of strengthening them' (Torres Carrillo, 2010: 196), and drawing these insights from the protagonists themselves. The following passage from Chilean popular educator Oscar Jara (2018: 196) demonstrates the relevance of systematisation for the study of social movements:

... the new scenario of this end of the (20th) century has raised questions over the practices and theoretical conceptions of Latin American social movements and social sciences. We are faced with new questions and challenges. It is a privileged historical

---

* See also Rappaport (2020) for a recent and insightful book on Orlando Fals Borda's PAR approach and the political commitment that underpinned it.

moment full of creation, but the answers to the new questions will not arise from any other place but from accumulated historical experience. Unfortunately, we have not yet accumulated the necessary learning contained in these (social movement) experiences. Systematisation, as a rigorous learning exercise and critical interpretation of lived processes, remains a pending task and today more than ever can decisively contribute to the re-creation of social movement practices and to renew theoretical production within social sciences, based on the daily experience of the peoples of Latin America, in particular those committed to processes of popular education and organisation.

The 'systematisation of experiences' entails a critical interpretation of an experience (process or event), beginning with its reconstruction and ordering, in order to discover the logic of the process, the factors that have influenced it, how they are related to each other, and why things happened as they did (Jara, 2018). It aims to reconstruct, to order or organise, in order to understand and interpret what happened and to then be able to draw lessons from that experience and transform practice (Jara, 2018). It is an investigative process that seeks to allow the experience to speak for itself, through all the voices of those who have been part of the experience (or at the very least a representative section) (Jara, 2018). According to Jara, one of the purposes of systematisation is to facilitate the exchange of knowledge and ideas, for example, between different social and pedagogical processes, because it allows the protagonists of a given process to communicate their experiences effectively. In line with this, our approach builds in ample space for critical, collective reflection and engagement in order to create spaces where the protagonists of the movements themselves can engage in dialogues and exchanges within their movements and between them. For this research, the process involved a series of dialogues between activists across the four movement organisations as well as extensive interviews and focus group discussions within the movements to capture reflective accounts of their systematisation processes.

Our systematisation process can be broken down into four interrelated phases that provide the dynamic for the collective reconstruction of the movements' learning and knowledge-making processes.

PHASE 1

The initial phase involved a process that sought to 'reconstruct' the lived experience of the movements, using any and every means of data available. In each of the countries, this involved individual interviews with key informants, archive and documentary analysis, newspaper articles, photos, videos, and much more. This phase required a process of organising and classifying information which facilitated a descriptive account of the evolution of the respective movements, based upon multiple sources. This is the foundational phase, and involved initial analysis in identifying emergent themes and points of interest, which were later fed into the subsequent phase of the process. This phase was carried out in a collective manner, involving many people who had been active in the movement who worked alongside the researchers and guided and supported the research process.

PHASE 2

This was the key moment of the systematisation process, which seeks to discover the logic of what happened in the course of the experience. Based on the initial framing of the systematisation process, this phase involved a collective process of reflection and analysis by those people who lived the experience. The point here is not to arrive at a single, unified viewpoint, but to access multiple voices in order to arrive at a deeper understanding of the lived experience. This necessitated engaging with a broader cross-section of constituencies than Phase 1, with multiple workshops and focus groups with leaders, activists, supporters. These participatory spaces allowed for a rich engagement between the researchers and the participants to develop research findings, check them with participants and in doing so refine and develop ideas.

PHASE 3

The systematisation processes then led to the production of a final written report, but also involved a number of other creative end products such as videos, leaflets, theatre productions and other dissemination events. One important consideration is the issue of communicating the knowledge produced in the process. This is not only a question of how it is going to be made available, but also to whom and in what languages and through what media. And why these audiences and not others? Also, some of the knowledge produced was for internal use only, not to be shared with broader audiences, on occasion to protect the security and confidentiality of activists. These important questions were decided collectively with movement leaders as the research progressed.

PHASE 4

In this phase, with the case studies produced, we deepened the dialogical process by attempting to explore whether the synthesis of the four case studies might produce more than its component parts. To what extent were the respective research findings geographically and culturally bounded? Can we develop insights that go beyond the particular? What collective insights can we draw from the cases on the nature of social movement knowledge-making and learning in the contemporary era? These outcomes emerged out of a process of intra and inter-team discussions, including a short retreat by the core research team to explore, debate, and discuss key emergent ideas from the research that underpin this final synthesis document. This then is a process of dialogue which started at the beginning of the research between the main researchers, and subsequently involved a process of dissemination and feedback with the movements themselves, which allowed for constant rethinking, reflecting and reformulating ideas. In that sense, this document is a working document, a work in progress, which is ready to be reformulated, revised and rethought as this dialogical process continues.

PROCESS

To clarify, there were two parallel, but interlinked processes taking place across the three-year research period. First, there was a *National Data Collection Process*. This 'systematisation' process took place in the respective country of each of the social movements. This included multiple workshops, focus groups, in-depth interviews with key movement activists, and review of movement documentation, in order to develop detailed narratives of their experiences and processes of movement organisation and develop the social movement case studies. Second, there were a series of *Inter-Movement Meetings and Engagement*. These research team meetings were held across the cycle of the project – and in the countries involved in the project. These meetings provided a moment for the researchers and activists to engage in a public event targeted at social movements and academic researchers in the respective countries, and an opportunity for the visitors to learn more about the particular history and struggles of social movements in the host country. Throughout the research period, research teams were also able to engage regularly and to share experiences, challenges and insights. In the latter stages of the research, we also deepened a process of dialogue between the main project researchers for each of the case studies in order to strengthen the collective synthesis findings. This final phase was slower than expected, due to the research being interrupted by the COVID-19 pandemic and the lockdowns, and lengthened the overall project beyond its initial timescale.

ETHICS

The study was conducted in accordance with the research governance framework of the University of Sussex* and ethical approval was granted from the Social Sciences Research Cluster. Three sets of ethical issues were specifically addressed in this project. The first

---

* University of Sussex Procedures for Staff Applications for Ethical Approval of Research (2016). Available at: https://studylib.net/doc/14974110/procedures-for-staff-applications--2015-16--docx-66.94kb-. Last accessed 4 April 2023.

concerns security for all researchers and participants in the project. Each country context, to differing degrees, has a history of violent conflict and repression against social movements. We worked closely with our research partners in each country to assess risk, and followed their respective security protocols for all travel and meetings. The risks were particularly stark in Turkey and Colombia. At the beginning of our research in early 2018, Dr Onur Hamzaoğlu, the then co-chair of the HDK and our main contact for the research, was arrested and detained, after signing a letter condemning the Turkish military incursion into Afrin, Syria. He was detained until July 2018, and this initial period brought home to all of us the constant pressure and danger that HDK activists faced in peacefully organising in Turkey. Similarly, in Colombia, NOMADESC and its partners faced a series of death threats and intimidation for their human rights work throughout the course of the research.

The second key ethical issue concerned protecting the identity of the participants and ensuring that their views were accurately reflected in the write-up of the project. In this regard, we assured all participants that any published material would not, in any way, identify the individual interviewed or observed, apart from cases where they asked specifically to be named in the research. We used standard research protocol in the writing up to make sure that this was the case. In addition, where appropriate, we released transcripts of interviews to participants individually so that accuracy could be verified.

Third, in dealing with vulnerable communities who have experienced trauma as a consequence of conflict, we paid particular attention to the principle of 'Do No Harm', and ensured that we were sensitive to the context-based experiences of informants and developed strategies accordingly. The research team in each context was aware of some of the dangers of pushback from dominant hegemonic intellectuals, given the focus of the study that aimed at investigating the struggle from activists' positionalities and with and for the benefit of marginalised communities. We also ensured a balance between local and international researchers to assist in the sensitivity of data collection. We were also conscious of the importance of not raising false expectations of the outcomes of the research, and developed sensitive feedback strategies to ensure that participants had access to research findings in formats that were intelligible to them (Goodhand, 2006).

In the write-up stage, we paid particular attention to ensuring that no individual information was fed directly to the respective governments, all findings were processed in an aggregated and anonymised manner, and that responsibility for any published materials was clearly in the remit of the authors. This was particularly important given that we were studying movements emerging from or in conflict, and which had delicate and often highly conflictual relationships with their respective states, as noted above. All participants were informed about the objectives and purposes of the study and provided with full details of Mario Novelli, the lead researcher, and the local lead researchers to facilitate easy and direct access to the team to raise any concerns. Key to all the above was an open and dialogical process and relationship with the movement leaders and coordinators, with whom we shared our dilemmas and challenges and collectively searched for adequate and ethical responses. Mutual respect and solidarity were and remain the central ethical tenets of the entire research process.

CHAPTER CONCLUSIONS

We hope to have provided a sense in this introduction of why we wanted to undertake this research, our objectives, our partners, how we conducted the research, and the ethics that have underpinned it. Crucially, it was a process of co-production, with a strong recognition and respect for the knowledge and insights of the activists themselves, and the need to produce 'really useful' knowledge for both a social movement and an academic audience. In the next chapter, we explore the foundational ideas and literatures that underpinned it.

1

Social movement theory, learning and knowledge-making in conflict contexts

INTRODUCTION

Having laid out the research questions and methodological approach, we now turn to theory and the key concepts we drew upon in the research. In this chapter, we will provide insights into the framing of social movements, the history of social movement research, the role and relationship of academics and activists in the production of research on social movements, and finally the role and importance of knowledge, learning and education within social movements.

DEFINING SOCIAL MOVEMENTS

For the purpose of this research, we drew on the work of Paul Routledge (2017: 4), who defines social movements as:

> organisations of varying size that share a collective identity and solidarity, are engaged in forms of conflict in opposition to an adversary (such as a government or corporation), and attempt to challenge or transform particular elements within a social system (such as governments, laws, policies, cultural codes and so on).

This particular interpretation emphasises the geographical nature of social movements, which sees them as:

> ... networks of people, resources and connections. Most operate at the intersection of a series of overlapping scales – from more local

municipalities, through regions to the nation-state and, increasingly, international forums. These different politics of scale – and their associated networks of activity – provide movements with a range of opportunities and constraints.

(2017: 6)

This geographical dimension has helped us both to frame the inter-movement relationships between the four case studies, and also to better understand and interpret the complex and multi-scalar nature of power and politics from the micro to the macro.

Essential for us is a definition of social movements that also incorporates their learning and knowledge-making dimensions. For that, we concur with Casas-Cortes et al. (2008: 20, cited in Della Porta and Pavan, 2017: 3), who note that:

In their effort to pursue or resist social and political changes, these actors do not limit themselves to protesting in the streets or the squares. Rather, they form collective spaces of knowledge production wherein collaboration and participation lead to the 'rethinking [of] democracy; the generation of expertise and new paradigms of being, as well as different modes of analyses of relevant political and social conjunctures'.

In line with this, and along with Hall (2004: 190) we see social movements as 'pedagogical spaces for adults to learn to transform their lives and the structures around them'. It is an exploration of these pedagogical, learning and knowledge-making processes, and their capacity to change individuals, institutions and societies themselves, that lies at the heart of our research.

SOCIAL MOVEMENTS, WAR AND PEACE

Moving slightly away from social movements to issues of violent conflict, in much of the literature on peace-making, peacekeeping and peacebuilding there is a recognition that the voices of civil society, and the social movements that emerge from them, are often insufficiently included in determining the nature of peace agreements and post-conflict development policies (Pugh et al., 2016; Richmond and Mitchell, 2011). In all of our case study contexts, the shadow and legacies of armed conflict are present, as is a generalised feeling that a just peace has yet to emerge. Too often, national political elites, armed movements, and international actors fail sufficiently to take into account the demands of civil society actors and social movements for access to basic rights, goods and liberties – demands and grievances that underpin many conflicts – favouring instead agreements that prioritise security, democratic elections and the promotion of markets (Paris, 2004). These peace agreements often result in what Galtung (1976) termed 'negative peace', characterised by the cessation of armed violence without addressing the underlying drivers of conflict that underpinned and fuelled that violence. Instead, Galtung argued for 'positive peace', which seeks to end both violence and the underlying causes of that violence.

At the heart of the drivers of conflict in many contexts is inequality, in its multiple economic, political, gendered and cultural dimensions (Cramer, 2005; Stewart et al., 2005; Stewart, 2010): unequal access to resources, land, food, housing, education, healthcare and unequal treatment before the law and/or the political system, particularly for different cultural and ethnic communities. As a result, for many social movements in conflict-affected contexts, the struggle for peace cannot be separated from the struggle for social justice – with many drawing on the discourse of 'peace with social justice' as the rallying call. For many analysts, failure to build 'positive peace' lies at the heart of why many peace agreements fail and relapse into violence.

Strengthening social movements and the organisations that they form, and seeking to pressurise states to redress inequalities, is therefore a crucial peacebuilding measure. How these organisations develop strategies, educate their members and build capacity, build new knowledge and understandings, extend contacts and solidarities with other movements, and impact national policy in these conflict/post-conflict contexts is central to the concern of our research, yet has often been overlooked by mainstream research on security, conflict and peacebuilding (Richmond, 2016).

A BRIEF HISTORY OF SOCIAL MOVEMENT RESEARCH

Whilst social movement research in the Global North has intellectual roots in the foundational work of nineteenth-century thinkers such as Marx, Weber and Durkheim, who provided broad theories for understanding social change; as a body of work, social movement research emerged from North America and Europe in the 1950s. The functionalist-inspired 'resource mobilisation theory' (RMT) became a dominant strand that focused on social movement organisation, resources, and opportunities (Tilly, 1985; Tarrow, 1999; McAdam, 1982). Resource mobilisation theorists have often been criticised for their overtly structural approach and their tendency to extract the struggles of social movements from the broader analysis of the socio-economic context (Choudry, 2015; Scandrett, 2012). They also tended to arrive at levels of abstraction and generalisation which inevitably produced reductive, simplified theory.

'New social movement' (NSM) theory emerged from Europe to challenge RMT (see Buechler, 2013; Touraine, 1981; Melucci, 1980) and the inadequacy of orthodox structural approaches, both functionalist and Marxist, to account for social movements which began to emerge from the 1960s onwards as significant subjects of struggle, but which could not easily be slotted into the traditional class analyses of earlier theories, e.g. the peace movement and the women's movement. NSM theorists tended to have a concern for questions around why new social actors emerge, and took into account cultural factors such as the construction of collective identities and lifestyles. Some strands sought to analyse the motivation, experience and communication networks of individual activists involved in social movements (Melucci, 1980). Such theories can be useful in helping us to grasp the internal dynamics and heterogeneous characteristics of social movements.

In development studies, the political and economic struggles of social movements have more recently been linked to battles over knowledge, coloniality and modernity, with alternative ways of knowing, being and producing at the heart of debates (cf. Escobar, 2004; Santos, 2007, 2014; Santos and Meneses, 2019). Whilst often critical of earlier framings of social movements, there are nevertheless strong lineages and linkages with anti-imperialist and anti-colonial literatures and struggles, which emphasised North/ South inequalities in their multiple economic, cultural and political dimensions (the works of Walter Rodney, Steve Biko, Samir Amin, Immanuel Wallerstein, Frantz Fanon and others) and often emerged out of the Global South. However, where there was difference, it was particularly in the challenge to the final destination, raising strong concerns about the ecological damage of industrialisation and a strong recognition of the wisdom of endogenous, and indigenous, knowledges, which could plot an alternative development pathway forward (c.f. Escobar, 2018, 2020). Finally, there are important literatures from human geography on the way social movements in the contemporary era of globalisation use space and operate across borders to strengthen their claim-making (Kriesi et al., 2016; Routledge, 2017; Halvorsen, 2019).

One general criticism which has been made of much social movement theory, is that it often lacked direct relevance for the movements themselves and 'often [has] little of substance to say about the struggles of the day' (Cox and Nilsen, 2014: 17). Two decades ago, Flacks (2004), surveying the ever-growing field of social movement scholarship, asked 'What is all this analysis for? In what way does the validation, elaboration, and refinement of concepts provide useable knowledge for those seeking social change?' (2004: 138).

From Flacks' critical starting point, a significant body of literature has emerged over recent decades which seeks to radically turn the mainstream trend on its head, challenging the detachment of the scholar from the movement by prioritising the aim of making research relevant and accountable to social movements themselves (Bevington and Dixon, 2005; Novelli, 2006, 2010, 2004; Choudry, 2015; Cox and Nilsen, 2014; McNally, 2013; Tarlau, 2014, 2019). Flacks and Bevington and Dixon's call for a new wave of 'movement-relevant theory' that is useful to those involved in struggles for social change (2005) has definitely been heard. This type of research represented an opportunity to increase both the academic utility and credibility of social movement research and its support for social impact. Whilst not without tension and contradictions (see Jasper, 2015; Cox, 2015), the scholar/social movement relationship was seen as having the potential both to produce insights relevant to the movement and to open up new academic debates and framings.

In a similar vein, Santos has argued, since the mid-1990s, that we needed to start by 'listening to the South' (Santos, 1995: 506) as the site where those suffering under global capitalism exist and resist. This necessitated a normative affiliation with the South, though one that neither implied the simple dissolution of the social scientist into the activist nor one that kept a distance between social science and activism (Santos, 2014). For Santos, the researcher was to become a translator, helping to bridge ideas and knowledge between movements.

In relation to and in support of this, the study of social movement learning and knowledge-making processes has been identified as one particularly relevant area for new directions in social movement analysis, which seeks to be movement-relevant and contribute to new challenges and debates (Zibechi, 2007; Santos, 2006; Della Porta and Pavan, 2017; Cox, 2015; Hye-Su and Tarlau, 2020). Key in this discussion is that radical and insightful knowledge emerges from those spaces at the margins of society, where the violence of contemporary global capitalism is most evident, and where innovations arise out of these sharp contradictions and tensions (Az et al., 2020).

SOCIAL MOVEMENTS AND KNOWLEDGE-MAKING

Linked to the role, nature and importance of social movements is also the role of knowledge within these movements. Social movement knowledge-making and learning has often been key to the historical evolution of social scientific thought, even if it is less often openly acknowledged. Central to this argument is both a critique of top-down knowledge, which presumes that academics theorise and social movements produce empirical evidence and receive theory, and a much more grounded understanding that social movements at the point of praxis build knowledge from below that can move social scientific thought forward and change the world. Cox (2018), Choudry (2015) and Shukaitis and Graeber (2007) argue that those at the coalface – suffering the harshest contradictions of contemporary neoliberal capitalist development – have privileged knowledge about the nature of the system under which we all reside.

Similarly, it is when academics engage with social movements that the most fruitful potential for breakthroughs in social science is provided. Critical theory owes its roots to intellectuals' engagement with social movements – not just Marxism, but feminism, poststructuralism, postcolonialism etc. However, from the 1980s onwards critical theory, particularly in the US and Western Europe, has often become distanced from grassroots struggles and has developed in very particular directions. This has made it less relevant and powerful – and also distorted its focus (Shukaitis and Graeber, 2007).

As Cox (2015: 956) notes:

In the period often taught as foundational, it was not only Marx and Engels whose thought was shaped by the movements that shaped their world. Weber, the conservative opponent of socialism, and Durkheim, the republican 'secular pope', both formed their thought in dialogue with movements. The same is true for the revitalisation of sociology from the 1960s: the arrival of feminism and Marxism within the academy, the growth of postcolonial and Foucauldian approaches, the struggles of scholars identifying as gay or lesbian, migrant or minority, and the methodological challenges represented by participatory, feminist and other approaches were all shaped by social movements.

Part of the argument being developed here also feeds into the broader debate around the 'decolonisation' of knowledge, that the subaltern knowledges of social movements, in their worker, indigenous, feminist, black and anti-racist forms, have been silenced, undermined or hidden through processes of both imperialism and elitism – which have prioritised Northern knowledge over Southern knowledge; University Knowledge over Social Movement knowledge; Elite Academic over Movement Intellectual; Middle-Class knowledge over Working-Class and Peasant knowledge; Male knowledge over Female; Traditional Intellectuals over Organic Intellectuals. To be clear, this is not a binary plea for the abandoning of universities as sites of knowledge-making, but rather for reconnecting and reinvigorating them by celebrating and mainstreaming epistemologies from the South, alongside a recognition and vindication of alternative modes of knowing and thinking. The aim is to produce what Santos (2007) called an 'ecology of knowledges' as a challenge to the process of 'epistemicide' that is impoverishing our capacity to see, think and move beyond our contemporary, highly unequal and brutal world.

Knowledge, therefore, takes on a particular importance in the pursuit of social transformation and social justice. The importance of education and knowledge-making in the contemporary era has not been lost on those engaged in processes of hegemonic neoliberal globalisation, and the last two decades have seen corporations talking of themselves as 'learning organisations', ' knowledge institutions' and discussing the 'learning society', the 'information society', 'the knowledge economy' and recognising the need to set up structures able to change and adapt to new circumstances, be that fast capitalism, lean production or flexible accumulation, which reflect the need for more mobile structures and a workforce skilled to adapt to a fast-changing environment (World Bank, 2007; Ranson, 1994; Jarvis, 2001).

In this context, it appears logical to ask how social movements are taking seriously the necessity to rethink strategies through processes of research, investigation and learning. Within social movement studies, there has been little focus on knowledge and education processes. However, more recently, there has been a renewal of interest (Cox, 2018; Choudry, 2015; Novelli and Ferus-Comelo, 2012; Della Porta and Pavan, 2017; Hye-Su and Tarlau, 2020) and an increased recognition that knowledge in social movements matters, and is worthy of deeper analysis. Della Porta and Pavan (2017: 300) call for the study of 'repertoires of knowledge practices', which they define:

> As the set of practices that foster the coordination of discon-
> nected, local, and highly personal experiences and rationalities
> within a shared cognitive system able to provide movements and
> their supporters with a common orientation for making claims
> and acting collectively to produce social, political, and cultural
> changes.

In relation to the above, Antonio Gramsci's 'philosophy of praxis' (Marxism) was always accompanied by a strong interest in a 'pedagogy of praxis' (Pizzolato and Holst, 2017), which saw the construction of both hegemony and counter-hegemony as fundamentally pedagogical and educational. Gramsci (1971) noted a distinction between 'common sense' (which reflected hegemonic knowledge) and 'good sense' (that knowledge emerging from people's own analysis derived from the everyday), and his work had a strong focus on workers' education.

Beyond a general cognitive framing, we also believe that social movements produce different types of knowledge. As Chesters (2012: 153) notes: 'social movements have long been bearers of knowledge about forms of oppression and injustice, expressing political claims, identifying social and economic grievances and bringing new or neglected issues to public prominence'. As Casas-Cortes et al. (2008: 42–43) note, this knowledge is often 'embedded in and embodied through lived, place-based experiences, [able to] offer different kinds of answers than more abstract knowledge ... situated and embodied, rather than supposedly neutral and distant'.

Classically, we can see that social movement knowledge-making has operated at three levels. First, all movements seek to provide a *thematic critique*: 'How can we understand the oppression we are suffering?' This might be specific – why are people being pushed off their land? Why do they face discrimination in legal, institutional and public domains? Why are their culture and language absent in their nation's education systems? – or more macro-societal, such as a critique of capitalism/feudalism, etc. Second, and emergent from the first, movements develop a *strategic critique* – 'How can we challenge the oppression we are facing?' This concerns both modes of resistance (strikes, protests, occupations, media engagement, etc.) and institutional forms (the centralised party, the umbrella organisation, popular front/united front, the trade union, the affinity group, etc.). Third, movements develop an *alternative vision*: 'What is our solution to the problem posed?' This might be thematic – solutions to social housing, right to citizenship and representation in decision-making bodies – or societal: the vision of a new society – communism/socialism, etc.

In summary, it is suggested that social movements produce knowledge on the nature of the system; the strategies, forms and tactics to transform it, and to defend the space once taken; and finally develop visions of what it might be replaced with: *Critique, Resistance, Alternatives.* According to Cox (2018), because academic/top-down knowledge has become increasingly separated from movements, it has been less able to address and explore Resistance and Alternatives, and therefore focused largely on Critique. However, to paraphrase Marx, the task is not just to understand the world (and critique it), but to change it. In order to do that, we thus need to reunite and bolster understanding of the trilogy of Critique, Resistance and Alternatives in order to build viable solutions in the here and now.

Antonio Gramsci recognised the need and importance of movement learning and knowledge-making and noted that every 'revolution has been preceded by an intense labour of criticism' (Gramsci, 1977: 12). Within this process, Gramsci talked of the important role of 'organic intellectuals', committed to an alternative counter-hegemonic project and able to articulate, strategise and transmit this to broader publics (Gramsci, 1986: 3–24). Whilst Gramsci often portrayed this function as rather mechanistic and unidirectional, another influential Marxist educator, Paolo Freire, would later provide a far more dialectical conceptualisation of this process, opening up the possibility of both creating a body of 'organic intellectuals' through serious educational strategies and enhancing the dialogical relationship between leaders and activists and movements and communities.

LEARNING AND EDUCATION IN SOCIAL MOVEMENTS

As mentioned earlier, Freire's 'popular education' emerged as a critique of formal schooling, or what he called 'banking education', which he argued was unidirectional and rooted in maintaining the status quo, rather than radically transforming it. For Freire, and others that followed in his footsteps around the world, this 'popular education' was the vehicle for producing reflexive, critical subjects from the grassroots movements that were forming to challenge injustice and inequality. The movement thus became the school, and those modes of learning and knowledge-making emerged out of both structured and unstructured learning processes and spaces.

Importantly, 'popular education' goes beyond formal educational events in social movements, and extends to much bigger processes which, though appearing 'informal' and 'arbitrary', are often deliberate. In this definition, both the 'popular education' events that take place, and the actual practice of 'strategy development' and 'protest actions', can be seen as examples of popular education, whereby the 'school' (the social movement) learns and makes knowledge. The first occurs when people consciously engage in educational practices (schooling), and the second occurs when people are learning through social action. Foley (1999) suggests that a broad conception of education and learning should include *formal education* (taking place in educational institutions), *incidental learning* (taking place as we live, work and engage in social action), *informal education* (where people teach and learn from each other in workplaces, families, communities, social movements) and *non-formal education* (structured systematic teaching and learning in a range of social settings). There is also a need to think through the relationship between individual learning processes and movement learning processes – which represent the transfer or fusion of individual experiences into collective or institutional learning. We also have to ask questions about the temporalities of that learning – the short, medium and long-term processes, and the way different forms of learning interact.

Clearly, if we are to explore these educational processes, then we need to extend our gaze beyond formal training courses for activists and develop an analytical framework that is 'open' and which allows for the conceptualisation of the rich diversity of ways that social movements (their organisations, activists and supporters) engage in learning and knowledge-making. In studying these different types of education and learning, Foley (1999: 10) suggests that these need to be firmly grounded in an analysis of the political economy, ideology and discourse of the focus of study. Earlier work has built on these foundations to theorise how processes of neoliberalism and globalisation have affected social movement learning and praxis, and the way movements are learning to operate transnationally in order to achieve their objectives (cf. Novelli and Ferus-Comelo, 2010). Similarly, Choudry's (2015) pathbreaking work, *Learning Activism: The Intellectual Life of Contemporary Social Movements*, provided both a vindication of the importance of social movements as sites of learning and knowledge-making, and an insider's view of the complex ways that education, knowledge and strategy development are built in and through the day-to-day struggles of social movements in diverse environments, and through what he called the 'grunt work' of activists. More recently, Choudry and Vally (2018) have deepened the historical aspects of this, to evidence the importance of learning from the history of previous struggles, through archive work, to inform the battles of today.

Becky Tarlau's (2014) important work on the relationship between education and social movement development is also helpful in trying to weave these different literatures together and make sense of them. She talks of how the 'critical pedagogy' literature inspired by Freire is often strong on the cognitive dimensions of agency, but often lacks the capacity to theorise the relationship between individual learning and social movement change. Similarly, she critiques the social movement literature for being strong on exploring the political opportunities and structures that movements are faced with, but much weaker on explaining the way individual agency and the micro-scale of everyday praxis is linked to more meso- and macro-scale processes of social struggle and change. Fusing the two fields, she suggests, might just open up new ways of overcoming each of their respective blind spots: 'Critical pedagogues need more organisational thinking and social movement scholars need a more pedagogical focus' (Tarlau, 2014: 369). The challenge of bringing those dimensions together similarly lies at the core of this research. In earlier work, Novelli (2006) developed the concept of 'strategic pedagogy' in work on the anti-privatisation struggles of the trade union SINTRAEMCALI, in Cali, Colombia. The concept sought to capture the links between the micro pedagogical processes of popular education and the broader and more public pedagogy of social movement strategy developed by the trade union in its defence of public services in Colombia's second city of Cali.

CHAPTER CONCLUSIONS

Having presented our framing of social movements, social movement research, and processes of knowledge-making, learning and education, we hope that we have given the reader a sense of the way we are conceptualising social movements as important 'laboratories of learning and knowledge-making', as sites where theory and practice intersect, sites that are often at the meeting point of some of the harshest contradictions of contemporary society, where alternatives are forged, as well as applied, experimented with and adapted, and where new ideas and ways of knowing, seeing and being constantly emerge. Whilst often underplayed and ignored in mainstream academia, we have traced the seams of influence that social movements have had on the evolution of social theory, and make the case for the necessity and importance of taking those learning and knowledge-making processes in social movements seriously. At a time of general global crisis (Fraser, 2022), 'where the old is dying, but the new has yet to be born' (Gramsci, 1971: 275–276), this is an urgent and essential task for the construction of better, more socially just societies. In the next chapter, we turn to exploring the social movements that lie at the heart of this research, exploring and explaining their contexts, evolution and central tenets.

2

Background to the social movements

INTRODUCTION

In this chapter, we provide a brief background to each of the movements, the context they exist and operate in, and their evolution, so as to assist the reader in understanding and processing the reflections on learning and knowledge-making that follow in the later chapters. The chapter concludes with some critical cross-case reflections on the four movements, their intersections and divergences.

NOMADESC AND THE INTERCULTURAL UNIVERSITY OF THE PEOPLES, COLOMBIA

The first social movement institution is NOMADESC, based in Cali, Colombia. Despite being one of the most dangerous places in the world to be an activist, Colombia is a country with a long and vibrant history of protest and organising in pursuit of social change. Trade unions, rural indigenous, black and peasant communities, students, urban dwellers, women, LGTBQ and many more sectors of society have formed social movements which have led important struggles in the defence and pursuit of territory, dignity, autonomy and equality. As the cradle of the country's indigenous and black movement, as well as a historical stronghold of the trade union movement, the southwest region of Colombia has provided more than its fair share of these emblematic struggles, and continues to do so today.* Despite, or perhaps because of this civic vitality,

---

* As we were initially writing up the synthesis report for this project in June 2021, Cali (the region's major city), where NOMADESC and the UIP are based, was the epicentre of an uprising which began on 28 April 2021. See Al Jazeera (2021) In Pictures: Cali

the region's social movements have also been widely targeted for violence and repression, and the Colombian armed conflict has provided a permanent backdrop to activists lives and their struggles.

NOMADESC is a radical grassroots human rights NGO, founded in 1999, based in Colombia, and operating in the southwest of the country. This organisation works with social movement activists from trade unions, black communities, indigenous, displaced peoples, women's organisations, students and environmental constituencies to help them build capacity, develop strategy and build synergies between the different movements to strengthen their ability to realise their rights as Colombian citizens. As a human rights organisation, NOMADESC is engaged in researching and investigating human rights violations, campaigning on human rights issues, supporting legal cases and processes, accompanying social movements as they advocate and defend their rights, as well as a broad engagement with processes of 'popular education', aimed at strengthening activists, movements and communities' capacities to defend and extend their basic human rights.

NOMADESC's conception of human rights goes beyond a narrow 'civil rights' framework, and encompasses a broad approach that includes economic, social and cultural rights. It also has a strong commitment to the notion of the 'rights of the peoples', best expressed in the anti-colonial Algiers Charter, signed in 1976 by a wide range of national liberation movements, social movements and public intellectuals, who met in Algeria to declare their commitment to national liberation, freedom from colonialism and imperialism, and the right of all peoples to self-determination and self-defence.* Within this broad-based and radical human rights focus, NOMADESC over the last two decades has run a Diploma Course in Human Rights for activists, accompanied different move-

---

– The epicentre of protests in Colombia. Available at: https://www.aljazeera.com/gallery/2021/5/14/in-pictures-barricades-continue-in-cali-the-epicenter-of-the-an Last Accessed 3 April 2023.

* Algiers Charter: Universal Declaration of the Rights of Peoples, Algiers, 4 July 1976. Available at: http://permanentpeoplestribunal.org/wp-content/uploads/2016/06/Carta-di-algeri-EN-2.pdf. Last accessed 3 April 2023.

ments in their advocacy and human rights struggles, and provided specialist advice on how to protect and extend the rights of marginalised communities in Colombia. In 2015, NOMADESC launched the Intercultural University of the Peoples (Universidad Intercultural de los Pueblos, henceforth UIP), a radical new mode of social movement learning and knowledge-making, which provided the central focus of our research.

NOMADESC's pedagogical-organisational strategy began in 1999, initially as an ad-hoc series of human rights workshops for trade unions in the Valle del Cauca region, which at the time were primary targets for paramilitary violence due to the militancy and effectiveness of the region's workers' movement. Leading on from these initial workshops, in 2001 a Human Rights Diploma programme was developed in coordination with trade unions and social movements, in response to the continued paramilitary expansion and violence against communities and social movements. These Diploma courses ran until 2010, when NOMADESC, and the social movements involved, decided to develop a proposal for a social movement-based and led popular university, which is now known as the Intercultural University of the Peoples, an alternative educational process that challenges Western notions of the university and brings together 37 diverse movements and grassroots social organisations in the Valle del Cauca, Cauca, Nariño, Huila, Chocó and the coffee region of southwest Colombia.

Throughout its history, this pedagogical-organisational strategy has been pursued alongside, and been engaged with, some of Colombia's most emblematic social struggles. The trade unions and social movements involved in the pedagogical process have led historic struggles of national and international significance, such as the 36-day occupation of the headquarters of EMCALI (Novelli, 2002), the regional public utilities provider, by SINTRAEMCALI trade union in 2001, in opposition to planned privatisation (see Novelli, 2006, 2010); the Social and Communitarian Minga led by the indigenous movement of Cauca, which brought together social movements from across the country in 2008 to oppose the government's militarised and neoliberal economic policies; or the 22-day civic strike in the predominantly black city of Buenaventura in 2017 to demand dignity, rights, respect and investment in Colombia's major port city on the Pacific Coast (Kane and Celeita, 2018). In all of these struggles, NOMADESC supported the movements, providing human rights advice and accompaniment, alongside the pedagogical workshops and activities.

It is in this context, characterised by vibrant social movement activity and high levels of repression and violence from state and paramilitary groups, that NOMADESC's pedagogical strategy has sought to strengthen social movements by connecting struggles and networks, providing tools and information for the defence of human rights, and developing an intercultural knowledge dialogue between the diverse social movements which converge within the pedagogical process.

Over the last two decades, hundreds of social movement activists in southwest Colombia, and from a variety of trade union, women, black, indigenous, peasant and student movements, have joined the educational programmes run by NOMADESC, and the imprint of this work is evident in the day-to-day practices and struggles of all of these movements. Delegates are nominated by their respective social movements to attend the training programmes. In return, they are obliged to feed back into their movement the knowledge and learning gained through the process, and to convey the challenges and perspectives of their respective movements in NOMADESC and the UIP's regular gatherings and events.

THE PEOPLES' DEMOCRATIC CONGRESS, TURKEY (HDK)

The second social movement institution is an umbrella organisation in Turkey, the HDK (Peoples Democratic Congress/Halkların Demokratik Kongresi). HDK was established in October 2011 and brought together various political and social movements, organisations and individuals around a broad-based agenda for peace with social justice, with a strong social movement focus. Since its inception, the HDK has come to provide a platform for sections of society that have long been excluded due to their political beliefs, ethnicity, religion, gender and sexual preferences. It also attracts a wider population that yearns for a more democratic, open and peaceful Turkey. As a result, in a short period of time, the HDK has built a significant movement across the country. Central to its political programme has been forging a link between Turkey's fragmented left movements and the Kurdish Liberation Movement.

The opening for this new broad oppositional unity was facilitated by changes in the strategy of the broader Kurdish Liberation Movement, including its armed wing, the PKK (Partiya Karkerên Kurdistanê). The armed struggle carried out by the PKK since 1984 expanded into multiple sites and spaces, and drastically changed both the scale and landscape of Kurdish resistance in Turkey during the 1990s. As a result, there was an increase in legal political parties, cultural centres, new social, cultural and political institutions, and solidarity networks operating in the public sphere, all of which have come to shape the daily life and politics of Turkey in significant ways. However, following the capture of Abdullah Öcalan, the leader of the PKK, in 1999, the Kurdish Liberation Movement made a significant change in its direction and aims: moving away from the goal of establishing an independent Kurdistan to calling for a democratically autonomous, self-governing social entity that operates within the Democratic Republic (Güneş, 2015).

Inspired by the work of Murray Bookchin (Bookchin, 1995, 1996, 2005), Öcalan proposed a new paradigm of radical democracy, as an attempt to go beyond what Öcalan calls the 'classical Kurdish nationalist line', but also 'a leftist interpretation of a similar tendency' (Öcalan, 1999: 10). Radical democracy has three fundamental projects that are interrelated and complementary to each other: Democratic Republic, Democratic Autonomy and Democratic Confederalism (Akkaya and Jongerden, 2013: 189). The notion of a Democratic Republic refers to a new type of state/society relation based on the recognition of diversity (religious, cultural, ethnic), and the representation of multiplicity (identities and cultures), materialised in the rearticulating of (equal) citizenship away from the notion of nationalism. Democratic Confederalism refers to 'democratic self-government' and direct rule of the people, who constitute their own institutions and a new socio-ecological-political system (Öcalan, 2013: 32) beyond the nation-state, based on direct democracy, gender equality, ecological sustainability and participatory economics (Stanchev, 2016). Democratic Autonomy refers to people's right to determine their own economic, cultural and social affairs within a newly created unitary structure that has its own administrative and power structure that can facilitate the diverse demands of peoples under the banner of the Democratic Republic. Whilst the Democratic Republic is a project of state reform, the projects of Democratic Confederalism and Democratic Autonomy embody the idea of a politics beyond and without the state (Akkaya and Jongerden, 2013).

Returning to the HDK, its founding Congress in 2011 brought together 820 delegates from 81 cities across Turkey, representing a range of diverse social actors, groups and organisations, including the Kurdish Liberation Movement, left-wing political parties and trade unions, women's movements, LGBT movement, environmentalist, labour and rights-based civil society organisations, and representatives of various religious minorities. Inspired by, and building on, earlier attempts to bring together the Kurdish Liberation Movement and socialist left movement as well as the dynamic social struggle of women and minoritised groups, the HDK was created as a new political form – 'the Congress' – with the explicit aim of capturing the dynamic momentum of the upsurge in social movement struggles in the 2000s and organising a broader opposition under one umbrella movement, on a long-term, sustainable basis. This required developing new practices and politics that could facilitate working collectively with diverse social groups, organisations and individuals on a common and shared idea, linking the peace and democracy struggle for a new alternative peaceful and democratic Turkey. The Congress structure was horizontal and egalitarian, and sought, in a prefigurative sense, to construct the future from today and in today, by building political, economic and social emancipation together and projecting it towards the creation of a new life.

In its openness and embrace of diversity in all its multiple forms, and its grassroots, bottom-up, democratic structure, the HDK represented a reverse image of a Turkey founded as a top-down, authoritarian, hetero-normative, mono-cultural and mono-religious nation-state. Modern Turkey, which emerged as a nation-state out of the ruins of the Ottoman empire after World War I, had been constructed on an extreme form of nationalism that sought to obliterate difference in a context that was and is culturally, religiously and ethnically highly diverse. Known as Kemalism (after the founding father of Turkey, Kemal Ataturk), this project had maintained hegemony for nearly a century, albeit on occasions by suspending democracy and instituting military rule. Whilst the rise of the AKP (the Justice and Development Party), an Islamist party which has been in power since 2002 largely under the leadership of Recep Tayip Erdogan, had challenged the 'secular' nature of the regime, the commitment to unity in sameness, rather than diversity, remained its hallmark. Both in the past and the present, the regime has never been averse to using overwhelming violence against any opposition and dissent. Both the Kurds and the left have been subject to massive repression over the years, as have religious, and other ethnic and sexual minoritised groups.

Despite this context of repression, from 2011, the HDK began to grow rapidly as it united and reinvigorated divergent social forces. The HDK created its own political party in 2012, the Peoples' Democratic Party (HDP), which in subsequent parliamentary and presidential elections gained over 10% of the national vote, and became established as Turkey's third-largest political party and its most steadfast and militant opposition party. Both the HDK and the HDP became known for their policy of appointing male and female co-chairs to all posts and for their democratic structures. This focus on gender equality has been strongly influenced by the Kurdish Freedom Movement's shift towards, and its commitment to, 'jineology', a feminist approach that emerged out of the Kurdish struggle. Beyond gender, it is extremely difficult to think of HDK/HDP's development separately from the collective achievements of the Kurdish Freedom Movement's long-term struggle. For example, from the Congress model to the HDK's gender equality practices, these all started to be implemented through the Democratic Society Congress (DTK), established in 2007, in the Kurdistan region of Turkey, which was the predecessor model for the HDK. For this reason, it is essential to consider the Kurdish Freedom Movement's post-2000 general political paradigm, and its commitment to radical forms of democracy, without denying the authentic and unique dimensions of the HDK, including the effect of its other affiliates in the socialist and identity/peoples' movements on its overall development.

Relatedly, the HDK and HDP were at their height when the AKP government was engaged in peace negotiations (2013–2015). During that period, the peace process provided a legitimacy for both the grassroots and parliamentary opposition that HDK/HDP offered. This enabled open gatherings, democratic debate and a public space for debates on issues of identity and democracy. After the collapse of these talks, and ensuing armed conflicts both internally and externally, HDK/HDP have become stigmatised and persecuted, and the space for public democratic debate and discussion has been severely curtailed.

Earlier political and electoral success was then met with widespread repression. The HDK and its members, and the HDP, have suffered brutal attacks from both state and non-state armed actors. Many of its supporters have been arrested, subjected to arbitrary detention, are in prison or forced into exile. How the HDK builds strategy and mobilises for social justice issues in this highly repressive and authoritarian context, and the learning and knowledge processes therein, represented the focus of this case.

THE HOUSING ASSEMBLY, SOUTH AFRICA

The third social movement institution is the Housing Assembly, which was formed in 2009 to address housing inequality in Cape Town, South Africa. They organise shack dwellers, back-yarders, people living in transit camps and those living in social housing. By 2020, the Housing Assembly was represented in over 20 communities and had 6,500 members and over 400 frontline activists. The Housing Assembly operates in contexts where the legacies of apartheid continue to divide populations, limit opportunities and shape the lived experiences of many South Africans. The struggle for housing represents one example of the broader disillusionment of millions of poor people who feel that the promise of better lives for all, made in 1994 when apartheid ended, has been broken. Across South Africa the legacies of apartheid persist in public and social life and whilst the ANC (African National Congress) has remained in power since 1994, it has increasingly become embroiled in corruption scandals and has failed to address the striking inequalities seen across the country. Disillusionment with the ANC and the failure of post-apartheid South Africa to deliver peace with social justice provides the catalyst for popular resistance amongst social movements, which organise the millions left out of the benefits of the 'rainbow nation'.

The Housing Assembly was itself born out of an eviction process. In 2008, a group of landless and homeless families had occupied land in Cape Town. They erected structures out of scrap materials on a piece of land without access to water or toilets. The families, including children and babies, stayed in these conditions for months. Every day they were violently and repeatedly evicted by the City of Cape Town's anti-land invasion unit. The powerful story of this experience is deeply embedded in the historical memory and DNA of the movement. It is the story that has formed the heart of their struggle.

The core group that was fighting the evictions joined a community activist course facilitated by an NGO, the International Labour Research and Information Group (ILRIG), based in Cape Town. During the course, they listened to other activists talk about their experiences of facing evictions, living in backyards, badly built RDP houses,* transit camps and informal settlements, and living in overcrowded conditions with little or no access to basic services. At first bewildered by alienating concepts such as 'neoliberalism' and 'capitalism', through this learning experience, the group came to the realisation that they were facing a housing crisis that was a direct

---

* Between 1994 and 2001 the Reconstruction and Development Programme (RDP) built over a million low-cost houses.

result of a system that benefitted the wealthy and powerful, and that the only way they could achieve decent housing was through building a grassroots and militant organisation.

After a year, in 2009, the Housing Assembly was born. Today it organises in five districts in Cape Town and one in Witzenburg, a rural area north of Cape Town. The movement organises across the different housing types of the working class, including those living in formal housing in former apartheid townships, informal shacks in townships and on occupied land, informal shacks built in the backyards of formal houses, and social housing either as RDP houses or high-rise buildings. The Housing Assembly has built its membership through visiting each household living in the areas in which it organises and through working with other community movements.

By 2010, the nascent movement was called in to deal with mass evictions that were taking place in the Western Cape. These evictions were directly related to South Africa hosting the football World Cup (Pillay et al., 2017). Many homeless people were moved off the streets in affluent areas where tourists were expected to visit; others were evicted off land where stadiums were being built to host the games. During this process, Housing Assembly activists met workers, unemployed people, young people looking for jobs and people in precarious employment. Realising that it was the same system which created unemployment, precarious work and homelessness, the Housing Assembly partnered with the South African Municipal Workers Union (SAMWU). The influence of working with a trade union can be seen in its working-class politics, democratic structures and accountability mechanisms.

By 2011 and 2012, it was clear that a movement was taking shape; the Housing Assembly had elected an interim committee made up of representatives from five districts and this would lead the movement towards its official launch in 2014. Its membership was made up of 50% women, and most of the district and executive leadership were, and still are, women who are active and vocal frontline activists in the struggle. The first Annual General Meeting of the newly launched Housing Assembly took place in 2015. The

Housing Assembly elected a woman as its chairperson – the first social movement in South Africa to be led by a woman.

Against the backdrop of the local government elections, 2016 became a critical year for the movement. The Housing Assembly started a two-month round of district meetings, ensuring that it was represented at all local government meetings to make sure that the housing crisis was on the political agenda. In that year they also launched the Campaign for Decent Housing along with other community organisations across the country. The Housing Assembly also participated, for the first time, in the city-wide Integrated Development Plan (IDP) process.* Despite their best intentions, they felt that their presence was used to legitimate the process and brought little concrete achievement. It would be the last time that the Housing Assembly participated in the IDP process, and an important lesson around state/social movement collaboration and the dangers of co-option.

THE NEPAL MADHES FOUNDATION, NEPAL

The fourth social movement institution is the Nepal Madhes Foundation (NEMAF), formed in 2007. The term 'Madhes' refers to the plains region of southern Nepal (also known as the Tarai) as well as some of the groups who live there. The Madhesi communities are very diverse, speak a range of languages and include Hindu caste groups and Muslims. Many of them have links to peoples living in the neighbouring states of India to the south. Historically, power in Nepal has been held by the ethnic groups based in the northern hills of the country, often referred to as Khas Arya. Groups from the northern hills who have moved into the Tarai are known as 'Pahadi' (or hill dwellers) to the Madhes people. The Madhesi ethnic groups historically suffered from the 'internal colonialism' of

---

* The Integrated Development Planning process was introduced during Mbeki's presidency. It involved a vertical and horizontal approach to planning: vertically, planning took place from the ward levels up to provincial level and horizontally, included a cross-government department approach. In theory it was supposed to democratise the government planning process; however, in practice it retained the space for elites as the IDP process was framed by the country's neoliberal economic policy.

the hill-based ethnic groups' dominance in political, economic and social domains. The Madhes' resistance erupted in 2007, following the peace agreement between the Maoists and the government of Nepal in November 2006. The resistance still continues in different forms, such as Madhes-based political parties, community mobilisation and self-organising resistance against structural inequalities, internal caste-based discriminations, lack of service delivery and poor life conditions of Madhesis.

The NEMAF is a non-governmental organisation that works as an independent intellectual and advocacy arm of the Madhes movement. Established in 2007, in the aftermath of the first Madhes uprising, the organisation's work broadly focuses on social, political and economic development in the most marginalised areas of Tarai/Madhes. In the past 14 years, it has implemented a wide range of programmes to promote social harmony, peace, security and good governance in Madhes. At the core of its work is the goal of social justice through the empowerment of the Madhesi people. NEMAF aims to help secure social, economic and political rights for Madhesis within the Nepali state. NEMAF conceptualises the notion of empowerment as a process of gaining critical knowledge about Madhesi history, language and literature, geography, and social issues, and promotes these through activism at grassroots, national and international levels. Located officially at Lalitpur, NEMAF conducts its activities both at the central and local levels, in collaboration with a broad range of stakeholders, including think tanks, human rights activists, NGOs and international development partners. NEMAF is committed to promoting inclusive democracy, social equality, social harmony, good governance and improved relations between Madhesi communities and the state.

NEMAF primarily operates within two interrelated domains of activity, the first of which relates to activism which supports and strengthens the gains of the Madhes movement and advocates for the protection of these gains – such as quotas for Madhesis in the civil service, legislature and security forces – as well as promoting good governance and protection of human rights in Madhes. It publishes opinion pieces in national newspapers and digital media, organises public discussion fora, and documents and archives knowledge about Madhes. The second domain is purely under the auspices of an NGO framework, operating with external funding to implement badly needed development projects in Madhes. It also carries out funded research to support programme implementation, advocacy and policy debate. All of these activities are interconnected and mutually reinforcing to the Madhesi cause.

The initial success of the Madhes movement in 2007 was when the term 'Madhes' and 'Madhesi' gained constitutional acceptance, which was a historic achievement. Many of the NEMAF members had been involved in the movement in different forms, including writing about Madhesi issues in the media, fighting legal battles against discriminatory practices and mobilising youth and cultural groups to join the Madhes struggle. Their backgrounds enabled the process of knowledge-making through continuous engagement with the grassroots populations, and by reporting their grievances and dimensions of struggle through publications. This systematic documentation has contributed to the legitimation of the struggle – helping to provide a theoretical rationale to the resistance based on intellectual ideas, social and political realities and the desperation and aspiration of the Madhesi population to achieve a dignified life in various realms of Nepali society. By engaging with public intellectuals, political leadership and the media, these grassroots narratives were translated into authoritative discourses to inform movement actions as well as to put pressure on the state to accede to social justice reforms.

In its early years, NEMAF concentrated its work on advocacy for constitutional issues such as federalism, social inclusion, state restructuring, citizenship rights and electoral reforms. It organised a series of discussions, dialogues and seminars, and began to document, compile and publish ideas emerging in these events. Aligning its activities with the agendas of the Madhes movement, it provided the urban elites in Kathmandu with evidence-based justification for the grievances of the Madhes. These events contributed to sensitisation relating to the prevalence of historical state domination and discrimination against the Madhesi people.

CHAPTER CONCLUSIONS: CROSS-CASE REFLECTIONS

In this study, we have four social movement institutions from four different regions and countries: Latin America (Colombia), Sub-Saharan Africa (South Africa), Europe/Asia (Turkey) and South Asia (Nepal). These distinct contexts include very different historical traditions, cultures of organising, and society/state relationships. They also share some similar challenges, such as the impacts of imperialism, predatory capitalism, environmental crises, authoritarian tendencies amongst elites, racism and patriarchal structures, and the challenges of constructing peace with social justice in highly unequal contexts. In terms of direct state repression, Colombia and Turkey compete in terms of brutality, assassinations, and imprisonment of activists, but in all of the contexts poor and marginalised communities suffer from repression by state actors. Recognising these convergences and divergences and keeping them in view is a crucial element of this research process.

Each movement is also institutionally distinct and operates at different scales. NOMADESC is an NGO providing popular education and support for the defence of human rights. Whilst it engages with issues at the national level, it is primarily focused on one region of the country, southwest Colombia. The Intercultural University of the Peoples (UIP), whilst created by NOMADESC, is made up of multiple representatives of social movements in this region, which have their own organisational structures and processes. NOMADESC and the UIP provide a node of contact for those movements, and a space for sharing and learning from other movements. The Housing Assembly is a grassroots organisation that emerged out of the struggles of homeless people in Cape Town, South Africa's most populous city. The Housing Assembly is perhaps the most grassroots of all the institutions under analysis, formed for shack dwellers by shack dwellers. Whilst it engages with issues at the national level, it is primarily focused on the City of Cape Town, and on the particular theme of housing and related social services. The People's Democratic Congress (HDK) is an umbrella institution made up of a wide cross-section of social movements, grassroots political organisations and movements representing the radical left, the Kurdish movement, gender, LGBTQ, ethnic and religious minorities across the entire territory of contemporary Turkey. Finally, NEMAF is an NGO that works on issues affecting the Madhes community on the Tarai plains of Nepal. It combines advocacy with running development projects to support a region that has been historically marginalised and population groups highly discriminated against. Whilst its focus and much of its practice is based in the Tarai region, it also has an office in Kathmandu which allows it to work on sensitisation and lobbying in Nepal's capital.

All our social movement institutions have complex links to a broader network of social movements and political parties. In Turkey, the HDK set up its own party, which is now a major political actor (HDP), so relations are extremely close. NEMAF in Nepal also has close relationships with political parties from the Tarai region. Both NOMADESC and the Housing Assembly have much more cautious and distant relationships with political parties. In recent years NOMADESC has engaged with both the Polo Democratico Alternative, a left-wing opposition party that emerged out of the trade union movement, and the Movimiento Progresista, but always at a critical distance. However, the Colombian general election in the summer of 2022 saw a shift in that strategy, with NOMADESC and its partners in the UIP supporting and endorsing the 'pacto historico' (Historic Pact), which now sees representatives of their movements in power. Finally, the Housing Assembly is the most sceptical of all of the movements in terms of its relationship with the main political parties in South Africa, particularly the ANC.

In the next three chapters, we explore the main findings of the research. In Chapter 3, we explore *how* these social movements learn and make knowledge. In Chapter 4, we explore *what* social movements learn and the types of knowledge they make. In Chapter 5, we explore the *effects* of this learning and knowledge-making on the movements and on the societies they operate in. Finally, in the Conclusion we *reflect* on the findings of the study and draw together some critical reflections.

3

How do social movements learn and make knowledge?

INTRODUCTION

Building on Foley's (1999) reflections on the way social movements and their activists learn, our starting point was to explore social movement learning as taking place through *formal education processes* (in educational institutions), *incidental learning* (as we engage with social movements in social protest and social action), *informal education* (where people teach and learn from each other) and *non-formal education* (structured systematic teaching and learning in a range of social settings), from workshops to conferences, to diploma courses, to reading groups. We later began to call these the 'spaces of social movement learning' and expanded the categorisation beyond the technical (formal, non-formal, informal, incidental) to understand the relational and situated nature of these diverse spaces and the subjects involved – because education is always a relational process, and occurs in particular contexts, with particular actors at particular moments.

Second, we explored the 'temporalities of learning'. This refers to the idea that both the capacity and the opportunity for members, leaders, and activists to learn is not flat and constant, but instead closely linked to the rhythms of the movements themselves, whose activities rise up and decline, in unpredictable ways. Moments of intense struggle, whether victorious or not, often represent tremendously important learning moments, whilst periods of low levels of activity and struggle might do the opposite. However, this might play out differently in the different movements. For example, massive repression might fragment, undermine and hinder collective learning processes, whilst periods of low social struggle might allow for space and time to engage and reflect on them. Similarly, in this understanding of the temporalities of learning, we homed in on the way movements often learn from their past (and from their older peers), learn in the present (through the day-to-day struggles and activities) and learn for the future. This includes learning about the history of their movements and their peoples' struggles, learning in the present in this multitude of 'spaces', and learning that is oriented towards the future. Linked to the temporality issue, across the case studies there is strong evidence of the importance of 'learning from key events' – which have the effect of focusing the movements' attention, providing concrete fora for debates around what has changed, and what it means for the movement, its present and its future.

Third, we explored the question of the 'Subjects of Learning and Knowledge-Making' – is it the leaders, activists, enemies, friends, the interested public, the general public, and what does that mean and imply? Depending on the nature of the movement, these constituencies were differentially targeted, as we shall demonstrate. Fourth, in thinking about how movements learn, an important issue emerged from our research related to the Emotional Dimensions of learning. Leaders, members and activists don't just learn with their minds; they also learn with their bodies and their emotions and feelings. How does that process happen? What are its catalysts and triggers? Fifth, we found that learning processes were not only taking place externally, as movements struggled against state forces, but also internally over the nature and shape of the movement being constructed. Finally, we explore the relationship between Activist Learning and Movement Learning; how do movements draw together lessons, learning, and insights from members and leaders and shape the institutional responses, what are the learning feedback loops between members and leaders?

Each of these issues: Spaces of Learning, Temporalities of Learning, Subjects of Learning and Knowledge-Making; Emotional Dimensions; Struggles Outside and Inside; and Activist Learning and Movement Learning will provide the framing for us to explore the question of how movements learn across the case studies. As we move through the issues, we draw on examples from the research to illustrate the different dimensions and nuance of the issues and findings. The evidence is meant to be illustrative, rather than representative of all the case studies, and hopefully will serve to stimulate further reflection.

SPACES OF LEARNING

NOMADESC's initiatives, from the Diploma in Human Rights that began in the early 2000s, to the Intercultural University of the Peoples that continues to date, reflect the fact that of all the social movement institutions under investigation in this research they are by far the most consciously pedagogical, and have made learning and knowledge-making a central pillar of their strategy for social movement renewal in southwest Colombia.

Theirs is a space of non-formal education that whilst evolving over time, revolves around some ongoing continuities: a strong commitment to building inter-movement, intercultural exchange, and an explicit programme of study that combines workshops and group learning with independent activist-led research rooted in exploring the challenges faced by their respective communities – for example exploring the relationship between resources, capitalist extraction and state and para-state violence. Support offered by NOMADESC and its members goes beyond the explicitly pedagogical, and includes accompaniment in their respective processes of community mobilisation, human rights support, guidance and ongoing solidarity. The NOMADESC team is in many ways a bridging organisation, whose networks extend geographically from the local to the global, and institutionally between human rights organisations, trade unions, lawyers, the media, diplomatic entities and international NGO partners and funders. It brings together both networks of contacts and expertise in the human rights domain and places them at the service of the social movements it engages with.

Within the pedagogical approach, there is also a strong drive to combine the theoretical/empirical with the experiential – in terms of engaging with and educating on the history, culture, politics and economics of contemporary Colombia in its relationship to global and national capitalist development. NOMADESC also seeks to provide technical skills and resources for the defence of human rights and social justice, whilst recognising that the tutor/teacher is not the holder of all knowledge, and that not all knowledge is or can be codified. That is to say that social movement knowledge is also tacit, sensory, instinctual and embedded in the bodies and minds of the activists, and revealing and unwrapping this tacit knowledge requires different spaces for knowledge sharing. The experiential knowledge is accessed not only by allowing participants to recount and be vindicated in their own praxis and activity, strategies and processes, but also by taking activists from different sectors, movements and cultures to physically visit their respective movement partners/colleagues to listen, to see, but also to feel and build empathy with the others' movement experience, their social reality and the challenges they face.

This pedagogical process, whilst taking place in these non-formal education spaces – workshops, meetings, field visits and so on – also very much takes place in those 'incidental' spaces around the structured events: in preparing collective meals, in sharing accommodation and socialising, in travelling to and marching in protests and solidarity events, in building friendships across divides, in participating in cultural events where participants are exposed to different cultures, values, histories, pain and joy. The pain often comes from remembering those that have been killed by state and para-state violence, of whom, in southwest Colombia, there are many. The joy is rooted in the rich cultural, artistic, musical offerings of participants and the famous and often sardonic Colombian sense of humour (see the section 'Emotional Dimensions' below).

Central to all of the above is the intercultural as the central space of encounter; and whilst the culture is indeed concretised around ethnicity and race (promoting 'contact' between black movements, indigenous and mestizo), it is also about geography, labour and gender – from the relationship between the trade unionist working in urban public services and the campesino, the sugar cane worker and the unemployed, as well as between the urban dweller and the rural, the highlander and the coastal inhabitant, the man and the woman, and the young and the old.

The space of intercultural encounter encompasses reflections and learnings on all these differences, not in the pursuit of unity through erasing these differences under the banner of commonality, but of mutual respect and understanding. This process is known as the 'dialogo de saberes' (dialogue of knowledges), in which people exchange ideas from different standpoints and resolve issues through self-reflection and dialogue. Similarly, whilst participants in the Diploma and UIP Programme – 'the diplomados' – are the major and direct beneficiaries of these learning and knowledge-making experiences, they are also transmitted to other members of their respective social movements through the compulsory implementation of replication sessions in a classical 'cascade' manner – where the 'trainee' becomes the 'trainer', and therefore extends the 'spaces of learning' geographically to their own social movement.

Similarly, the connection between the 'diplomados' from the same organisation, and between years, further builds that institutional learning process. This is further strengthened by NOMADESC's direct support for these movements – at an institutional level – as they engage in the process of struggle and resistance. The 'space of learning' for NOMADESC thus becomes holistic, geographically expansive, multi-site and non-formal, informal and incidental – and in the initial Diploma, which was offered in partnership with a local university in Cali – also formal.

For the Housing Assembly in South Africa, the 'spaces of learning' are intimately implicated in the foundation of the movement. Founded by a group of homeless individuals facing daily evictions from occupied lands, they began visiting ILRIG (International Labour Research and Information Group), a local, popular education and trade union support centre – not so dissimilar to Colombia's NOMADESC. In ILRIG, and through the powerful presence of Michael Blake, a leading ILRIG activist and researcher, they were eventually inducted into an educational process, rooted in popular education techniques, influenced by Freire, but equally by the South

African struggle against apartheid, and iconic figures such as Steve Biko and his Black Consciousness Movement. ILRIG provided them with the space and orientation to start analysing their own situation, how to change it and the destination of travel. In that process they learnt about self-organisation, Marxism and capitalism, apartheid and its resistance, and the role of solidarity in building a better world.

Central to the Housing Assembly's pedagogy is the space of the home: as a space of organisation, but also a site of memory. The foundational event for the Housing Assembly, which is recounted again and again, was the founding members' initial experience of land occupation, daily eviction, police brutality and state neglect. As a space of organisation and of learning, the home became the central site of organising and building the movement. Activists would visit each and every house/structure in an organising area before building up to local 'speak-outs' where residents would share their stories, struggles and aspirations. These 'door-to-door' and 'speak-outs' were organising mechanisms directly derived from the civic movement's struggles against apartheid, and transmitted through ILRIG's historical memory – a good example of inter-generational learning.

In these learning processes, participants would not only share their realities, but also learn about the law and their rights – to housing and basic services and how to access them, evictions and how to resist them – both legally and physically. The home as a site of organising, as Benjamin (2021) notes in the full study, was a gendered space, and it was women that were often at the forefront of the movement as they defended their family's right to exist, subsist and flourish. As a result, the Housing Assembly's struggles and learning processes were not only external – state, police, local government – they were also internal, about changing patriarchal attitudes to domestic chores, childcare responsibilities and the broader gendered division of labour, within their own family structures.

For NEMAF, an organisation that emerged out of the early struggles and political reawakening of the Madhes community during the Maoist uprisings in Nepal, their spaces of learning and knowledge-making have been both in the Tarai region and in Kathmandu, the administrative and intellectual capital of Nepal. For NEMAF, the Nepali state's national cultural homogenisation project (Onta, 1996) had long repressed Madhesi cultural identity, language and way of life, and whilst the restoration of democracy in 1990 reinstated the powers of political parties, Madhesis were once again sidelined and their legitimate grievances ignored, which gave rise to new forms of resistance across the Tarai region.

In Kathmandu, after processes of research and writing, NEMAF sought to present information about the Madhes, their history, their struggles, and the discrimination they have faced historically in the popular press, in the media, and in public meetings and events.

> In the early years of its inception, NEMAF concentrated its work on advocacy for constitutional issues such as federalism, social inclusion, state restructuring, citizenship rights, electoral reforms etc. It organised a series of discussions, dialogues and seminars and began to document, compile and publish ideas emerging in these events. Aligning its activities with the agendas of the Madhes movement, it provided evidence-based justification to the grievances of the Madhes among the urban elites in Kathmandu. These events contributed to the sensitistisation of the prevalence of historical state domination and discrimination against the Madhesi people.
>
> (Pherali and NEMAF, 2021: 79)

NEMAF's work, alongside many others from the Madhesi community, is a good example of what Santos (2001) calls the 'sociology of absences', researching and telling the stories of those that have been written out of history, absent from the national narrative, victims of what he calls 'epistemicide'. NEMAF's work in this process of cultural recognition and vindication involved both trying to raise awareness amongst non-Madhesi intelligentsia and strengthening the self-identity of Madhesi youth in the Tarai region. In that process, there are echoes of Steve Biko's 'black consciousness' movement in South Africa, with Madhesi communities recovering a sense of collective identity, collective dignity and a framing of the multiple dimensions of the discrimination they have faced at the hands of national Nepali elites. In this sense, NEMAF's focus was on both an 'internal' Madhes learning space, and an 'external' one that extended beyond Nepal to the international sphere: proclaiming that as Madhes, we are oppressed, we exist and we resist!

NEMAF, therefore, served as a *dialogical bridge* between the dominant political discourses in the centre and the struggle for Madhesi democratic rights, the question of equity and civic engagement. This could be understood as a process of *political translation*, 'a disruptive and communicative practice developed by activists and grassroots community organisers to address the inequities that hinder democratic deliberation, and to entreat powerful groups to work more inclusively with disempowered ones' (Doerr, 2018: 3). NEMAF plays a role not as a neutral facilitator of the dialogue between the marginalised Madhesi voice and elites, but as a *disruptive third* that is able to utilise its persuasive power drawn from its understanding of 'the values of the privileged groups and the needs of marginalised ones' by '... directing attention to power imbalances and drawing on the egalitarian commitments of those who otherwise would be unlikely to recognise their own structural privilege' (Doerr, 2018: 4). The *dialogic bridge* is built not only through the translation of Madhesi grievances into evidence-based persuasive narratives that rupture elitist approaches to purported grassroots representation, but also as a process in which the dominant political actors are compelled to listen to the lived experiences of Madhesis in discussion fora. Hence, NEMAF's intellectual endeavours are not limited to mitigation of linguistic or cultural subordination of Madhesis, but seek to go beyond in order to generate and exercise agency for transformative change.

For HDK, the movement itself had a built-in spatial and strategic pedagogy, constructed as the mirror opposite to the homogenous state – 'one nation, one religion, one flag'. HDK's core identity was the cultural, political, linguistic and ethnic diversity of Turkey's rich landscape. By bringing together such a diversity of movements under the umbrella of the Peoples' Democratic Congress (HDK), every space of engagement was a potential learning and knowledge-making site, and an intercultural encounter. From the women's movements to left-wing revolutionary organisations, to the Kurdish Liberation Movement, Alevi, other minority ethnic groups and LGBTQ, young activists and old, all had to learn to interact with each other, to learn with and from each other, and to build common agendas and platforms. In contrast to the construction of Turkish hegemony as unity in homogeneity, the HDK was a call to arms for unity through diversity.

Working through the space of the 'Assembly' became a key mechanism for the expression of this horizontal, inclusive, democratic aspiration. Michael Hardt and Antonio Negri see the assembly concept as the vehicle 'to grasp the power of coming together and acting politically in concert' and regard the assembly as 'a lens through which to recognise new democratic political possibilities' (Negri and Hardt, 2019: 23). For the HDK, Article 16 in their founding statutes (HDK, 2012: 4) notes that 'Our Congress regards assemblies as the fundamental tool for democracy to win and for the oppressed to become the subject of politics'. The assemblies were the space where this intercultural political dialogue would take place, a site of intense learning. These assemblies were both geographical and also thematic (labour, health, women, ecological) in bringing together different constituencies. There were also special commissions, such as the 'Rights and Beliefs Commission', which worked on developing a counter-memory to the official narrative, and like the NEMAF work in Nepal, highlighted both the cultural richness and diversity of Turkey and the historical oppression and repression of minorities.

Whilst by no means the only 'space of learning', the Rights and Beliefs Commission is an important illustrative example of the types of opportunities for learning that were created within the Congress. One of the most exciting dimensions in the formation of the People's Democratic Congress is the wide range of struggles encompassed within it, from identity to class, gender and ecology. Whilst the official state perspective was associated with the denial of ethnic and religious variety in Turkey, as well as 'discipline and expulsion' policies based on this denial, the HDK's approach in contrast defied this monistic state, and encouraged various oppressed groups to align themselves with the HDK.

As an illustrative example, the Rights and Beliefs Commission, as a 'space of learning', made two extremely important contributions to HDK. First, it provided the opportunity for a shared space for different groups that have had little opportunity to engage with each other. This allowed for the sharing of knowledge of each other's history, religion, culture and language. Interactions between people with different beliefs and ethnic identities, such as Kurds, Alevi, Arabs, Cherkess, Pomaks, Armenians, Georgians, Laz, Muslims, Rum and Assyrians, created a transformative experience for activists in many ways. Out of this emerged a Panel Series entitled 'Peoples and Beliefs Are Talking about Themselves'. These panels allowed representatives from one ethnic or belief group to talk about themselves, enabling activists in the Congress to hear about the cultural diversity in Turkey directly from those groups. For example, in 2019 alone, eight panels were organised and, in these panels, Alevi, Arabian Alevi, Assyrians, Armenians, Cherkess (Abkhaz, Osset, Ubykh), Hemşin and Laz people talked about themselves. In these events, diversity was considered as a resource, and valued as a fundamental part of the common struggle of ignored, oppressed, suppressed and degraded minorities, and these were crucial learning processes for the activists involved.

Second, the Rights and Beliefs Commission made a central contribution to challenging official/public memory that had been built on the basis of the official historical narrative in Turkey. In doing so it drew together alternative historical narratives, exchanged them between different groups and through inter-generational exchange, creating a powerful counter-collective memory. These *counter-memories*, entirely excluded in the public domain, were included in the HDK and presented as a new form of collective memory. Violence, resistance and mourning in the history of each group was introduced to other groups in the Congress, and progressively evolved into a common memory. For example, the accumulated learnings of the Rights and Beliefs Commission concerning the commemorations and celebrations of each group were gathered together and included in a Peoples and Beliefs Calendar. Memorial practices to commemorate events such as the Armenian and Assyrian (Seyfo) genocide, Pontus genocide, 6–7 September pogrom, Maraş, Çorum, Sivas and Gazi massacres; various commemorations and celebrations such as Easter, Eid al-Fitr and Eid al-Adha, the Armenian grape celebration, Arabian Alevi Gadir Hum celebration, Alevi Muharrem fasting, and Yezidi celebrations were all organised by the HDK Rights and Beliefs Commission, and these activities collectively formed a challenge to official history. This collective memory shows the determination and wisdom of the current struggle. This learning space provided a unique venue for exchanging hitherto silenced cultures and traditions, vindicating their existence and celebrating their rituals and practices. As activists engaged in these spaces, they both taught and learnt of the rich diversity that exists in Turkey, and in doing so laid the foundations for a different future reality.

Similarly, there was also a vibrant women-only assembly, which provided a space for women collectively to address issues and develop strategies. This was both a space through which to work out an agreed women's position on issues within the HDK, but also a space for dialogue between groups, where the urban-based feminist movement engaged with the Kurdish feminist movement (also see the section 'Gender as a route to liberation' below).

The organisational form of the HDK, its repertoire of struggle, and the diversity of its members affected both the means and forms of learning within the movement. In contrast to the central and hierarchical structure of the classical party-type organisation, taking part in a horizontal, pluralist and consensus-based Congress-type organisation generates a different type of learning experience. Eyerman and Jamison (1991), with their concept of 'cognitive praxis', draw attention to the 'cosmological', 'technological' and 'organisational' effects of organisation in social movements on movement actors (and society). 'Cognitive praxis', according to them, refers to a process whereby activists as movement intellectuals collectively transform the historical trajectory and collective memory/identity and 'rewrite' the cognitive understandings of the social environment in which they operate through engaging in various forms of 'knowledge practices' ('cosmological', 'technological' and 'organisational') (Taylor, 2013). Thus, the institutional form or structure of social movements, the form and style of work within the movement, the nature of internal communications and decision-making processes are all integral parts of this process of rewriting cognitive praxis. To this extent, the HDK's new strategy of social transformation as outlined in its programme, its new political form that brings together the rich diversity of peoples in Turkey on the basis of equality and recognition, its organisational structure, decision-making process and libertarian radical pedagogy are fundamentally geared towards constituting a new 'cognitive praxis' that can bring about the desired societal transformation by the practices and articulation of its movement actors.

The highly dynamic nature of the inter-generational learning experience and transfer within the HDK has also become an important arena for the process of constituting this collective 'cognitive praxis'. Indeed, by bringing those activists who have been part of the struggle since the 1960s together with those young activists whose first experience is joining in the struggle of the HDK, the movement created an 'inter-generational pedagogical space' where rich knowledge sharing takes place. No doubt, the co-existence of various activists coming from different generations at the HDK commissions, governing bodies and assemblies and their participation and engagement in everyday struggle increases the interactions and encounters between these different generations and provides an opportunity for them to learn from each other. Taking part in the struggle alongside each other enables the transfer of knowledge and practice about history, culture and daily life. The range of diversity between and within these generations in terms of class, education, culture and sexual orientation further enriches the content and nature of this process. For this reason, the HDK exemplifies an important space as well as a means for rich inter-generational learning and knowledge transfer.

Similarly, the experience of being together and engaging in the struggle with a range of political parties, people from alternative

media, foundations, platforms and individuals from different political traditions provided an important learning experience in terms
of creating a common sense of belonging and a collective movement
(the HDK) identity. The HDK, as an organisation of commoning based on the idea of a 'new life' that is imagined as classless,
non-exploitative, gender egalitarian and sensitive to social ecology,
builds a new emotional and discursive 'cognitive praxis' amongst its
movement actors. As we will see in the following sections, this new
'cognitive praxis' is being woven not only through *material labour*
but also by *non-material affective labour*.

TEMPORALITIES OF LEARNING

The second dimension of the 'how' of social movements learning, is
related to temporality. We define this, following McLeod (2017: 13),
'not as a fancier word for time, but as signifying the messy, moving
relations between past, present and future'.

In the HDK case, Kutan and Çelik (2021) talk about *Learning in
Struggle*, *Learning from Struggle* and *Learning to Struggle* to highlight
this dimension. Whilst inevitably there is some overlap between this
'temporal' focus and 'spaces of learning', there is something useful
about framing this in terms of 'in', 'from' and 'to', in allowing us to
capture the interactions between time and space, whereby the first
is rooted firmly in the present, the second looking back to the near
or far past, and the third projecting forward to the future. Centrally,
the classification of these three forms of learning processes emerges
out of our aim to draw attention to the *forms* (structured, unstructured, latent), *temporal* (short-, medium- and long-term), *spatial*
(inside-outside, central-local) and *situational* (instant, under difficult conditions, need-based) contexts of the learning processes.
However, it is important to note that these three processes are interrelated, intertwined, and reciprocal, and each mutually constitutes
the other.

Learning in Struggle represents the process whereby activists,
and by default the movement, learn through the day-to-day actions
that are produced through engagement in social movements. These

unstructured learning processes include going on marches, preparing for marches, attending press conferences, attending meetings, what Aziz Choudry often called the 'grunt work' of movements. These are learning processes where you are both learning by doing, but also learning from others around you. As one HDK activist notes:

> Of course, you learn a lot of things. For example, you learn how to write a press release. You learn how to read a press release, how to negotiate with the police, how to act towards the police when your friend is detained, which actions will cause you to be beaten or what you need to do to avoid being beaten etc. ... You learn by experience and from the environment. Of course, there are people more experienced than you and you are more experienced than others. You share all your experiences. As if some of our friends are born to write press releases. Some were good writers and others were not.
>
> (Individual Interview T4, HDK Youth Assembly Activist, cited in Kutan and Çelik, 2021: 82)

The nature of this Learning in Struggle process is not generic, but dependent upon the context and the organisational/movement structure. As a 'Congress', the HDK model of organising was itself explicitly open to participation, engagement, interaction. Similarly, its openness to all the diversity of Turkey's left-out majority (Kurds, the left, women's movement, LGBTQ, religious and minoritised groups) meant that the space for Learning in Struggle was rich in diversity and experience, facilitating intercultural and inter-generational learning and knowledge exchange.

Whilst rich in learning potential, HDK spaces were also sometimes challenging, for both individuals and movements that were perhaps not skilled and experienced in relating to different social groups and might lack the knowledge and language to respectfully engage with the 'other'. It is in these spaces that the 'traditional' Kurdish activist might encounter a member of LGBTQ for the first time, or where a Turk, politically schooled in orthodox leftist class struggle, is confronted with issues around ethnicity and identity in challenging ways.

Relatedly, new Learning in Struggle opportunities were also presented by the HDK in the special commissions, which went deeper into specific issues such as 'gender; rights and beliefs; education etc.'. Within these examples of Learning in Struggle there is also a sense of dynamism in the content of learning, dependent upon the nature of the struggles that the movements are involved in at particular times. From 2011 onwards, activists in the HDK were engaged in struggles related to supporting the mother-tongue language for Kurdish political prisoners, engaging with the hunger strikes in support of demands to end the solitary confinement and harsh treatment of PKK leader Öcalan, the Gezi Park protests, support for Rojava, and the HDP election campaigns. Each represented moments through which new skills, insights, knowledge and learnings were gained, exchanged and developed.

Similarly, from all of the other case studies, we can see ways in which Learning in Struggle took place. The Madhes movement provided a remarkable level of political consciousness to ordinary Madhesis. It helped them rupture historically imposed hegemonic discourses about what counts as being a 'Nepali' (Lal, 2012). By engaging in the movement, Madhesis not only learnt about their economic, political and social marginality within the state but also learnt how to resist marginalisation. In this process, the widespread experience of discrimination and injustice became an entry point for learning about the 'generative mechanisms' (Bhaskar, 2008) that produced those experiences. It provided them with an opportunity to engage with much deeper causes of discrimination, such as the history of the country, political system, and state policies on education, language, civil service recruitment. A female activist in a town near Birgunj stated:

I was in the college during the first Madhes movement. The Federal Socialist Forum Nepal [FSFN] had organised an interaction programme in our college. There, for the first time, I got to know how Madhesis were being marginalised. Their agenda deeply interested me. In the college hostel, we, Madhesi girls used to face discrimination but had never thought about it from a political perspective. Slowly, I came to realise broader structural issues in our society. Then, I began to participate in various interaction programmes at schools and colleges. I also received training on how to politically educate and mobilise people for the struggle.

(Madhesi Woman Activist 4, Birgunj, cited in Pherali and NEMAF, 2021: 162)

For Housing Assembly activists in South Africa, we can see how the direct experience of evictions allowed them to develop a sophisticated knowledge of laws, and the limits of what the state can and cannot do. It also brought into sharp relief the nature of police forces and their priorities. This seems to be a cross-case commonality, that when 'in' the struggle, activists begin to see the reality of the state forces that are supposed to protect them, but instead often brutalise them. A powerful example of this occurred in the HDK case, whereby a female interviewee talked about how her mother joined her at the Gezi protests, and witnessed first-hand the brutality of the police, and their violence against both property and protesters, which changed her perceptions forever. All of these examples give flesh to the notion that activism is itself an important learning experience, whereby through putting 'body and soul' into the movement, you learn experientially in often deep and profound ways.

Learning From Struggle provides a lens on how learning and knowledge-making develop through the specific struggle knowledge that emerges out of critical and collective reflections on specific movement protest/historic events. In the case of HDK, there are pivotal events in the evolving history of the movement that led to spaces of reflection emerging in the wake of the Gezi Park protests, in the wake of elections, in the aftermath of the collapse of the peace process, the failed military coup. All of these rich movement/societal events present themselves as 'learning from' key events.

In the case of the failed peace negotiations, one HDK activist noted that the movement really failed to do what was necessary to sustain and support the process:

There is one thing clear; we clearly wasted the peace period. This is true for Turkish politics, Turkish leftists and Kurds. Because during peace meetings, Öcalan said the following specifically from İmralı; peace can be earned with the society. Something earned with social struggle. This is what we call the socialisation of the peace. The public should demand peace. Of course, there will be tables and I will tell everything; but this should have power behind it. This power should be civil society power. In this sense, we need to openly and clearly see that we should have self-criticism for the peace period because we were unable to create a mass movement for peace. I mean, we did not have millions of children, women, elderly on the streets demanding peace. We needed to do that during peace negotiations. For example, millions or hundreds of thousands of women should have marched to support this peace. Children should have walked and said they no longer wanted war. We should have transformed it into a social demand. It should have turned into a demand beyond PKK, Öcalan or the Kurds being tired of war, into a demand for the whole of Turkey.

(Individual Interview T53,
cited in Kutan and Çelik, 2021: 93–94)

Similarly, and not unrelated, rich learning processes – both positive and negative – came out of the Gezi Park protests, which emerged out of popular attempts to defend a conservation site targeted for redevelopment by the Turkish government in 2013. On the one hand, Gezi represented a concrete bottom-up manifestation of the aspiration of the HDK Congress model: a diverse, mass participation, multi-sectoral movement, which was prefigurative in its construction, imaginative and powerful. Whilst many HDK activists participated in the protest, and were directly involved in constructing the horizontal organisational forms that emerged, the HDK itself initially was not, due to multiple organisational constraints and failures. At the time, the peace process negotiations were in a delicate state, and one of the main components of the HDK, the Kurdish Liberation Movement, felt constrained. This led to deep tensions within the HDK components, particularly those who saw in Gezi a potential revolutionary moment, and a chance to build a new movement.

In a similar manner NOMADESC and the UIP note that:

> we learn from the organising processes of the movements we work with, and I could give three examples: the struggle of SIN-TRAEMCALI was a school for us from which we learned so much; the Minga of Social and Communitarian Resistance of 2008 was a school which we learned from – we learned to walk the word; and the Buenaventura civic strike [2017] was a school.
>
> (NOMADESC founding member and currently
> a leading member of the organisation, interview,
> 2018, cited in Kane and NOMADESC, 2021: 104)

Each of these big 'events' marked a turning point in the movement's evolution, where NOMADESC and later the UIP would reflect on what happened, what they did or didn't do, the activities of the state, alliances constructed or fractured, which would lead to new trajectories and thinking. For example, in the SINTRAEMCALI event, there was a strong recognition of the power of the trade union/community alliance. There was also a strong reflection on the power of the symbolic: hundreds of masked workers occupying the headquarters of public services in Cali, Colombia's second city – 'Nos Cubrimos El Rostro Para Que Nos Vieran' (we cover our faces so that we can be seen). Ultimately, there was also a recognition that despite the massive odds, the violent repression, ordinary people can do extraordinary things and prevent injustices (Novelli, 2010). Crucially, the SINTRAEMCALI experience provided the foundations for the intercultural pedagogical logic that has since provided the central organising principle of NOMADESC in both the Diploma in Human Rights and the UIP.

For the Housing Assembly, the first eviction experience became the event that has shaped their whole approach:

> The Housing Assembly was born out of an eviction in post-apartheid South Africa. In 2008, a group of landless and homeless

families had occupied land in Cape Town. They erected structures out of scrap materials. On that piece of land there was no access to water or toilets. The families, including children and babies, stayed in these conditions for months. Every day they were violently and repeatedly evicted by the City of Cape Town's anti-land invasion unit. Every day, the homeless families would dismantle and bury the materials used to build their shacks. In the evening they would dig up their materials and reconstruct their houses. This was the only way they could prevent their daily evictions and destruction of their homes. As if this was not enough violence and cruelty, one of the families lost their baby, and had to bury the body of the baby in the same place where they would bury their scrap materials for their homes. This powerful story has been told so many times by the founding members of the Housing Assembly and is deeply embedded in the historical memory and DNA of the movement. It is the story that has formed the core of their struggle.

(Benjamin, 2021: 52)

For NEMAF, the series of Madhes uprisings provided the 'event' material for their reflections.

On 16 January 2007, a group of Madhesi activists representing Madhesi Janadhikar Forum Nepal led by their leader Upendra Yadav burnt copies of the interim constitution at Maitighar Mandala in Kathmandu. They accused the government of ignoring the Madhesi people's demands for federalism. The leader and the activists were detained and charged with a public order offence. This triggered a series of protests in the southern plains of Nepal leading to the death of 16-year-old student, Ramash Kumar Mahato in Lahan. The mass demonstration following the killing turned into the first Madhes uprising which lasted for 21 days. The following year, the second Madhes uprising erupted demanding reforms in the electoral system to address the problem of underrepresentation of Madhesis and their equitable access to state mechanisms such as the bureaucracy, judiciary and security domains. The third uprising in 2015 was linked with the declaration of the 2015 constitution of Nepal which undermined the inclusive rights of the Interim 2008 constitution of Nepal and various historical agreements between previous governments and the Madhes movement.

(Pherali and NEMAF, 2021: 22)

Each uprising represented both a claim and a stage in the ongoing struggle for equality – from the 2007 recognition of existence as a collective social subject, to 2008, where the Madhes called for electoral reform to redress under-representation, and 2015 when they demanded constitutional inclusion, each uprising event providing a set of new and adapted demands that were then carried forward as a legacy of the events.

Regardless of whether these 'learning from' events demonstrate hope, pain, or regret, they are without doubt crucial laboratories of learning, where theory meets practice, where the organisation/movement is tested in real-time and aspirations often meet the cold realities of the Realpolitik. Reflecting on these movements provides the impetus to revamp, tweak or overhaul their respective strategies and move their struggles forward. Each of the above examples are illustrative, and many more could have been discussed that have equally shifted the respective social movements' strategic practice and form part of the historical memory of the movements.

Learning to Struggle speaks to the process of deliberately constructing learning and knowledge spaces, an explicit process akin to Foley's non-formal education processes, and with a future-oriented trajectory. These Learning to Struggle processes are asking the question, what does the movement, its members and activists, need to know, what are the learning needs of the organisation, and how can we develop them?

Whilst since its creation in 2011, the HDK was clearly a forum and laboratory for learning and knowledge-making, it was nevertheless slow to formalise learning within its organisational structures and processes. However, educational events that first started for activists within the movement eventually evolved into HDK Schools, with the idea to make the 'new life' perspective of the HDK accessible to a broader section of society who shared libertarian perspectives and were open to critical pedagogy.

One-day education modules set up by the HDK Education Commission at the local organisation level, annual summer camps and thematic conferences, an Ata Soyer Health Policy School (working together with the HDK's Health Assembly), and plans for HDK Schools, all aimed at radically questioning neoliberal global capitalist modernity, the nation-state paradigm, the patriarchal gender regime and inequality-based human-centric society–nature relationships. These programmes drew on a libertarian pedagogy based on critical consciousness that sought to cultivate the realisation of an alternative 'new life' ideal.

For NOMADESC, central to both the Diploma and the UIP was a future-oriented approach aimed at providing participants with the tools to deepen their political knowledge and praxis. The intercultural dialogical space of the UIP sessions would allow for collective learning about different movements, the history of the country and the region, strategies and tactics, and human rights protection measures. The UIP also provides the participants with research skills that they would apply to researching their social, political and economic environment, exploring the practices of corporations, of patterns of violence, etc. Similarly, for NOMADESC/UIP leaders these were moments where they themselves would learn from participants, gain insights and build knowledge that could provide new ways of thinking about strategy.

Learning to Struggle, thus appears as the most strategic and interventionist dimension and its most explicitly educational. In those future-oriented pedagogical spaces the research and planning, the skills and abilities that movements perceive necessary for the struggles to come are developed, discovered, refined and sharpened.

SUBJECTS OF LEARNING AND KNOWLEDGE-MAKING

It is evident from the case study research that knowledge and learning in and through social movements is complex and involves a range of constituencies or subjects. From the activist to the leaders, the engaged public to the general public, to friends and enemies there are a range of relational learning and knowledge processes taking place. We should also recognise that our different social movement institutions operate on different scales, from the local, the city, the regional, the national and international, and this is reflected in the targeting of different audiences. Common across all the movements is a breaking down of traditional knowledge hierarchies and a recognition that ordinary people are also knowledge bearers. Clearly, these hierarchies between leaders/activists/intellectuals/masses are never completely erased, and some have more time than others to focus energy on learning, reading, thinking and acting. However, there is a strong sense across the cases that every activist inside the movement has the potential to become a leader, and that formal education is not the only indicator of wisdom.

For NOMADESC/UIP, there is a strong focus on building up a cadre of new leaders, often young, who will then return to their movements and, through replication workshops and through modelling leadership will spread the ideas and thinking built into both the earlier Diploma programme and the subsequent UIP. Through active work on social media and the production of audio-visual materials, they also reach out to a broader Colombian activist community, but with a distinct focus on southwest Colombia. NOMADESC, as a human rights organisation, also spends time advocating with and educating international human rights activists, organisations and networks on the situation in southwest Colombia, both through the production of materials (written and audio-visual), and also through delegations to and from these constituencies (international delegations to the region, sending delegates to US and Europe). This would include both mainstream human rights organisations, and solidarity/social movements. Its work on human rights violations also leads it to engage with 'victims' of human rights abuses, not all of whom are necessarily actors and members of social movements. The process of accompaniment, defence and informal processes of education about the situation in Colombia, often transforms these actors from passive victims into active subjects, as we shall see in a later section.

For the HDK in Turkey, subjects of education and knowledge-making range from the development of leadership cadres to the broader membership, national social movement fora, and media and the general public. Access to the general public has reduced markedly in recent years after the HDK/HDP was de-facto criminalised, and access to national media drastically curtailed. This contrasts markedly with the peace negotiation period, when access to national media was much more fluid. Ironically, it is during the period when there are fewer possibilities to engage broadly that the HDK has begun to develop a more overt education strategy, through the HDK Schools etc. One important constituency and social subject that has been visibilised within the HDK since its foundation is the 'independent', that is those individuals engaged with the political left and social movements, but not affiliated to a political party. By incorporating a quota system for the representation of 'independents', the HDK created a space for the engagement of a 'new' political subject.

For NEMAF, Madhes leaders and potential leaders, the broader Madhesi community, and Nepal intellectual elites seem to have been the targets of its interventions. Evident in the case study findings is the recognition that more needs to be done to engage with grassroots Madhesi populations as NEMAF moves forward. Finally, for the Housing Assembly, the focus has been on building a cadre of movement activists ('everyone a leader'), emerging from the community, and more generally to raise awareness amongst precarious shack dwellers of their rights and their situation.

Across the movements, we can see the emergence of a desire for more horizontal relationships and broad education processes. For the Housing Assembly, this is captured in the phrase 'everyone an organiser'; for NOMADESC and the UIP, there is a recognition of the wisdom of the people, captured in the notion of the 'dialogo de saberes' – that everyone has something to give, and everyone can learn from each other. Common in this is the idea of 'leyendo el territorio': an illiterate peasant can 'read the territory', a black community activist and an indigenous activist carry 'ancestral knowledge' that is passed on through oral histories, stories, songs. Engagement between different types of knowledge has the potential to produce new, productive ways of understanding and changing the world.

In all of the case studies, the most intense learning processes are experienced by the activists of the movements. Whilst NOMADESC is the only one that has called itself a university (UIP), there is a sense that for all activists joining the movement, engaging with the movement is an intense learning experience that is often more educative and transformative than that of a formal university – a process whereby activists learn about their history, learn new skills, have their previous opinions and perceptions challenged, and build self-confidence. For many, it is life-changing. For the HDK activists the transformative power of the movement is apparent, as it is for Madhes movement activists who reported that participation in the struggle had built their confidence to verbally and physically resist discriminatory treatment of Madhesis by authorities and dominant ethnic groups in Nepal. In both countries, where difference is denied, where cultures and histories and religions are suppressed, the space of the HDK and the Madhes movement comes across as a radically transformative one for activists.

Beyond activist learning, for all movements there is an education/ knowledge function that the movement performs for the public: educating, engaging, informing, enraging – through media, through public events, press releases, festivals, protests and mobilisations. For NEMAF, a key initial target has been the Kathmandu intelligentsia, who through literature, public events, debates, have been made aware of the existence of the Madhes community, its historical marginalisation and the inhumane treatment it has received. Just as mobilisations and protests in the Tarai created a space for the recognition of the Madhes as a social subject – and put them on the political map – so these engagement processes have created an intellectual space.

For the Housing Assembly, the 'door-to-door' and 'speak-outs' as well as being 'spaces' of education are also potential recruiting processes for activists, as well as fora for teaching and learning in which

Housing Assembly activists can convey the knowledge they have, but also learn of the different experiences of communities in order to further build their own understanding of the situation. When activists turn up outside the house of a minister, with banners and placards, and talk about the crisis of housing in Cape Town, they are targeting different audiences – both the civil servant and MP and the general public are being told 'we are here, we exist, we demand this'. In this sense, the demonstration, the picket, the protest, the riot, are all educational events – with a pedagogy to communicate a message to a range of audiences; a message that is oral, written, visual and symbolic.

For NOMADESC, supporting the victims of human rights violations' next of kin after an act of violence (for example, an extra-judicial execution) is a key activity. This engagement implies not only the human rights and humanitarian aspect, but also a peda-gogical process in helping relatives to understand the systematic criminal behaviour of the state, and how these crimes are part of the modus operandi of the security forces. This also serves as a process of collectivising and sharing the sense of loss among the activists, becoming a pedagogical tool. In this way, the category of victim is transformed from one of passivity to a political category and spur to activism. During the period under analysis, the category of 'victim' emerged as a social and political subject in itself, with its movements, its cognitive framings and its repertoires of struggles and actions – embedded in, but also alongside intersectional trade union, peasant, and Afro-Colombian movements and identities.

EMOTIONAL DIMENSIONS

Becoming an activist is a dangerous undertaking, particularly in contexts of authoritarianism and repression. To think that people do this purely based on a logical analysis of the facts feels illogical at best. In the Latin American context, the notion of 'senti-pen-sar' (feeling/thinking) captures the complex relationship between emotions and thought processes, and the dynamic relationship between thinking and feeling. For NOMADESC and the UIP this concept of 'senti-pensar' runs across the whole pedagogical process. The link between thought, action and emotion is often expressed through the concept – central to 'social humanism'* – of an 'ethical position in the face of the conflict'. Wrapped up in this is an appreciation and remembrance of the fallen, through the ritualisation of their memory. These 'martyrs' are often called upon before the beginning of events, or at the end of events: 'Companero Eduardo Umana Mendoza, presente, presente, presente', then followed by vocalising another victim, and another. Visual 'galleries of memory' that exhibit the names and pictures of murdered comrades, play a similar role in recalling the past but also triggering powerful emotions of connection, commitment and continuity of struggle: summoning the fallen and carrying them with you in the struggle.

In NOMADESC, they also draw upon the concept of 'mistica', which has emerged in Latin America, to explain a bonding process that emerges out of a fusion of endogenous cultural rituals, liberation theology and left-wing popular resistance. The process of 'mistica', as Hammond (2014: 372) notes, in relation to the Brazilian social movement MST (the Landless Workers' Movement):

> refers to an expressive performance, mainly nonverbal, that incorporates themes central to the goals of the movement and affirms confidence in the achievability of those goals. It is a regular practice of the MST. It is intended to promote a sense of identity as a separate group and commitment to the group's purposes. The term mística refers not just to the performance, however, but to the whole world view that underlies it, drawing on traditions of Christian mysticism to affirm unity with a transcendent reality. Mística is sacramental in that its manifest physical reality is taken to represent the deeper meaning. It is impossible to separate the enactment of mística from the engagement with transcendence.

---

* Social humanism can be understood as a praxis-oriented, people-centred ideological approach that is highly influential within some sectors of Colombian social movements. It is discussed further in Kane and NOMADESC (2021, Section 5). Social humanism emerged in Colombia from critical scholar-activists who were influenced by Marxism, but critical of orthodox Marxist-Leninist approaches to organising.

Through participating in or observing mística, people express their ideals and believe that they come closer to attaining them.

For the UIP, 'mistica' is embodied in a range of practices and rituals that bring together symbols of all the different movements and cultures, music, dance, but also collective pain and memory. It is highly symbolic and powerfully emotional – serving to bond participants together: a form of militant spirituality, that links liberation theology with the cultures and symbols of resistance of labour, women, indigenous and black movements. One recurring phrase, drawn from the iconic lawyer and activist Eduardo Umana Mendoza, who was assassinated in his home in 1998, 'Mejor morir por algo que vivir por nada' (better to die for something than live for nothing) – captures the emotional power of the pedagogical process. As one UIP activist noted:

> There are possibilities for cooperation and exchanges which are outside of the logic even of the university itself, so that people get to know each other in their resistance processes, and emotional bonds are created and behind these links there can be new exchanges and collaborations, new solidarity, affection, and that for me is a fabric of solidarity, the weaving is done at the emotional level, then later the head is what explains and justifies it.
> (Activist expert in participatory action research,
> UIP facilitator, interview, 2018, cited in Kane, 2021: 116)

The emotional power of this process is evident across all the movements, and serves to link body and mind, thought and emotion. The listener's response to the foundational story of the Housing Assembly, which we first heard from Faeza Meyer, then chair of the Housing Assembly and a founding member, is a further case in point. The story of false promises, police brutality, the abandonment of the poor and the death of a baby penetrates both mind and body, heart and soul in ways that can't be understood without reference to the visceral emotions that it triggers. This anger at injustice is part of the learning processes that are triggered through activism – part of the way activists connect with each other, and convey the indignation they feel, and the justice and righteousness of their cause.

Similarly with NEMAF, the Madhes have a strong collective experience of being 'humiliated' and this process of almost ritual humiliation becomes the rallying call for recruitment and a target to overcome. Humiliation becomes countered through 'dignity', refusing to accept humiliation as a daily occurrence, and the demand to be recognised, respected and to be fully integrated as citizens into the Nepali state.

In the case of HDK in Turkey, there is a calmness and dignity amongst many activists in the face of massive state brutality and injustice, which seems to perform a similar emotional function. As part of the research, we both gathered and listened to the court testimonies of HDK members and other activists charged with a range of political offences. These were often delivered quietly and calmly, but with a powerful emotional force that refused to accept wrongdoing, and used the platform to legitimate the movement's actions.

There is a strong sense in the HDK of the power of being together, imbued in collectivity – 'feeling not alone' – which allows activists to overcome the difficulties that they face when they are arrested, imprisoned, etc. It allows them to see what happens to them not as an act against them as an individual but rather as a form of political violence against their political ideas and those of their collective (i.e. the politicisation of violence – moving beyond the 'individualisation' of crime). The former co-chair of the HDK, who was imprisoned at the beginning of this research, talks about the importance of the politicisation of violence when he deals with questions of 'why me and why we' in facing such intense criminalisation:

> There is no personal retribution for the state violence directed against us. What is deemed as dangerous (therefore under attack) is our thoughts and our politics, not us as a person. Thus, it is necessary not to 'personalise' violence and individualise what is happening here whether it is positive or negative ... I thought a lot about it. Because I didn't personalise these experiences. I thought there was something wrong with that. The prison conditions force

us to personalise and individualise the situation we are in as the system is set out to detach a person from their collective environment where she/he belongs to. But I came to realise that ... this is not done because I'm a father, spouse, or HDK co-spokesperson, but rather because of what I/we stand for: our politics, ideas, visions ... because I'm one of the left opposition ... and the state and governments have always done this sort of thing to anyone who stands up to them and produces an alternative politics ... The Marxist and socialist understanding of violence not as an individual phenomenon in fact helped me to protect myself in the harsh conditions of the prisons and allow me to see prisons as an extension of struggle where I came to engage in creating a better environment for me together with those whom I shared my cell with. This protected me as I came to think that I am not afraid and I will not back down ... and it made me not focus on questions like what will happen to me, how will my trial be concluded or will I go to prison again, and how will I cope, all those concerns lose their importance when you think differently ... I know what that feeling can do to a person. I met some people in prison who were there because of their involvement in Fetullah Gulen who thought individually ... They seemed to feel defeated, dissolved and shrunk ... But I've never felt anything like that personally.

(Individual Interview T50, cited in Kutan and Çelik, 2021: 168)

One should also not underestimate the emotional power of the HDK project itself, and its capacity to bring diverse movements together. Talking about how this was felt at the first Congress of the HDK, a co-spokesperson of the HDK says:

I remember our first general assembly. It was so inspiring. It was the first time in Turkey's history where we saw different people and groups coming together with their own identities and beliefs. We came to realise that our difference and diversity was a positive thing that we could learn from each other. Everyone was in shock to see so many diverse opinions, beliefs and identities, that for so long had been denied and excluded. Ahmet Türk, a veteran

Kurdish politician said 'I have been waiting such a long time to see this scene. Now that I have seen it, I will not die in disappointment'. I will never forget his comment, as he has played such a key role in the Kurdish movements and continues to pay a heavy price for that work.

(Individual Interview T50, cited in Kutan and Çelik, 2021: 212)

As our analysis shows, the HDK's imagined utopia was far from being a singular homogenising and universalising one, but rather plural utopias that could co-exist alongside each other in a different Turkey. As mentioned by one activist, despite all the tensions and challenges, the fact that the HDK still retains such strong commitment from its members is testimony to what the HDK 'means' and 'what it continues to offer' for their future:

... if there are still so many people here at the HDK, it means the HDK still promises something for people ... Nobody wants to continue in this struggle if the HDK was not offering something different ... Perhaps this is the reason why we keep going under these extremely difficult conditions. For this reason, I think, the HDK still remains a projector for our future and a future hope that we hold onto ... a radical hope that gives emergence to a radical bottom-up movement. It is this radical hope that gives a new direction to this new bottom-up movement ... the kind of hope that I am referring to here is not just something that is related to optimism or about being optimistic in every situation. But this hope refers to a particular mindset that makes us think that there is always another way no matter what and asks us to act upon this thinking despite all the fear and repression. Thus, this hope is not just a matter of courage, but rather a life potency (power), a political drive that acts as a driving force and leverage for organisation and mobilisation. I think, HDK still signifies this hope and that is why it is still a home for many of us standing here under these conditions.

(Individual Interview T3, cited in Kutan and Çelik, 2021:
214–215)

When exploring social movements in contexts of high levels of inequality and repression, it is easy to drift into pessimism and rage about injustice, inequality and suffering. All of these are of course important, true and necessary, but we should also not forget that being engaged in radical and revolutionary politics can also be a great source of joy. Part of this is the discovery of a collective home which can provide a source of comfort for the activists; part of this is knowing that despite the challenges, activists are consciously engaged in challenging the status quo – rather than passively accepting it. Other aspects are the friendships forged in struggles, the dreams shared, the solidarities expressed, and the new value systems developed. This resonates with the ideas of Massimo de Angelis (2007) and others around the notion of 'commoning', of creating or reclaiming space 'outside' of capitalism where different values and norms apply. This process of 'commoning' harks back to a pre-capitalist era, where processes of commodification of people and land had not taken place – where exchange took place 'outside' capitalist relations. However, unlike in previous revolutionary thinking, that 'outside' does not have to wait for the end of capitalism, but is lived in spaces that are actively transformed into anti-capitalist and prefigurative spaces where we can live in the present as we would like to live in the future. Part of that is expressed in the joy of resistance, and the emotional power of resisting in the present to build a better future for all of us.

One early co-spokesperson of the HDK describes this as follows:

> The enthusiasm and excitement I enjoyed at the establishment congress is at the top of the exciting moments of my life ... In the end I was giving lectures on mother-tongue language and defending education in the mother tongue, I was working for socialist magazines, feminist magazines, I mean I knew those movements, but I should say that it was really fulfilling to be able to come together with people who were part of these movements ... I already knew the region [Sinop] and what was going on there; but being together, cooperating and even being persecuted together was unforgettable ... This richness is really priceless. And it

has impacted people I knew, my students, half of my doctoral students attended the Education Council. And nobody made a special effort to make them come there, they just came by themselves. That dynamism was just created.

(Togetherness and Unity in Diversity, Workshop 2, cited in Kutan and Çelik, 2021: 264)

One of the founders of HDK, and prominent revolutionary of the 1968 generation, similarly expresses this joy in resistance:

You notice that all those moments, years of struggle where you almost gave up hope during this revolutionary process, all those efforts weren't for nothing. Not on earth would I have imagined it like that. For instance, I didn't know that those very young Kurdish children, youngsters and women knew that much about the Turkish Revolutionary Movement and that they held it as their own achievement. It is very important to me to see that this revolution is not placed at a higher place than theirs but they still embrace it. This wide historical standpoint occupies an important place among these people; seeing that your efforts weren't in vain is of great importance. For instance, wherever I go in Kurdistan, everybody knows me, they are with me, I know it. And it's true that I cannot say the same thing for all Turkey but that's a fact for Kurdistan. Because a society which is in process of revolution understands and involves other revolutionaries. When Turkey will look to its own revolution, it will start to appreciate Öcalan, they already started to learn. That's why these issues are important to me. In other words, it was important to see what it meant living in a place with multiple peoples, beliefs and experiences; it was also important to notice all the potentials and evaluate them. And secondly, it was important to see that our revolutionary truth continued its existence in other languages, forms and minds. It was important knowing that we were organising this. We met with very valuable people we wouldn't have met in other circumstances and that's a great richness. And these things continue, it's not over yet. In other words, the doors of the dungeons will be opened and those people will come out and we'll be meeting again. I should say that, there hasn't been any other period in my life where I felt that everything is in the realm of possibility. Forty years ago, I was expecting to get killed by a firing squad, but now I can say I've seen it all. I've seen that those who wanted to execute you became those hoping for a solution, hoping you provide the solution. Nothing is impossible. Now I am even more convinced with my more than seventy years of existence on this earth. Just one thing, you might not live long enough to see the consequences to materialise. But unfortunately, human life is too short, I wish I had seventy more years to live.

(Individual Interview T45, cited in Kutan and Çelik, 2021: 283)

We have similar evidence from the Colombia case, of the joy that is generated from struggle, and the way that this joy keeps people engaged, open to learning new things, and building trusting relationships:

... an important element, we came together and connected and we really made possible the right to joy even in the midst of conflict ... we knew that we were living in the midst of a terrible conflict, and when we got down to work we worked very seriously and for hours on end, but the 'recocha'* was vital.

(Participant, territorial workshop, Cali, 2018, cited in Kane and NOMADESC, 2021: 175)

This friendship and solidarity was key to sustaining relationships: 'there was chemistry, a lot of fraternity, we started celebrating birthdays together, and in December we always got together ... I think that was the fundamental factor' (participant, territorial workshop, Cali, 2018, cited in Kane and NOMADESC, 2021: 175). Rooted in this friendship and fun, was Colombian dry and sardonic humour, exemplified in the following quote:

---

* A rough colloquial translation of 'recocha' would be 'horseplay'.

As an anecdote of that time, when we used to go to get the bus to go to Cauca [to a territory acutely affected by the conflict], before we took the bus we always went to get a sandwich from Sandwich Cubano, and we would always ask for the most expensive sandwich and say 'screw it, the English [funders] are paying, and if we get killed at least we ate well!'

> (Participant, territorial workshop, Cali, 2018, cited in Kane and NOMADESC, 2021: 175)

These emotions, of togetherness, hope, joy, pain, fear and nostalgia circulate across the movements, and in many ways seem to represent the glue that binds activists together. For the activists the fear and the danger of challenging powerful enemies intensified the relationships forged, and deepened their meanings.

STRUGGLES OUTSIDE AND INSIDE

In all of the movements, one key finding emerges, that in every process there is simultaneously a struggle against the state but also a struggle inside the movement; and each of these struggles is a crucial learning process. As the Housing Assembly struggles against a brutal state that denies people a dignified existence, they are also often women (and men) struggling against patriarchy within the home and in the movement. Changing the world also means changing social dynamics inside the house, in terms ranging from domestic violence to domestic labour. The Housing Assembly has similarly had to struggle against the mentalities produced by a post-apartheid society that has failed to move beyond the racialisation of society. There is no better (or worse) example of this ongoing racialisation than the maintenance and reproduction of the geographically segregated nature of housing in South Africa. The divide-and-rule strategies of racial division constructed through apartheid continue to implant themselves in the present, through suspicion and mistrust between the differently located ethnic populations across Cape Town's racially segregated terrain. Challenging both patriarchy and racialisation inside the movement and outside are therefore central to the Housing Assembly's ongoing challenges to build a unified and powerful movement.

For the HDK, it is similarly a struggle against the Turkish state, but also an internal struggle to challenge patriarchy, left-wing chauvinism, the historical subordination of the rights of Kurds and other minorities to the broader struggle for social justice. Struggles over internal democracy, but also to ensure parity of focus for different types of oppression and recognition of different types of subjectivity and agency. These internal struggles might be sacrificed if activists do not become permanently vigilant, and this likelihood is not just about agency and action but also the broader political environment. As we have seen in the case of Turkey, renewed state repression and violence puts strains on the HDK's praxis of inclusion, and on the priorities of both individuals and movements. In the face of massive repression, it is easy for some movements that form part of the HDK to revert back to their historic and closed political structures as they seek protection from persecution. Similarly, for the Kurdish Liberation Movement, which bore the brunt of both political and military attacks after the breakdown of peace talks with the Turkish state, it has often felt isolated and abandoned by some of its HDK partners. These internal struggles threaten to undo all the hard labour of building inter-movement solidarity that went into the creation and consolidation of the HDK, and no doubt their fragmentation forms a central plank of the Turkish state's strategy.

In Colombia, for NOMADESC/UIP, the challenge is the constant labour of 'weaving' the diversity of resisting actors together, in a society where leadership of the state and of social movements has long been dominated by the mestizo population. Battles to get indigenous voices heard by the state, are mirrored in the national social movement debate. Similarly, for NEMAF in Nepal, a challenge that they are just beginning to face up to is a recognition of the need not only to work for Madhes inclusion in the unequal apparatus of the Nepali state, but also to engage within the Madhes movement over inequalities between different 'Madhes' subjects.

All of these internal movement struggles are crucial learning spaces, where activists seek to find ways to overcome difference, build cohesion and internal solidarity and move the struggle forward. In all of the case studies, this is not seen as a linear developmental process, but more so as a constant process of movement-making. Learning is central to these activities.

FROM ACTIVIST TO MOVEMENT LEARNING

Back in 2017, Della Porta and Pavan (2017: 300), called for the study of 'repertoires of knowledge practices', which they defined as:

the set of practices that foster the coordination of disconnected, local, and highly personal experiences and rationalities within a shared cognitive system able to provide movements and their supporters with a common orientation for making claims and acting collectively to produce social, political, and cultural changes.

This production of a 'shared cognitive system' leads us to reflect a little on the interaction between activists (and between activists and leaders) that builds this collective and institutional learning. In all of the case studies, we can see this dynamic process of collective learning, where the 'sum' becomes more than the 'parts', but what are the learning feedback loops that can help us better understand how a movement learns? Whilst the next chapter helps us reflect on the content of these shared framings, in this part, we will reflect more on the processes.

For NOMADESC, the Diploma and later the UIP courses provided the central mechanism through which political education takes place, and is targeted to movement militants, from the different affiliates, and often young members. But targeting these individual activists was always part of a collective objective. NOMADESC and the UIP required that only affiliated movements can nominate attendees, and attendees are obligated to carry out 'replication' workshops with movement members in their home space, thus passing on learning beyond the individual activist. Over the years, this has meant that each movement will have sent a significant number of activists to the pedagogical events. Similarly, numerous 'replication' workshops will have taken place. NOMADESC would also be regularly visiting the respective movements in their own territories and accompanying them on demonstrations and protests. Through this process, which Kane and NOMADESC (2021) call 'ripple effects' as learning processes, we see a process of dialogue and engagement linking teaching and practice, and embedding that learning within the respective movements. Furthermore, as we saw above, through NOMADESC's engagement with the individuals, the movements, and the protests, the organisation itself learns more about those movements and develops its own strategic thinking. It learns from and lives the realities of the movements; it engages with the participants in the Diploma or UIP and the research that they carry out in their own contexts. Through this process, we can see NOMADESC learning, reframing its language, its ideas, and its strategies. This is most evident in a notable shift in NOMADESC over the last decade towards a much stronger appreciation and respect for 'ancestral knowledge' and endogenous movement thinking. It is also reflected in its shift towards indigenous and black movements as spearheads of the region's social movement revival. In that sense, there is a shared process of learning – with the PCN (Black Communities Process) as an example of an organisation developing its thinking as it engages with NOMADESC/UIP, and NOMADESC similarly learning from engagement with these other movements. That collective process also happens across the different movements as they try to construct a common 'southwest Colombia' position, rooted in dignity, respect, anti-capitalism and anti-imperialism. In that sense, we can evidence individual learning and political development, social movement institution learning, and a broader social movement learning that incorporates a sense of collective wisdom being developed through the interaction and struggle of the different organisations.

For the Housing Assembly, feedback learning loops between communities, members, activists and leaders are evident across the case study, and as in the case of NOMADESC work at a number of levels. First, the movement learns through the political action it is involved in. The Housing Assembly was not only a movement of shack dwellers and homeless people that worked to pressure the state; it also engaged in direct action to claim land. This process of occupation and commoning, in which activists shared the space, resources and a vision for a better life, was a central learning platform for the movement. From the experiences of the activists, the movement learnt about the nature of the state and its forces of legal and often violent control (anti-land grab units, Council Housing teams etc.). It learnt its rights and how to defend them – both legally and also through power and mobilisation. As the movement expanded across the city, it learnt about different housing types, different challenges and conditions of existence. In doing so, it learnt how to develop an analysis of the broad housing situation in post-apartheid South Africa, to be able to incorporate the diverse living conditions. Beyond the collective experience recounted above, the movement also learnt through 'door-to-door' campaigning and 'speak-outs', which provided the platform for the exchange of both leaders' and activists' knowledge on how to fight for decent housing, and peoples' knowledge of the particular conditions under which they lived. This two-way dialogue was instructive for all, but allowed the movement to build up a class-based analysis that could incorporate this diversity of experience of different types of housing, distinct communities, distinct needs and perspectives. This was particularly important, and challenging, in a post-apartheid South African context where the geography of housing remains segregated along racial lines and therefore fuels inter-ethnic suspicion and tensions. The movement also learnt through its engagement with trade unions, with city council processes, and with national organisations, tested out its strategies and cognitive frameworks, and pushed forward its agendas.

For the HDK, the organisational structure of the Congress, Assemblies and Commissions allowed for the expression of both particularity and diversity. Commissions and Assemblies were able to drill down into issues and develop positions, whilst the Congress provided the representational delegation that allowed for the collective development of policy. As Rasit and Kolokotronis (2020) have noted in discussing Rojava, which was similarly formatively influenced by the Kurdish Liberation Movement's post-2000 political evolution, the HDK model provided a hybrid form of organisational structure that mixed elements of Marxist democratic centralism and anarchist direct democracy. The combination allowed for the gathering of diverse opinions and positions whilst facilitating centralised decision-making processes – a complex learning process that allowed HDK to be both receptive but also directive. Clearly, this was not without its tensions, but those tensions also created a dynamic learning environment, with spaces both for thinking through issues in particular identity groupings, for example, in the women's commission, but also for inter-group dialogue and discussion. Again, commonality at a level of abstraction – anti-capitalism, anti-authoritarian, anti-imperialist, class solidarity – whilst engaging directly with the specificities of diverse histories, ideas, positions and concerns.

CHAPTER CONCLUSIONS

In summing up this chapter, we can see that these distinct social movements learnt and made knowledge in a variety of spaces, which were located in, and targeted towards, particular temporal moments. Learning and knowledge-making processes that looked back into history, forward to imagined futures and at the present, and involved multiple and complex interactions between activists, communities, leaders and movements, which were both embodied and embedded in particular relations of time and space. Central to this learning and knowledge-making were emotions and emotional ties that bound actors together, raised their spirits, shared their pain and strengthened their resolve to carry on, often in circumstances where futures were unclear, and the present was fraught with personal risk and danger. In all of the movements we can sense that there are simultaneously external and internal struggles taking place, which facilitate the movements' learning, development and transformation. Old ways of doing things were often challenged by alternatives, new ways of thinking and framing suggested, and often challenging proposals and suggestions put forward. These internal processes could be difficult for all involved, but crucial to social movement renewal. Furthermore, whilst individual activists clearly learnt a great deal, there were also processes of collective learning within, between and beyond the movements which translated into social movement strategic change and development. In the next chapter, we will delve deeper into the content of this learning and knowledge-making, and explore the interconnections between the different movements.

4

What types of knowledge do social movements produce and what are they learning?

INTRODUCTION

In Chapter 1, we made the case for a renewed recognition of the importance of social movements in the production of social theory. We traced the way dialogue and engagement within, between, and with social movements have contributed centrally to social theory advances from Marxism to feminism, to postcolonialism and beyond, but that these intellectual activist roots often went unrecognised. Similarly, drawing on the work of Boaventura de Sousa Santos, we noted that this epistemological silence extended beyond professional hierarchies between academics and social theorists, activists and movements, to a broader process of 'epistemicide' that privileged Western, Modernist knowledge and undermined and ignored non-Western, non-traditional modes of knowing and being – from the ancestral knowledge of indigenous elders and black movements in Colombia, to the shack dwellers of Cape Town and the historical knowledges of anti-apartheid struggles, the rural Madhes, the Kurds in Turkey and subaltern and workers' knowledges the world over. Knowledges that weren't commodified, standardised and produced in universities (particularly in the Global North) seem often to be excluded, trivialised and ignored.

This poses challenges not only for social movements which struggle to be heard, but also for critical theory, which has often become increasingly divorced from critical practice, particularly, but by no means exclusively, in the Global North. For Santos, Zibechi, Escobar and many others, this is a civilisational crisis, whereby

88

'we have modern problems for which there are no modern solutions' (Santos, 2014: 73), and a route towards these solutions lies in listening to the Global South – as the metaphor for all those resisting global capitalism, colonialism and patriarchy. In those spaces, old knowledges long repressed and new knowledges emerging from the struggles of ordinary people provide some orientations towards possible new trajectories in social thought, social life and social futures. This dual process of excavating hitherto marginalised knowledges and drawing upon the experiential knowledge of activists provides a potential mechanism through which this social and societal renewal can emerge. As you will see, in most of our case studies, the experiential and the ancestral are often fruitfully brought into dialogue with critical theory, particularly in its Marxist, anarchist, postcolonial and feminist modes, which open up new and interesting hybrid directions, solidarities and mutual understandings for the advancement of critical theory and social movement praxis and practice.

Whilst theory, and its advancement through this praxis, is clearly important for activists, leaders and movements, there is also an array of practical knowledge that social movements and their members acquire during processes of social struggle. This practical knowledge would also feed into theory building, but should also be recognised as 'really useful knowledge' (Johnson, 1979) in itself for social movements and their members and activists. Such knowledge could be a fact-based understanding of particular issues. As Cox and Flesher Fominaya (2009: 1) note:

A crucial aspect of movement practice is making known that which others would prefer to keep from public view, be that practices of torture and extra-judicial executions, the effects of individual pollutants and the costs of global warming, levels of rape and sexual abuse, the facts of poverty and exploitation, caste oppression and racism – the list is long.

Similarly, members often learn useful information about defending their rights from knowledge about particular laws (on housing law, protest, land rights, etc.). Beyond that, activists are continually learning new skills: how to organise a meeting, write a pamphlet, set up a press conference, use different communication media and tools to mobilise people, or develop strategies to organise a demonstration or protest. They are also often learning new social skills – speaking in public, engaging with different groups/communities, participating in meaningful dialogues with fellow activists and leaders, presenting their perspectives and arguments during meetings, and managing tasks – all of these things can build self-confidence and self-respect for the individual whilst simultaneously strengthening the collective organising power of the movements.

Drawing on this recognition of the different dimensions of learning and knowledge-making processes, and recognising that the uniqueness of social movement activism is its praxis, its application of theory to practical challenges, its ability to test out theory, strategy and aspiration in its everyday practice; in later sections, we will explore a number of 'knowledge' themes that have emerged over the research period. When exploring each theme, we will endeavour to touch on the intersections between critique, resistance strategies and the aspirational destination point, to provide insights into the dynamic ways that social movement knowledge-making takes place through the praxis of learning in and through struggle. Prior to this, we will lay the foundations for those selected themes by reflecting a little on the particular way social movements in the Global South are building theory in the contemporary era.

KNOWLEDGE AS CRITIQUE, RESISTANCE AND ALTERNATIVES: SOME INTRODUCTORY REFLECTIONS

As we settle into the third decade of the twenty-first century, there are evident shifts in social movement thinking and theorising in the Global South, a renewed interest in endogenous knowledge, and a reinvigorated scepticism about Northern solutions to Southern problems that is often symbolically linked to the image of the Zapatistas, but more recently demonstrated in the 'decolonial' turn and a renewed recognition of the legacies of colonialism and the ongoing impacts of imperialism. A strengthened commitment to the environment, and a resultant questioning of industrialisation and urbanisation as necessary or inevitable developmental trajectories. A questioning of the privileged revolutionary subject, whether that be the working class or the peasantry, and consequently a renewed interest in identity and its relationship to social struggle (black movement, women's movement, indigenous movement). Our case studies are not all telling us the same stories, but there is evidence in all of them of a new endogenous self-confidence, a new looking inwards – as well as outwards – for struggle resources. Furthermore, when movements look outside for inspiration, then these days they are less likely to look to the Global North and more likely to look to other movements in the South for innovative ideas, strategies and new directions. Similarly, whilst solidarity was key to all the case study movements, it was often focused primarily on the inter-movement and intersectional, rather than the international. Where it was international, it was often regional, and less focused on linking to centres of global capitalist power in the North. Perhaps this is a further demonstration of the decline of the Global North as a 'beacon of progress' (even if this was always a myth), and a reflection of its moral and intellectual decline. Nor is there any evidence, unlike during the Cold War (see Prashad, 2017), that social movements are looking to either China or Russia for new and fresh thinking, resources, support and solidarity. If anything, the inspirational transfer has been in the other direction, with Western social movements inspired by the Zapatistas, the Piqueteros, Rojava, the Bolivarian and Venezuelan revolutions and others. Finally, the endpoint is much less teleological than earlier movements and struggles, encapsulated in the phrase 'We make the road by walking'. From the mode of post-capitalist existence – socialism, communism or something else – to the target of power: the state; social movements are reimagining and rethinking goals, destinations and endpoints that reflect concerns arising out of historical reflections that start to reframe what success looks like, and what victory means.

In the rest of this chapter, we now explore four knowledge themes, that emerged out of our research, which demonstrate the new, innovative contributions to social theory that these social movements are developing as they struggle for their diverse objectives in vastly different contexts. The first, 'Theorising society: beyond Western/ modernist lenses', reflects on the nature of contemporary theorising in our movements. The second, 'The praxis and challenges of building unity as diversity', explores the way movements are producing new ideas and ways of bringing together diverse oppositional subjects together within movements. The third, 'Gender as a route to liberation', explores the way social movements are thinking about gender within their distinct struggles. The fourth, 'Building the future in the present: prefigurative politics and social movements', explores shifts in thinking amongst many social movements around the relationship between current practices and end goals, and the increasing importance of living our movements values in the present as we build for the future. Each of the themes came out of our workshops and collective data analysis as key issues where new ideas and thinking were emerging, and that these ideas were transforming practice.

THEORISING SOCIETY: BEYOND WESTERN/MODERNIST LENSES

For NOMADESC, and the Intercultural University of the Peoples, from its inception in the early 2000s to the current UIP, there has been an evolving critique of the brutal status quo of Colombia. Rooted in a strong critique of capitalism and imperialism (and their inter-relationship), there is a strong structural critique of the Colombian conflict, tracing its origins in the parasitical behaviour of both national elites and international actors, from the US military to multinational corporations, in a country that is geo-strategically important and resource-rich. The UIP analysis links resource extraction and capitalist exploitation to mass displacement of populations, massacres and widespread political violence against communities. Whilst the above fits a broadly Marxist/neo-Marxist analysis, this critique has evolved and been nuanced over time. It builds on a historic analysis of Colombia and Latin America's violent and particular integration into the world system, and is sensitive to the experiences of oppressed and exploited peoples in this process and the dynamics of these relationships.

NOMADESC is intellectually building on an endogenous form of critical thought that emerged out of the debates of three activist intellectuals in the 1960s: Camillo Torres, Orlando Fals Borda and Umaña Luna, over the need for social change in Colombia and the suitability of orthodox Marxism. All were committed to popular education and participatory research, and all had a strong sense of responsibility towards the people and what they called 'compromiso social' (social commitment). They were the founders of the first Department of Sociology in both Colombia and Latin America, in Bogotá in 1959. Each made their mark in historic ways: Camillo Torres, known as the 'revolutionary priest', eventually joined the ELN (National Liberation Army), a guerrilla movement inspired by the Cuban revolution of 1959. The ELN were also influenced by the shift in the Catholic church to 'liberation theology' and its 'preferential option for the poor'. Umaña Luna was a lawyer and human rights defender who laid many of the foundations for a radical understanding of human rights in Colombia and across Latin America today. Third, Orlando Fals Borda, often referred to as 'Colombia's Paolo Freire', was a sociologist and historian of violence in Colombia, a popular educator, and the founder of what would become known as 'participatory action research', a methodology that recognises the knowledge present amongst the people and a strategy to nurture that knowledge through collective research aimed at radical social change.

They all saw the need for the development of popular consciousness amongst the people, were sensitive to a particular Latin American route to socialism, and were committed to radical transformation. This bottom-up approach to knowledge and theory production from its inception sought to go beyond Marx's maxim of 'the philosophers interpret the world, the point is to change it', to 'the people can both interpret the world and change it'. This sensitivity and respect for local, situated, bottom-up knowledge also led to Fals Borda's engagement with critiques of Western intellectual hegemony, including within Marxism, and the need for Latin American solutions to Latin American problems (Fals Borda, [1970] 1987) and for a socialism with Colombian roots ('socialismo raizal') (Fals Borda, 2013).

Emerging out of this was a mode of thought known as 'social humanism', which forms both a theoretical and ethical framework and guide for action, that underpins NOMADESC/UIP and many other social movement organisations in Colombia:

[You could understand social humanism as] an ecosystem of ideas shaped ... in the 60s by several basic problems – the problem of what to do with Marxism and with socialism and its inability ... to see the stories from below, the history from below but also its inability to see beyond the structure, then a series of theories emerge [in Colombia], because [Eduardo Umaña Luna] comes from the discipline of law, and Orlando Fals Borda comes from the world of sociology and Camillo [Torres] also with strong influence of theology, so let's say it was an ecosystem of people concerned about social change and social justice who came together, but also aware that much of the deficiency of social struggles in Colombia had been the failure to propose a strong and solid alternative paradigm based on our reality ... so that spurred them to seek to generate ideas on how to understand that reality and in the case of [Eduardo Umaña Luna] there was a very specific problem ... so he said, 'I want a social humanism that intends to think about the centrality of human rights but based on the agenda of the Rights of the Peoples [Algiers Charter]', that is, that allows us to see the collective: Human Rights are rights centred on individuals, as understood from a liberal perspective – individuals included in the social pact, included in the forms of social organisation, whilst collective rights are rights geared towards collective social claims of peoples who have been marginalised and who seek inclusion [within the social pact] but also transformation, then and that is the interesting part about the Rights of Peoples, it was a way of saying 'yes, human rights are very important for those who are included and those who are outside have to look for an inclusion

94

which in itself implies transformation, it is not simply inclusion: it is, include me but also [seeking broader] transformations, so I think that was their concern and the difference'.

(Scholar-activist, facilitator on the UIP, interview, 2018, cited in Kane and NOMADESC, 2021: 128)

We can see clear evidence of these roots in the Colombia Case Study: a fusion of Marxism, a sensitivity to local knowledges, and an abundance of ethical responsibility and commitment to social change. What we can also see is the evolution of that thinking over the two decades under analysis, moving from a largely trade-union-centred focus, with black movements, indigenous, campesino communities and urban poor linked together, to a much more indigenous/ Afro-centred focus over recent years.

This reflects changes in both the rhythms and subjects of social struggle in Colombia during that period (what the Colombians would call the 'coyuntura' or political conjuncture), and how NOMADESC/UIP has itself transformed its thinking. This transformation itself reflects a sensitive pedagogy, which is listening to and learning from participants (movements and individuals) – who are articulating and researching their own social reality and sharing it with the broader group. It is from this praxis and the dynamics that this produces that we can begin to explain the changes. In the process known as 'dialogo de saberes' mentioned above, this reflects a bottom-up process, rooted in respect for diverse knowledges, needs and aspirations and which has social struggle and resistance at its heart. One of the things that emerges from the case study that evidences the dialogical nature of this process is that it did not just change the perceptions and behaviours of the participants, but also the behaviour of the leaders and tutors of the pedagogical process, who became far more attuned to the relationship between society and nature, ancestral knowledges, and indigenous or endogenous knowledges. But we should not just see this as a bottom-up process, arising only from the participants. Rather, it was a process of exchange, where the NOMADESC/UIP team and educators are also bringing their political, and intellectual skills and background to the dialogue. Perhaps it could be seen as more akin to a process of 'assemblage' (Deleuze and Guattari, 2012), connecting analysis of capitalism and revolutionary traditions with diverse endogenous and experiential framings, to construct new framings of analysis and solidarity between movements in the southwest of Colombia.

Social humanism's centring of the human subject, which is understood as a *collective being*, provided the basis for an activist praxis which could open itself up to the epistemologies and cultures of the social movements involved. With the expansion of the pedagogical process to include more social movements and territories (particularly indigenous and Afro-Colombian movements), the knowledge-making processes have been transformed by the epistemologies and struggles of these movements and have brought about a deeper paradigm shift, as the demographic character of the participating movements has shifted away from the early predominance of trade unions, with their leaderships tendency to adhere to fairly rigid Marxist class politics with clearly defined ideological route maps for the struggle, and to reproduce the knowledge hierarchies associated with modernity:

> It was difficult for many of us at the beginning, or for me particularly, the break that we see very clearly today at the time it was very blurred, very tangled because we were so rooted in Western thought … epistemologically for me it was very complicated …
> (Interview with trade unionist organic intellectual who has been involved in the process since the early phase of the Diploma until present day, interview, 2018, cited in Kane and NOMADESC, 2021: 128)

With this paradigm shift, the knowledge-making processes have become even more bottom-up and dialogical in which teachers and learners, old and young, leaders and activists, engage in a collective process of meaning making that transforms both participants and organisers in new, exciting and innovative ways of creating intellectual resources for their struggle. The 'ancestral' rationalities of indigenous and Afro-Colombian social movements, which have

become increasingly influential, are rooted in alternative conceptions of social relations (including between humans and nature)
based upon interdependence; collectivism; solidarity; and the indigenous concept of 'buenvivir'.

> Within our thinking we do not understand the need to accumulate
> – why accumulate? Because we don't live with what is necessary to
> live well and be in harmony with nature, be happy and grateful to
> be able to feed ourselves, to have a roof, to have clothes, what we
> need but without having to accumulate and destroy ...
>
> (Indigenous activist and university academic, facilitator
> in UIP, cited in Kane and NOMADESC, 2021: 148).

Within the Afro-Colombian epistemology and discursive con-
structions, the concept of 'renaciente' is often employed, and holds
connotations relating to the Colombian black population's African
heritage and history of slavery and resistance. A veteran activist in
the black movement described how it relates to the underlying consciousness and resistance of the black community:

> ... there are people who say that the black struggle was invented
> in 1990 [with the struggle for recognition of black communi-
> ties] but I believe our people already had their consciousness ...
> I remember so much that my grandmother whenever we had an
> argument she'd say 'you are white!' and with that she closed the
> discussion ... they were clear on things and what had happened,
> that is my story but we've picked it up all over the place ... maybe
> they didn't express it in the same way that we can express it today,
> it was expressed another way and what we did was understand
> that that was there ... in that sense my generation ... those of
> us that had the opportunity to go to the university and study,
> all we are is translators, that was in the language of the people
> somehow we got some things out of here we translated them into
> the other language, and other things we translated and took them
> to the communities ... but this consciousness was already there,
> for example I remember so much a word which they use in the

Pacific, the word 'renaciente' for me that is what I'm going to tell you is like the holy grail, a conversation we had in Yurumangui [remote Pacific region jungle river community] and we started talking about what the word 'renaciente' meant and the elders told me 'it is as if we were before on one side and now we are here, as if we had an accident and now we are reborn in another place' and I asked the old men, 'and where were we before?' And they said, 'in Africa', and 'what was the accident?' ... Blacks have always known what happened ... That day, talking to those elders, I came to understand that when they speak of renaciente it has two senses, that we are not *from* here and that we are here because there was slavery ... it was already there in the memory of the elders, it was there hidden behind the word, of course it is the same as we know now, but they already knew it and what we did is translate it in another way ... we weren't the first to say that we must defend our territories as black communities, our people have been saying that for a long time.

(Early leader of the black movement at the regional and national level, an early ally of NOMADESC and the pedagogical process, interview, 2018, cited in Kane and NOMADESC, 2021: 54)

For indigenous ethnicities such as the Nasa people, their episte-mology is closely tied to their language, and the preservation and recuperation of the language has formed an important part of their struggle over recent decades. The central role of territory, and the human relationship to territory, within the thinking of indigenous, Afro-Colombian and peasant communities has been increasingly influential within the NOMADESC pedagogical process in recent years, and differs from Western notions of territory:*

For me, territory means everything ... a space that is the territory, not seen as something material that I can sell it and leave it and

---

* For further reading on Latin American conceptualisations of territory, see Halvorsen (2019).

turn it into an asset, but as a living space, a space for dignified life, let's say that for me that is the territory, Leila Arroyo says that for others the territory is a space of the accumulation of wealth, for us the territory is a life space and not only human life, but of life in the sense of all the beings that are there, for me that is the territory, we have risked life itself for our territories, these are where our culture has been reproduced, where we have reproduced life and dignity despite all the systematic and structural violence imparted by the state against us, in spite of the structural racism of the economic, political and legal system, we have lived together as a community, we have made community in our territories.

(Rural Afro-Colombian community leader, former student in later phases of the Diploma, interview, 2018, cited in Kane and NOMADESC, 2021: 146).

Through these processes a new language has emerged, based around 'territory', 'ancestral knowledge', 'life plans' 'territorial and transformative peace', 'pluriverse' and 'historical memory', which simultaneously looks back and projects forward. But within the UIP, this emergent language builds on, rather than replaces, a language of critique of capitalism, imperialism, multinational corporations, elites, etc. What we see instead is a fusion or assemblage of neo-Marxist and decolonial analysis and experiential/contextually grounded reflections which represent a clear example of the power of this intercultural/inter-movement praxis to begin to produce new, hybrid thinking. A hybrid thinking that reflects the coming together of the different political subjects, in all of their complexity. A fusion of histories, struggles and strategies of resistance that become more than the sum of their parts and sculpts a new collective identity that gives power and meaning to the collective.

This theoretical fusion, itself reflects the intellectual evolution of the Critique, Resistance and Alternatives challenge that NOMADESC and the UIP set themselves when they were created. NOMADESC was seeking a strategy that could go beyond the fragmentation of oppositional movements whose lack of collective action, empathy, solidarity between themselves was hampering the achievement of radical social change. By bringing leaders and activists of the respective movements together under the Human Rights Diploma and later the UIP they were able to listen to each others' ideas and respective situations and begin to develop a common intellectual grammar of resistance that became more than the sum of their particular organisational parts. This new grammar also provides a potential route and vision towards the construction of a new pluri-cultural society beyond capitalism and movement fragmentation. A new revolutionary 'good sense' in the Gramscian framing was clearly emerging.

From a very different geography, a not-dissimilar transformation of thinking and acting has appeared in the HDK in Turkey. From a left social movement and oppositional culture that often saw the Kurds as marginal to the overall class struggle for social justice, homogeneity as the norm, and modernity as the destination (albeit with socialist economics), the HDK has brought in a radically new approach to social movement struggle. Their intercultural, intersectional stance approaches diversity as a resource to be celebrated and learnt from. Where the Turkish state had sought to obliterate difference, the HDK's strategy has been to recover, cultivate and celebrate it, both historically and contemporaneously. Rather than being an adjunct to the broader national struggle, the Kurdish Liberation Movement has become central, and its post-2000 intellectual rebirth is highly influential. The Kurdish movement's development of a conception of radical democracy that saw 'politics beyond the state, political organisation beyond the party, and political subjectivity beyond class' (Akkaya and Jongerden, 2012), has underpinned the HDKs approach to diversity and struggle.

As expressed by the imprisoned leader of the PKK, Abdullah Öcalan:

I offer the Turkish society a simple solution. We demand a democratic nation. We are not opposed to the unitary state and republic. We accept the republic, its unitary structure and laicism. However, we believe that it must be redefined as a democratic state respecting peoples, cultures and rights. On this basis, the

Kurds must be free to organise in a way that they can live their culture and language and can develop economically and ecologically. This would allow Kurds, Turks and other cultures to come together under the roof of a democratic nation in Turkey. This is only possible, though, with a democratic constitution and an advanced legal framework warranting respect for different cultures. Our idea of a democratic nation is not defined by flags and borders. Our idea of a democratic nation embraces a model based on democracy instead of a model based on state structures and ethnic origins. Turkey needs to define itself as a country which includes all ethnic groups. This would be a model based on human rights instead of religion or race. Our idea of a democratic nation embraces all ethnic groups and cultures.

(2017: n.p.)

Furthermore, the Kurdish movement's rethinking of patriarchy and feminism – encapsulated in 'jineology' and '*men*tality' has centred gender equality alongside interculturality as one of the foundational pillars of the movement. At the core of these notions is the conviction that society cannot be free unless women have an equal share in social, political and economic spaces and their freedom is central to the realisation of social justice. One dimension and concretisation of this has been the appointment of women co-chairs and representatives in all sections of the HDK and the HDP, women's quotas, and genuine efforts at a reformulation of gendered relationships. Interestingly, just as we saw in the case of UIP/NOMADESC, where there is a fusion of endogenous knowledge and thinking with liberation theology and Marxism, so the Kurdish Liberation Movement has been strongly influenced by the ideas of Murray Bookchin, a US anarchist/environmentalist and libertarian socialist who developed a critique of capitalism and its destructive effect on both humans and nature, and a pathway forward rooted in decentralised, radical democracy (see Stanchev, 2016).

Bookchin's championing of radical democracy, Democratic Confederalism, and an autonomous, democratic and decentralised mode of governance has been contextualised, adopted and adapted through the process of struggle and praxis in both Kurdish areas of Turkey and Rojava, Syria, an experiment that has attracted global attention and admiration. It has also transformed the Kurdish Liberation Movement from an overwhelmingly top-down and militarised model, to a much more bottom-up, mass participatory process, which has been reclaiming control of territory through democratic politics and protest.

Whilst the Turkish left have undoubtedly undertaken a learning process through engaging in the HDK, the Kurdish Liberation Movement has equally been on a cognitive journey, which has forced it to re-evaluate its own political trajectory, and led it to engage with the myriad of oppositional social forces in Turkey in very different ways to previous pacts and alliances. This can be extremely challenging, but exemplifies the way social movements work out theory on the ground through engagement – a praxis that is tested out through struggle.

As noted, the HDK is producing a hybrid form that draws together anarchist and Marxist ideas and modes of organising, fusing democratic centralism and direct democracy in new ways, in a form of top-down and bottom-up democratisation that creates the conditions for the empowerment of historically marginalised groups and opens up diverse dialogues and standpoints between different social groups. Within the HDK, the Kurdish Liberation Movement acts as the spearhead to provide confidence for other groups to assert their autonomy and identity. The Turkish state and its capitalist and homogenising project provides the counter-point against which modes of collective unity and action can be mobilised through this diversity. In this process, there is a strong focus on local knowledges. This was noted by some activists as an important methodological necessity to problematise those ahistorical theories and debates that bore little resemblance to the national context. As mentioned by one activist, this refocusing on 'going back to the roots' necessitated looking at local histories and knowledges rather than 'limiting ourselves to the daily conflict, contradiction, confusion of locality'. This, he suggested, led them to move away from more 'centralised and hierarchal political forms' (Individual Interview T28, cited in

Kutan and Çelik, 2021: 283), which was the key to the success of today's social movement.

NEMAF, as an NGO that emerged out of the Madhes post-2007 struggles, and embodies its aspirations, has carved out an intellectual space for itself to support the broader movement. It has done this by helping to strengthen the intellectual basis for the Madhes movement. The hegemony of a particular ethno-state imaginary projected by the Nepali elite based on four key principles: Nepali language, Hindu religion, monarchy and the tradition of writing the national history (Onta, 1996; Burghart, 1994; Shah, 1993), had led to the systematic marginalisation of Madhesis over centuries. This has resulted in the normalisation of existing and extremely unequal power relationships and the erosion of the capacity of Madhesis to critique that system of oppression.

As NEMAF's founder mentions:

We worked on three areas to support the movement. We developed a practical approach in which we worked with public intellectuals to produce literature and evidence-based narratives about discrimination and marginalisation of Madhesis in Nepali society and got them to train Madhesis lawmakers who were involved in the constitution-making process. The Madhesi leaders represented the emotions of the Madhesi people but they lacked the robust political substance to assert and justify their positions.

(Madhesi Civil Society Leader 1, Kathmandu, cited in Pherali and NEMAF, 2021: 81)

In this process, they sought to target both the Madhesi and non-Madhesi communities and vindicate the cruel, marginalised and oppressive situation of Madhesis. As one activist noted:

I felt that non-Madhesis were unable to understand the notion of ethnic domination and therefore, could not make sense of Madhesi agitation. Likewise, Madhesis lacked in ability and sophistication in presenting well founded arguments about structural domination. In other words, they were unable to articulate their feelings and experiences of discrimination when challenged about the rationale for their discontent towards the state.

(Madhesi Civil Society Leader 1, Kathmandu,
cited in Pherali and NEMAF, 2021: 80)

NEMAF's programmes were designed to systematically articulate the Madhesi agenda by working with political analysts, sociologists and human rights activists who engaged in analysis of the history, geography, politics, culture and identities of Madhesis. As this work developed, they were able to explore the multiple dimensions of oppression that the Madhes had faced and continue to face, but also to vindicate their existence as a political subject, with a distinct culture, language and identity. In this sense, there was both a negative and positive dimension to the process. The latter was crucial work for a community that had been dehumanised and degraded through a process of systemic humiliation. A people who, up until 1952, were only allowed to visit the capital of Nepal with a permit, and continue to have very restricted citizenship rights and be looked upon as 'less than' Nepali. Whilst the dehumanisation of the Madhes is extreme, we can see in all of the social movements a response to this process through the reaffirmation of marginalised and oppressed identities, and the building up and vindication of the participants as sovereign and dignified subjects.

For NEMAF, which itself is composed of Madhesi activists, the task they undertook was to gather data, experiences, facts and figures to demonstrate the particular nature of Madhesi marginalisation, and simultaneously to draw upon these experiences to work towards the forging of a particular Madhesi experience, which was composed of different socio-economic and cultural groupings. This cultural labour was both a tool for unifying the Madhesi movement – involving local workshops and dissemination, and for projecting the Madhesi community as a sovereign subject, with a particular history, and set of grievances, to a broader Nepali audience. This provided important ammunition for the activists of the Madhesi struggle and represented a very particular intellectual contribution to that movement.

In the case of the Housing Assembly, they moved from practice to theory through engagement in a struggle which for them was also a politics of survival. The group of activists that arrived at ILRIG were there as much to clean their clothes and wash, as they were to learn about defending their rights. They were embraced by ILRIG's leaders and inducted into a language of critical analysis through a form of endogenous South African popular workers' education that was rooted in the practices of the anti-apartheid civic movement. A process of dialogue where the homeless activists began to work out why they were in the situation that they faced, the deeper structural drivers, and the unfinished business of the anti-apartheid movement. This was as much an inter-generational dialogue as it was an inter-movement one, and eventually led to the founding of the Housing Assembly.

One of the founders of the Housing Assembly recounts those first contacts with ILRIG:

> The first time I was taken to ILRIG I met Michael Blake. If ever I was confused it got even worse. It sounded like the comrades were speaking a language I would never understand. Michael is a wonderful teacher. He introduced me to new things and new people like Koni, and together with the staff of ILRIG and Worker's World Media I began to see light at the end of the tunnel. Don't get me wrong, the light is faint, but at least I see it now. From what I have learnt and experienced this far, there's not much new in our immediate struggle, most of what we are going through and experiencing had already happened to others, even worse … Learning from all the other struggles and comparing it to ours taught me a lot. I could learn from the mistakes others had made. To always put me ahead of where I'm supposed to be.
>
> (Benson and Meyer, 2015)

Central to Michael Blake's and ILRIG's work was that change would only come from the people themselves and that practice – the struggle – was where ideas got worked out. These fundamental precepts underpin the Housing Assembly's approach to knowledge and knowledge-making. They have developed a detailed analysis of the different types of housing and the varied challenges in different parts of Cape Town, and built an overarching and unifying critique of the housing crisis as a failed legacy of post-apartheid agreements and neoliberal policies. Information gathered through 'door-to-door' and 'speak-outs', coupled with the experience of occupations and evictions, has built up a broad critique that has managed to transcend the particularism of different personal housing challenges, as noted by Levenson (2017: 154):

> (it) is grounded in two major strategic developments that distinguish it from many previous housing-oriented organisations: the active construction of a novel agent of struggle – the subject of a generalised housing crisis, as opposed to distinct and fragmented housing identities; and involvement in decommodification struggles instead of acting as a pressure group on the municipal state.

Intellectually, we can see in the Housing Assembly the coming together of detailed grassroots knowledge and experience of the realities of the housing crisis in Cape Town, the inter-generational wisdom of leaders and activists of the anti-apartheid civic movement, and the organisational logics of the trade union movement. From these hybrid influences the Housing Assembly has articulated an intellectual strategy of both emergency defence, whilst simultaneously cultivating a platform for a broader vision of housing for all. In doing so, they have rearticulated the 'home' as a central terrain of social struggle. In doing so, they have turned what is often seen as a private concern, into a very public issue, which requires collective solutions.

In all of the cases, we can see the complex and dialogical relationship between the experiential knowledges of activists and communities, and their interactions with movement leaders and theories of society and societal change. As evidenced above, we should also recognise that these knowledges cannot be seen as time-bound, but instead build on historical struggles and ideas, involving inter-generational and inter-movement processes that build the present from the past and for the future. All of the movements form a part of a broader historical story of oppositional struggle and social change in their respective contexts. There are also clear differences in the geographical scales of operation of the different movements as they construct and maintain these new cognitive frameworks.

THE PRAXIS AND CHALLENGES OF BUILDING UNITY AS DIVERSITY

The relationship between building a unified movement and incorporating a diverse membership within it has been a perennial challenge for many social movements. For national liberation movements, it was often the national issue that became prioritised; for socialist movements, it was social class. In both cases the legitimate demands of other constituencies were often deferred for a later date, and this has induced scepticism and the pillarisation of movements into separate entities. Our case studies have much to say on this, and the way these challenges have been worked on through the praxis of struggle.

For the HDK in Turkey, a powerful critique emerged on the relationship between diversity, unity and struggle. In Turkey's highly mono-cultural and assimilationist national structure, which was created on a foundational myth of 'homogeneity', the HDK both recognises and vindicates diversity and difference as a source of power and strength.

As stated in the HDK Foundation Bulletin (2012: 3)

Our Congress sees the spaces of struggle of all democratic oppositional forces as a common space of struggle and draws its strength from that. Our Congress is the common struggle space for all those oppressed and exploited; workers, laborers, immigrants, women, peasants, youth, retired people, disabled people, LGBT individuals; all those excluded and ignored ethnic minorities and faith communities as well as those people whose living spaces are being destroyed.

As highlighted by several activists, 'being together while respecting each other's individuality', 'recognising their difference' and 'standing side by side with differences' is not intended to create a new universal difference nor sameness or uniformity, but rather to bring together and unite 'these "irreducible differences" whereby they can be "in a constant state of flow" as they struggle to create a new alternative world in which differences live freely while in "common"' (Togetherness and Unity in Diversity, Workshop 2, cited in Kutan and Çelik, 2021: 142). The unity of these diverse social actors can perhaps be better described as a process of 'commoning' – engaging in a process of 'commoning of common values and goods', where the focus is on engaging in new forms of 'biopolitical power' that underpin a new alternative future for all.

Indeed, this radical reconceptualisation of unity in diversity as 'commoning' challenges not only the Turkish state, but also the orthodox conception of the 'unity' of activists in progressive social movements in Turkey. A brief historical analysis of these movements shows that unity was normally seen as a 'united front', as an oppositional response, and as a temporal/conjunctural tactic to challenge sovereign power. Secondly, the issue of diversity and difference was often seen as an afterthought, as a negative resource that could hinder the struggle over the control of production (class). Similarly, it was often suggested, explicitly or implicitly, that the differences would disappear with the coming of the revolution. These practices were the reason many activists left those groupings and organisations and formed their own identity-based collectives and movements. Hence, this new HDK 'unity in diversity' approach challenged the negative and often sectarian perception of unity within the left, and opened up new possibilities through 'commoning'.

Central to the HDK's practice was a prefigurative position, whereby a diverse, democratic, more inclusive Turkey was not just envisioned in some future utopia, but practised in the present through the Congress representational model and its organising strategies. In that process, representation was not just seen as a form of long-awaited justice, but also as a resource for the production of a more imaginative future. Through diversity we can imagine new futures and co-construct new trajectories.

Kutan and Çelik (2021: 132) evidence a dynamic process of praxis that occurs as HDK develops its position on this and other issues. They suggest that:

> This dialectical relationship is shaped by the experience whereby a prefigurative political future horizon constantly collides with the existing political realities and demands of everyday life. This is important as it shows us that the type of knowledge being produced sits at the frontier of the emerging tension between 'what is actually being produced (what is)' and 'what is being imagined (should be)' by the HDK and what effects this newly learned knowledge has had in the transformation of subjectivities (individual and collective) and social relations.

That collision of aspirations with the everyday realities of existence, means that this new 'unity in diversity' is constantly challenged and requires protection and nurturing. The materiality and brutality of the Turkish state presents challenges, limits and possibilities of solidarity, as sectors come under the purview of the state.

In this sense, we see the importance of social movement knowledge, as the HDK example shows, which doesn't just theorise the need for unity in diversity, but also acts upon it, with all the challenges that it entails: the challenges of trust, of unequal power relations between groups, and of conjunctural trials, and we can see attempts to overcome this. Across the case study, we can see multiple examples of these challenges whereby the 'prefigurative political future horizon constantly collides with the existing political realities and demands of everyday life' (Kutan and Çelik, 2021: 132). For example, we can see the limits of solidarity between groups, when the peace process collapses, and the Turkish military began attacking Kurdish regions. The polarisation, the fear and the limited tools for defence that social movements had, meant that Kurds felt isolated, targeted and unsupported. After the failed coup, the ensuing militarisation created a similarly hostile environment, unconducive to open and collective gatherings, whilst the increased incarceration and targeting of activists and communities led to a degree of atomisation. For some movements it was just a question of prioritising their own survival – whether of the movement or the individual; for others, it challenged their confidence in the HDK idea. This is not to say that the idea of unity in diversity was totally fractured, and there were numerous inter-movement acts of solidarity during these times – not least the now famous 'Academics for Peace' letter, whereby progressive academics signed a letter condemning the attacks on the Kurdish areas, and were then subsequently persecuted, imprisoned and/or sent into exile.* But what is clear from the example of the HDK's experience is that there are real practical obstacles that face the political project of building an alternative and diverse society and the power of the state to undermine it.

Yet perhaps it is precisely the brutality with which the Turkish state has targeted the movement that evidences the fact that it represented a real threat to the status quo. In such a short time it had galvanised the population, created a political party that became the main opposition, and transformed the future imaginaries of where Turkey could go and what it could be. Never before in the history of social struggle in Turkey had a political movement been able to bring together such a diversity of social forces under one open banner. That memory and knowledge remains strong, even if many of the movements leaders and activists are holding on to that memory from behind prison walls or from outside its territorial borders as they live their lives in exile.

For NOMADESC and the UIP, a similar commitment to building intercultural dialogue has been central to its political and pedagogical work over the last two decades. From the early Human Rights Diplomas to the founding of the UIP, there has been a strong commitment to the 'dialogo de saberes'. For many, the UIP has been the midwife for a new relationship in the southwest of Colombia between trade unions, women's movements, and black and indige-

---

* See Academics For Peace (2016). 'We Will Not Be Party to this Crime'. Available at: https://barisicinakademisyenler.net/node/63

nous organisations that, like the HDP in Turkey, goes well beyond the utilitarian politics of 'unity in diversity' as a conjunctural necessity. The intercultural 'dialogo de saberes' involves a central place for the exchange of ideas, histories, cosmo-visions, life plans, and utopias; a process through which culture was no longer seen as a deficit to be eroded through the march towards socialism, but rather as a resource for understanding the past and guiding the struggle towards the future. The concept of 'ancestral knowledges' emerged out of these debates to evidence a renewed respect for the historical and experiential struggles of historically marginalised communities in Colombia, and this knowledge and tools for struggle were embraced and incorporated into the critique. For the more orthodox revolutionaries this opening up to these cultural and historically embedded framings has often been a difficult process of 'unlearning', particularly of the often-racist stereotypes of marginalised communities in Colombia.

For the Housing Assembly, reflecting on two decades of post-apartheid social policy, a huge question mark is raised as to what the benefits of post-apartheid peace really are, and for whom? Their critique is located in the failed housing and social policy of post-apartheid South Africa, where a 'leaning in' (Fraser, 2013) model of social inclusion, has meant a small number of non-white citizens have accessed power and prosperity, whilst the physical and geographical barriers of apartheid remain intact. Theirs is a critique, built from the bottom-up experience of homelessness, land evictions, social exclusion, that is firmly rooted in working-class politics, and the need for radical social transformation.

Interestingly, whilst in the cases of all of the other social movements under analysis, ethnicity has been elevated, reconceptualised and vindicated as a carrier of social struggle, the Housing Assembly has from its inception emphasised class politics and class struggle. Perhaps this is precisely in reaction to a South Africa where post-apartheid racial politics is hegemonic, and where the discourse of the 'rainbow nation' has concealed ongoing class differences. But despite the surface orthodoxy of the focus on working-class politics, built on the shoulders of the anti-apartheid civic movements, the radicalism of the Housing Assembly is located in their construction of the home as the site of organising, and a recognition that those familial and neighbourly ties constitute a powerful nucleus of organising power and strength. In this, the centrality of women in that struggle is also clear – with the home as the site of control by women, whilst also a site of patriarchy and domination.

Having said that, whilst a discourse of working-class unity is their organising framework, the Housing Assembly has recognised that the challenge of identity in a highly segregated and racialised housing market is central to their concerns. Their strategy has been to engage with dwellers in all different types of housing – which reflect ethnic divides – and build an overarching discourse that can bring different ethnic groups together under this critique of capitalist and neoliberal housing policy and the commonality of exploitation across housing types.

NEMAF, in a similar manner, has sought to create an overarching identity rooted in 'Madhes' identity that cuts across ethnic and social divides across the Terai region. This has been both a resource that has strengthened the power of the movement and mobilised diverse social groups, but also a challenge as there are clear and unscrutinised differences between different social groupings that exist within the Madhes, differences that might undermine the movement's development if not addressed. The movement not only asserted the historical marginality of Madhes but also exposed these intra-ethnic divisions along with caste discrimination and political representation.

All of the above examples highlight the importance of the cultural labour of social movements, and most importantly the dynamic nature of building unity amidst the diversity of communities that compose different social movement struggles. Here we can evidence not just the abstract call for unity in diversity, and for the imperative to build a pluri-cultural movement, but the messy day-to-day struggles of bringing this aspiration into reality. In these processes we can learn from the rich experiences of both success and failure, of movement forward and back. We can identify strategies, and developments that forge new intercultural subjectivities and subjects. In the case of NOMADESC and the UIP, we see these changing subjectivities not only in the linguistic shifts towards greater incorporation of indigenous and black 'ancestral' thinking, but also in forms of dress and mobilisation strategies. In the case of the HDK, we can see it in the way different social actors, from distinct social movements, become champions and advocates of the rights of other marginalised communities. Inside those seemingly micro-processes of transformation might be much to learn for other social movements across the world seeking to build their own unity and diversity.

GENDER AS A ROUTE TO LIBERATION

One of the central components of domination, and sites of injustice, in all of the contexts under analysis is unequal gender relations and patriarchy. Just as contemporary social movements are taking cultural diversity and race more seriously – and reject waiting until after the revolution for their resolution – so gender relations are a central terrain of struggle across all of the case studies, both internally and externally. For some movements, it is a privileged concern and explicit focus; for others it is more implicit, but for all it is a major concern, and terrain of struggle.

The programme of the People's Democratic Congress (HDK) is based on a critical and radical pedagogy of 'the epistemology of the South' and seeks to create a democratic and egalitarian modernity in opposition to capitalist modernity; a democratic confederal life based on the people's right to self-determination against colonialism and its dominant form of the sovereign nation-state; and gender equality based on a new equal life opposed to the male-dominated patriarchal system by bringing together the jineology perspective (science of women) of the Kurdish women's liberation movement (Öcalan, 2013) and other feminist movements. On this basis, gender constitutes one of the top priorities in the HDK's agenda. The HDK's main aim is to build an intersectional feminism that focuses on multiple dynamics (class, identity, religion and sexuality) by uniting the feminist movement that emerged from an internal critical approach to the epistemology of the North with the jineology movement emerging from the reflexive transformation of the epistemology of the South. One emerged from the mountains in Kurdish areas, the other from the urban cities of Turkey, and their coming together sparked intense counter-hegemonic, collective learning processes which would have a huge influence upon the HDK's organising praxis, as together they re-imagined gender issues in new and exciting ways. The following discussion provides a sense of these collective learning processes and the way that they have shaped the HDK's praxis and organisational culture.

The organisational structure of the Congress and the decision-making processes are all built according to this new perspective. This includes a 50% quota for women's representation in all committees and co-chairs: one woman and one man in all leadership positions. These are the *sine qua non* principles for all the decision-making and representation processes of the Congress. That this political approach has become a fundamental principle both for the HDK and amongst the Kurdish freedom-oriented social movements is one of the main achievements of the struggle against the patriarchal order in Turkey.

Based on the general perspective of the Kurdish Freedom Movement, the HDK's new democratic and egalitarian means of participation have had significant impacts on changing gender dynamics in the country. From the co-spokesperson to equal quotas, from the councils to LGBT perspectives, strategies that didn't exist up until now in any other organisational structures were implemented, and those principles inspired many movements and institutions in Turkey. Many HDK affiliates have carried these strategies back to their organisations over time. As a result, the HDK has not only influenced the subjective transformations of its own activists and the institutional-level perspective of its components, but also paved the way for these policies to have broader and more widespread social effects. This process reflects the 'ripple-effect' learning processes that social movement practices have, which spread out beyond the immediate social movement space to influence new constituencies.

A female activist from the New Life Association tells how the HDK's gender-based work does not only affect and transform activists at the level of the movement, but also generates learning processes which bring about change at the family and community level, including within the homes of HDK activists:

> We do not do all this struggle in vain, we do not waste all this effort, and people do these things in their own homes too. We have many friends and we can go to their houses. This auto-control also began to happen in their homes. For the classic Turkish leftist or Kurdish leftist, the free woman is out of reach for him all the time. They give her great value but don't want her as their wife. We are trying to change it. We are developing a very serious resistance in that regard. We make it to our red line and it is really effective. They are really changing. For example, many married female friends have said to us, 'after my husband came here, he changed a lot. He comes home and helps with chores, he changed the way he speaks'. These are important things to one person, even to two people. The problem with leftism is that we already talk a lot about the problem but we do not put it out in our lives. We will do it with such little things ... So we feel very good as women. We know that we have a serious weight on men. Men sincerely pay attention; The way they act and behave. For example, they wash the dishes in the kitchen. Let's see them not doing it and they will see what is coming at them (laughs).
>
> (Individual Interview T33, cited in Kutan and Çelik: 301)

Just as gender is being conceptualised as a holistic concept, so too is the concept of power. Within this feminist thinking, the HDK defines patriarchy, capitalism, nationalism, religion and authoritarianism as interrelated and mutually inclusive forms of domination rather than as separate phenomena. As stated in the HDK Foundation Bulletin (2012: 6):

> Our congress recognises that the male-dominated system (patriarchy) is a systematic form of domination that is touted in all spaces of society. It believes that male sovereignty (patriarchy),

against all other forms of domination and exploitation (class, national, faith) is a specific form of oppression and exploitation.

Intersectionality has become a key heuristic device for analysing/conceptualising multiple intersecting dynamics in the making of gendered identities, and multiple intersections of social structures in the making of injustices (patriarchy, capitalism, nationalism, etc.) – gender injustice being just one particular expression. Intersectionality also functions as a strategy of emancipation and struggle – connecting gender struggles to other forms of struggle. Besides drawing on the intersectionality of these situated diverse gender identities (class, ethnicity, race, religion and sex, etc.) and intersectionality of various sources and structures of domination and injustice (capitalism, nationalism and patriarchy), the HDK's radical gender politics also draws attention to the intersectionality of diverse struggles as the key factor for transforming new subjects, organisations and society. This is done both by connecting those diverse feminist praxis and women's struggles and also by linking them to other forms of struggle through a common shared idea to bring forth an equal, free and democratic society.

Thus, at the centre of this framework lies a strong commitment to bringing about a new gender-based equality which is understood as an important component of broader social emancipation and transformation. The horizontal institutional form, adopting new practices of inclusion and equality (such as the co-presidency and quota system) and adopting and creating new autonomous women-only struggle spaces are all seen as means to unleash the radical potential of this emancipatory political framework. These distinct and *autonomous spaces* for collective action (such as women's assemblies, women's commission and women's congress), whilst at the same time having equal representation (under the quota system) in every political space within the HDK and the co-chairing, sharing of power equally in every political unit, are thus seen as crucial mechanisms that provide spaces where women can engage and practice democracy, utilise their equal rights and develop a new politics. All of these practices are aimed at inclusion and equal representation of the most marginalised voices in a horizontal and diffused form of power, and providing spaces to allow women to develop their own mechanisms of power that provide real security, protection, defence and prosperity, not just for them but also for their communities.

Many of the women activists described the crucial importance of these practices and having their distinct and autonomous polit- ical spaces, which have allowed them to talk about their unique and distinct issues, as well as other broader issues, and make deci- sions away from the 'male gaze'. Elsewhere this has been called a 'positive boundary making process' (Taylor and Whittier, 1992). However, 'intentional autonomous political spaces' are not just places of 'democracy in action' but also 'emotional spaces', 'spaces for new subject formation', 'spaces of freedom', 'spaces of solidarity', 'spaces of learning', 'spaces of knowledge-making' (as our inform- ants noted again and again); where multiple encounters take place, where women touch each other's lives in different ways, where they develop new concepts and knowledge, where they share, learn and construct. Talking about these autonomous political spaces, one women's movement actor argues that these spaces are:

> our space of freedom, our field of sovereignty, a space where we were confident that we would not experience anything that we may experience in a mixed environment. Of course, women coming from social organisations had some concerns. But after a while, once we have known each other, we began to trust each other.
>
> (Woman, Gender and Change, Focus Group 2, cited in Kutan and Çelik: 239)

The female activists with whom we spoke gave a sense of exciting processes of prolific learning which took place in these intercul- tural, female-only spaces within the newly formed movement. With the forming of its own party – the HDP, these measures were also incorporated into the political form and politics of the new elec- toral vehicle, which made it the only political party that included gender-based equality politics right from its creation rather than including women later. This is particularly important given the reality that political parties and representational politics are increasingly gendered spaces, where women's roles are seen as secondary and often as a 'showcase' for gaining wider female support.

In the HDP's historic first electoral success in June 2015, under these practices, out of the 80 HDP members of parliament elected (out of the total 550 MPs), 32 were women. This, indeed, not only changed the proportion of female representation in parliament, which historically has been very low, but also made it more diverse, particularly by including women from the most marginalised communities. Representation of those women in parliament has been significant. Women began to form their own autonomous groups and had equal representation in every other mixed group that formed on particular issues. These secured women's central role in the debate and decision-making process not only on issues directly related to women but also on broader societal issues. It was also the first time in history that those marginalised women had taken centre stage in political debate, with their diversity (of colour, ethnicity, religion and vision) alongside each other, bringing their histories and experiences to the fore and making themselves and their communities more visible. In doing so, they challenge the hegemonic conception of women and gender roles at the heart of mainstream political power and propose an alternative politics that changes the conditions in which all their community lives.

Through all this, they are not only creating new subjects but also changing the public perceptions and stereotypes of themselves in which women are often seen as 'uneducated', 'traditional', backward' or as a 'threat', which has given hope to many women. Constituting a new gendered subject is central to this emancipatory framework. This new gendered subject announces herself as a radical subject (as described by several women activists), one that is willing to organise and 'resist' and 'fight' rather than one that is a passive 'recipient', one that 'demands' the impossible against all the odds.

This resistance is seen as an important strategy to develop women's power, and is constitutive of this new imagined subject. It is argued that it is only through learning processes which occur through struggle that women become 'self-confident' and empowered and it is this form that can destabilise the 'deep-seated patriarchal patterns' (Cemgil and Hoffmann, 2016: 64) and (re)configure the existing 'historic imbalance of power' between men and women (Gupta, 2017). Creating such enduring social structures, given that women are working within and between highly hierarchical forms of power, can only be sustained by a 'double axis of struggle'; an internal struggle against all forms of existing (patriarchal) domination and injustice within the 'safe space' of the HDK; and an external struggle against the various hegemonic dominations and injustices in society. It is only through this intersected double strategy that one can destabilise and challenge those embedded and internalised patriarchal forms of domination under the hegemonic form of *men'tality* and create a new form of *women'tality* (gained through a situated philosophy of the praxis of women) that allows women to remove all those 'enslaving emotions, needs and desires for their husband, father, lover, brother, friends' (Öcalan, 2013: 52). These are all powerful learning processes for women and men alike: indeed, we understand the process of creating this new *women'tality* as essentially a pedagogical process which is manifested as the HDK's alternative gender praxis.

This gender equality and women's empowerment is linked to the equality of the commons. The central aim being not just strengthening individual women's power and increasing gender equality for women but also reproducing the collective power of women (developing the women's movement), whose role is seen as crucial for the emergence of a new alternative world against and beyond hegemonic power (Federici, 2012). Thus, gender equality and freedom is not just an aim, but an important strategy that can be practised at the level of 'the fleshy, messy, and indeterminate stuff of everyday life' (Katz, 2001: 711); it is not something that will be achieved in a democracy, but rather it is democracy that is being made into reality through the collective action of diverse women. Since the body is seen as a collective entity, it combines the 'body politics' with that of the 'politics of the commons'.

Rejecting the unnecessary division between private and public and individual and collective, this framework combines the struggle of the 'personal is private' with that of 'struggle for equality, representation, recognition and justice' in order to create the spaces and necessary conditions for the body to live, act and perform freely without any forms of domination. This approach indeed requires a radical rupture with the existing social structures. It goes beyond most feminist analysis in which body politics seems to be separated from that of the commons. Thus, gender equality is not seen as a political end in itself but rather as a technology of change through which new subjects are being constituted, a new sense of belonging and a new social pact are being developed.

Talking about expanding the body and body politics beyond the periphery of skin, Silvia Federici (2020: 5) reminds us of the importance of different forms of being and living together:

> for what it finds, in going beyond the periphery of the skin, is not a culinary paradise but a magical continuity with the other living organisms that populate the earth: the bodies of human and the not-humans, the trees, the rivers, the sea, the stars. This is the image of a body that reunites what capitalism has divided, a body no longer constituted as a Leibnizian monad, without windows and without doors, but moving instead in harmony with the cosmos, in a world where diversity is wealth for all and a ground for communing rather than a source of divisions and antagonisms.

Thus, the freedom and equality of women is tied to the freedom of their communities as we are related and interrelated with humans and non-humans for multiple reasons and have a duty of care and responsibility for each other. Judith Butler explains that whilst the family may be a source of vulnerability, it can also be a source of love and protection and care (2016). This is nowhere more true than in the context of Kurdish and other marginalised communities; families are at the centre of this care and protection for their children and communities that have suffered an extreme form of violence by the state. Thus, what is required is not reforming those structures, but completely transforming and creating a new reality.

In this sense, this HDK gender equality approach transcends liberal gender equality in which equality is seen as an individual matter, where the aim is to get women to occupy certain social positions equally with men (leaning in), without challenging the existing uneven power structures that are the source of those inequalities in the first place. Furthermore, the horizontal nature of power with the HDK contrasts with conventional political party structures (including those of progressive political parties) in which power is often embodied in one person or a group of people and decisions are made at the top. The positive discriminatory strategies (quotas, safe spaces, etc.) that are aimed at securing equal representation and power-sharing between men and women are seen as crucial given the context of the political parties in Turkey, where leadership and power are dominated by men. As Gültan Kışanak argues, 'when there were many chairs, men like to share them with women, but when there was one chair, they did not want to give that to a woman' (Kışanak, 2018: 38).

The HDK radical gender politics challenges the existing hegemonic meaning of gender, roles, womanhood and femininity profoundly and generates new meanings and new understandings, as the coming together of women from diverse cultures and backgrounds produces counter-hegemonic semiotic processes. It has gone beyond being a mere critique or challenge, as through various technologies and practices it has engaged in the process of (re)constituting new radical gendered subjects, new values, new relations and relationality. Thus, the HDK's new gender politics was not just conducive to creating a new epistemological understanding but also an ontological one, a new world beyond the existing system of powers.

An HDK activist who was from an Islamic tradition joined the Democratic Islam Congress and HDK's Peoples and Beliefs Commission. She talks about how she has learnt from coming together and working with the diverse women of the HDK:

I met today at HDK with the Women's Council which continues to grow stronger and bring together all different women's structures within it. This is one of the examples that had an impact on me, both politically and socially. It is very local and small sized; in the past I had been in charge of projects where I was a founder and president of an association; but here it is really different; here you see women from so many different backgrounds under the same roof. Women's councils are authentic and autonomous, independent; the decisions that are taken here are not debatable, you see here women's self-confidence, power and freedom ... I went to such a meeting once, the Middle East Women's Conference, this was way before HDP. It was organised by Kurdish women. After that meeting when I got back to Istanbul I remember having discussed with my women friends, members of our women's movement in Istanbul, we said to each other 'we have always looked at and talked to women's movement in Europe, but we haven't even noticed that movement which was right under our noses'. This was really striking. There are so many steps that develop them and bring them to maturity.

(Individual Interview T41, cited in Kutan and Çelik, 2021: 274)

Another woman activist underlines the importance of the autonomous and separate structure of HDK's council:

For instance, I know very well now that I should not take any decisions about women in a mixed structure. In other words, following the journey with women and not letting any women's competences be discussed. We have witnessed this a lot at all management levels. Women's competences are subject to discussion while men's competences are never put on the table. I can discuss any matter related to women with even a woman whose opinions differ from mine but can never do so with men. I had this experience thanks to HDK.

(Women, Gender and Social Change, Focus Group 2, cited in Kutan and Çelik, 2021: 274)

Another woman activist emphasises the dimension that made it meaningful for her to engage in this political praxis which generates 'human and conscientious depth' in the HDK's activists:

From my point of view, I can say that HDK pulled me from dry and shallow politics and put me in a place where politics have a meaning, something deep. And I am not talking about political depth, it is more about human and conscientious depth. You can learn political depth from books, here and there. HDK allowed me to wipe myself clean of all this androcentric state policy and opt for a more social one.

(Women, Gender and Social Change, Focus Group 2,
cited in Kutan and Çelik, 2021: 274)

The existence of LGBTI within HDK and their visibility and their politics of demand in HDK's big organisations is an important dimension that has had a transformative effect on many activists:

First, HDK involving LGBT movement is really awesome. I mean they couldn't prevent it, stop it. Although there was some resistance, it didn't happen. Because Gezi Park protests had already happened, LGBT was, I say it in quotation marks, Gezi's hero. The LGBT movement had established themselves and pride parades were going on smoothly. Therefore, there was HDK and HDP's LGBT Commission. For instance, that commission organised a meeting together with Sabahat Tuncel. I'll never forget that meeting. It's engraved in my mind. Here at that meeting I've seen Kurdish brothers with their beards and stuff, you'd never believe that they were gay, and they made demands. They said to Sabahat Tuncel: 'I want to see an Ahmet Türk talking about queer politics', 'I want to see at the Parliament a Selahattin Demirtas who is talking about gay rights', they said stuff like that. This was radical for me, you know, addressing those things to the representatives of the Kurdish movement. I remember his face but I don't know who he was or which movement he belonged to. But that was important ... There was another congress of HDK in Ankara. A trans friend, also a member of the General Assembly, said out loud from the lectern 'Where are you darling? Here I am darling'. And then he said, 'I see you all from here and can see who didn't chant the slogan' and repeated once again compelling the protocol to do the same. The fact that LGBTI chanted the slogan and that everybody joined was important to me.

(Individual Interview T8, cited in Kutan and Çelik, 2021: 275)

Another woman activist explains how being together with the Kurdish movement and leading a women's struggle made her stronger:

I was politicised at university over the Kurdish issue. I was reading and doing studies on Kurdish issues. I was at that time following BDP. I wasn't part of a feminist organisation but I would describe myself as a feminist. Therefore, HDK was the only organisation I was part of, and I like that feeling of being part of an organisation. It's something to do with the sense of belonging. Here I defend people's right to self-determination and for that reason I am together with the Kurds. I had thought on many issues before too but HDK is where I noticed it, if there is a struggle for labour, ecology, if there is an issue on people's right to self-determination, well, it is in here, at HDK, that I noticed I was part of it. I would sound arrogant if I said I support them, instead I prefer saying that I am a subject who is leading a struggle there with them. In other words, I am a subject, a part of this struggle for peace. When I joined them, I wasn't that young nor part of an organisation. I noticed that here women are very strong; for some time, there were a lot of crisis and problems. I got kind of depressed, and I remember crying in the women's room. Then a woman approached me and said to me that 'if we cried each time we faced a problem we wouldn't be able to have all those achievements'. She was angry with me, she said 'come with me' and took me out of that room. That's just one souvenir, we have many more like this. I noticed there that we, women, are part and partner of this organisation. We are the founders, the subjects. We have, or at least I have learned from women colleagues of the Kurdish Movement that we cannot leave the positions to men each time there is a negative situation.

(Togetherness and Unity in Diversity, Workshop 2, cited in Kutan and Çelik, 2021: 276)

The learning processes generated by the HDK's gender-based praxis do not only affect its organisational form and the subjective transformations of its own activists. They have also contributed to the creation of new organisations, participation and decision-making mechanisms of the women's struggle and LGBTI struggle in Turkey.

Whilst less dramatic, and at a smaller scale, the Housing Assembly's organising has seen similar transformative learning processes:

> When I joined the Housing Assembly I realised it's a two way thing. This is not only one way and a woman needs to cook, work and you give your wages [to your husband]. So I learnt a lot that late one night I came home and I said to my husband, 'We need to talk. I can't work for you. You need to work for me'. He said what is this you are talking about. I said, 'we need to do both. You come from work, I come from work, and if you are first you clean, you start making food. If I come first, I need to clean and make food'. I said it's not a man in the roof and a woman on the floor. And since to date, both of us share the work in our house.
>
> (Participant, Focus Group, Cape Town, 13 June 2019,
> cited in Benjamin, 2021: 99)

A few of the women interviewed told similar stories of changes in their households. Whilst this learning has not yet generated a change across the movement or spread throughout the communities, it has the potential to bring about this change. This can be done if the prefigurative politics that we see emerging in the visioning of a 'decent house' begins to include an intersection with gender equality and the role that women play in the household; and if the Housing Assembly starts to embody this in the way care roles in the movement are redistributed. This will then have the effect of influencing the political agenda of the movement such that the call for decent housing and basic services is done from a gender-responsive angle that also seeks to redistribute the care work in the household.

However, despite shifting their struggle to be more intersectional, gender is yet to make an impact on the organisation in terms of how the struggle for housing is articulated. Whilst a large number of women are represented in the movement's structures, they have yet to influence the movement to include gender and the patriarchy as another system of oppression alongside race and class. This is an unfortunate legacy from the anti-apartheid movement, which also put race and class struggles ahead of gender. The effect of this is that the struggle for housing has not engaged with the unequal social and power dynamics that exist between men and women in the home and in the community, with the majority of women members still carrying the burden of care responsibilities. And so the fight for housing has left out the fight for gender equality or the rights of women.

There are a few women within the movement who have been trying to push this agenda and have been successful in achieving small changes. They have done this through setting up a women's collective for women members to gather and share experiences and using that space to introduce new knowledge on patriarchy as a system of oppression. Whilst it has not been adopted across the organisation, this knowledge and learning has brought about changes in some members' household dynamics.

The women's collective that women in the Housing Assembly set up presents an opportunity to shift the movement's political agenda to one that is an intersection of race, class and gender. 'A women's collective is a good thing, and we really need that space because it would take us away from our male comrades, and there are things that would be easier to discuss if they were not part of us'. (Member of Housing Assembly, Individual Interview, 21 May 2019, cited in Benjamin, 2021: 100). But this is not going to be easy as gender equality is constantly in a battle with the class and race struggle within the movement. The class struggle always takes priority, in the same way as race took priority in the struggle against apartheid, and the struggle for gender equality carries less importance and is not prioritised: '... We haven't really done anything aimed specifically at women. I would say do more focused activism, maybe even a bit of feminism' (Member of Housing Assembly, Individual Interview, 21 May 2019, cited in Benjamin, 2021: 100).

For NOMADESC, despite being a rare example in Colombia of a human rights organisation run exclusively by women, during the early years of the organisation's work in the southwest region there was not an explicit construction of a gender perspective to the organisation's work, perhaps inevitably given that NOMADESC found itself in the context of extreme violence which had spread across the region and was driving social movements into a defensive survival mode. 'I think at the beginning when I came in it was there, but it wasn't so prominent or so signposted; it was part of the political focus and the human rights work, and part of the knowledge dialogue ... but the theme of gender wasn't so strong' (current leading NOMADESC member, and Diploma student during early years, interview, 2018, cited in Kane and NOMADESC, 2021: 139).

From 2006 onwards, NOMADESC began to develop a more explicit, structured and themed approach to its work with women, initially through two particular bespoke pedagogical-organisational support processes with communities:

It was from 2006 onwards that the work around women and gender became a more explicit part [of our work]; that year we began the two pedagogical processes in human rights in the Triana and Cisneros communities. In Cisneros, the process was aimed at the wives and mothers, etc., of the victims of the mass detentions which [the state] had carried out in the community, 64 people in a total of 600 inhabitants, under the 'Democratic Security' policy of Alvaro Uribe's government. The process with Triana was aimed at the mothers, wives, and relatives of victims of the massacres and murders committed by paramilitaries in the rural areas of Buenaventura. (The process would later be extended to include men.)

(Current leading NOMADESC member, and Diploma student during the early years, interview, 2019, cited in Kane and NOMADESC, 2021: 140)

From 2010, NOMADESC's work with women would become even more prominent within their own organising and pedagogical work, as well as amongst the social movements of southwest Colombia, when it began to organise the Women's Forum for Economic, Social, Cultural and Environmental Rights, an annual event which has become something of an institution on the social movement calendar in the region. Each year the forum brings together 200–300 women activists from social movements and organisations across the southwest region:

> [The event] puts into dialogue the experiences and processes of struggle of organised and unorganised women in southwest Colombia. The event has three aims: first, to come together and meet via a dialogue of experiences, struggles, realities, knowledges, and imaginations … second, to advance in the recuperation and respect of the dignity and the rights of women, as well as of the different social sectors and peoples, and strengthen their organisational capacity in the region. Third, to strengthen the links and networks, and seek to create solidarity and a common agenda between women from different sectors, urban and rural, from across the southwest region.
>
> (Current leading NOMADESC member, and Diploma student during the early years, interview, 2018, cited in Kane and NOMADESC, 2021: 141)

> I think it is a really interesting initiative … because it opens a space where women can build together, can build Resistance and Alternatives, and also make visible what they are doing.
>
> (Participant, territorial workshop, Cali, 2018, cited in Kane and NOMADESC, 2021: 141)

As the quotes above demonstrate, the event has several political and pedagogical objectives, the first of which is linked to the inherent value of providing a forum for women from diverse struggles, movements and territories to come together and share experiences, learn and build from each other. As with all events organised by NOMADESC, these events are always full of the symbolism of the social movements involved, art and culture, along with the political element in which all of the participating organisations have a chance to make a declaration about the context and realities which they face as women and as members of collectives which are engaged in social struggles against a multitude of injustices. The fact that the event is staged in one of the city centre's busiest plazas is a political statement in itself, an attempt to make visible what has been kept invisible by the state and the mainstream media, both in terms of the realities faced by women in southwest Colombia and also the struggles of their movements. Men are invited to attend the events, but the focus is on giving a voice to women and highlighting their roles within the struggles of the region, and in generating solidarity and collaboration between them.

NOMADESC's experience of working with communities and movements across the territories of southwest Colombia provides them with a unique insight into the intersectional effects of the armed conflict. During the past two decades in Colombia, the particularity of the way that women have experienced the armed conflict has increasingly been recognised and debated within social movements as well as in broader civil society:

The social and armed conflict in our country leaves deep marks on lives and particularly on generations of women; that is to say that, aside from the fact that women's bodies are used as war trophies, the war also brings about modifications in individuals and collective lives, and since women tend to have the role of caretakers of life (cuidadoras de la vida), they are at the forefront of the search [for actions] to prevent the repetition of these violent situations which snatch life away.

(Current leading NOMADESC member, and Diploma student during the early years, interview, 2019, cited in Kane and NOMADESC, 2021: 142)

As the quote above points out, this debate has finally led some sectors to recognise the role which women have played historically within families, communities and collectives seeking to survive within the context of the armed conflict. In a socially conservative

Catholic society in which female suffrage was only achieved in 1954, NOMADESC's concrete experience of working with communities has confirmed to the organisation that the struggle for women's liberation begins at home:

> On an individual level, we consider that the difficulties derive from the daily lives of women and our own spaces, because historic, structured machismo has been naturalised in its many forms, impeding the effective, active, mass participation of women in organising and mobilisation processes. The struggle begins at home, where the idea that women have absolute responsibility for the home and to raise the children has been naturalised. This is the first barrier that the vast majority of women find.
>
> (ibid.)

Within the internal political organising spaces of social movements, communities and activist collectives in Colombia, the past decade has also seen increasing attention paid to overcoming practices which serve to reproduce patriarchal social relations, in the search for a prefigurative organising praxis which can begin to build social relations in line with the emancipatory visions which are being fought for. Despite increasing awareness and debate, NOMADESC's organising experience has demonstrated that much work remains to be done in order to achieve equal participation and recognition within the struggles for social change of the diverse movements and communities which NOMADESC works with:

> In the collective political sphere, the barrier which women must overcome is that they are usually given menial tasks and chores, which then limit their participation in spaces for debate and decision-making within social movements, despite the fact that their collective action is at least equal to that of men. Despite the fact that progress has been made in this respect in recent years, there is still a certain resistance in terms of valuing the importance of the ideas, proposals and contributions of women in the struggles for social transformation.
>
> (ibid.)

The conception and praxis of gender contained within NOMAD-ESC's work have been forged as a result of the collective learning processes generated through two decades of intercultural organising and pedagogical work with diverse social movements across the conflict-affected southwest region of Colombia. As has been discussed extensively elsewhere, the praxis of the pedagogical process is influenced by popular education principles such as 'knowledge dialogue' and learning through doing; and at the same time is rooted in the philosophical principles of social humanism, which dictate the importance of recognising the diversity of social subjects and sensitivity to their different experiences of oppression.

> If we're talking about social humanism, which was a really strong element of the diplomas and even stronger now … in the UIP and the focus on 'buenvivir' … then gender has to be an important element of the work in order to be able to talk about that harmonisation between humans, and with the natural environment and everything that surrounds us.
>
> (Current leading NOMADESC member, and Diploma student during the early years, interview, 2019 cited in Kane and NOMADESC, 2021: 143)

NOMADESC's work with communities, and indeed with women's collectives, has been based on the recognition that women experience the repressive context of human rights violations and the armed conflict differently, and that women's oppression takes on added and different dimensions than that of men in all spheres of society, including within communities and social movements. Political subjectivities are understood to be defined by this diversity of experience. It is this diversity of experience which provides the fundamental elements for the intercultural knowledge dialogue which occurs within the process. A key aspect of facilitating and developing this dialogue has been the Annual Women's Forum events, which have provided a space in which this intercultural dialogue can take place between women from the diverse movements and territories of the region.

Within NOMADESC's pedagogical work, the starting point for this approach to gender is around recognising women's contribution to communities, movements and social struggles (including self-recognition of women in order to recognise the role they play within broader struggles and the gender dynamics which operate): 'We start from a key element which is very simple, it is about recognition … the recognition of women, of our struggles, our contributions, our ideas, everything that we have offered and which often isn't recognised, that is the starting point' (ibid.).

This approach has also determined NOMADESC's approach to working on issues relating to gender, and has seen the gradual development and deepening of an attempt to build an intercultural, class-based feminism which is sensitive to diverse cosmo-visions, identities and cultures of the movements involved, and which at the same time is able to empower women and challenge practices which reproduce patriarchy both within and outside social movements. As set out above, the approach is still in the process of construction:

We have been elaborating it and debating it, not only in the university … [the debate] has also fed off many other processes … we have a permanent dialogue with the communities, with the black community, the indigenous, the peasants, what are they all thinking … this has fed into the process, we are building together … so our approach to gender is strongly linked to the territorial characteristics of the areas that NOMADESC works in … [the work] … has suggested the inclusion of certain particularities when thinking of a feminist conception which could respond to the ethno-territorial diversity, the different cultures.

(Current leading NOMADESC member, and Diploma student during the early years, interview, 2018 cited in Kane and NOMADESC, 2021: 143)

Clearly, this approach has potential tensions, given that patriarchal structures and social relations can be even more deeply rooted within rural communities in Colombia, where social conservatism can remain strong. Key here is the dynamic notion of culture: the different cultures of the movements and sectors involved are not viewed as fixed, static phenomena but as social processes which can be transformed and enriched through contact with each other. Hence the potential tensions, which are undoubtedly latent within the process, can at the same time be viewed as potential learning and transformation processes within the intercultural dialogue which occurs within the UIP:

> For example, with sexual diversities ... take the peasant movement, without being disrespectful, within its cultural aspects there has been a lot of conservativism and the university allows this sector to meet with urban spaces and the new identities of new subjects which are emerging, and which have new revindication struggles ... and in this process together they start to understand why these perspectives are important ... also the question of female leadership which has become stronger and more common [in social movements], before they were less visible and this is, they are making themselves felt in the UIP.
>
> (Activist, an ally of the pedagogical process, interview, 2018, cited in Kane and NOMADESC, 2021: 144)

Set within the intercultural pedagogical space, and the broader objective of seeking to build thematic and strategic unity and collective identity between the diverse collective subjects involved, the broader aim of NOMADESC's gender work is around creating more just, harmonious and equal relations between men and women. Within a repressive context in which generations of both male and female activists have been murdered, disappeared and exiled, concrete experience has taught the organisation that only an intercultural feminism rooted in a class-based analysis of the broader structures which create and sustain patriarchal oppression can be of use in the struggle for emancipation. They are critical of what they perceive to be academic, urban mainstream approaches to feminism which have become influential within Colombian civil society, academia and some social movements, and which are deemed to be too focused on public policy and insensitive to the intersectional dimensions of the diverse female experience across Colombia, as well as the realities of women in poor urban or rural communities and conflict-affected territories.

One interesting learning point within NOMADESC's pedagogical praxis has been the central role of women in knowledge processes within communities, for example, in the preservation and repro-duction of historical memory and 'ancestral knowledge' contained within communities. The emphasis upon the revindication and weaving of different knowledges within the UIP, as well as within NOMADESC's broader work, has meant bringing to centre stage this vital knowledge role which is often played by women within communities and social movements. For example, rural communi-ties would historically have a vast knowledge of medicinal plants, which has been gradually lost over recent decades. In many commu-nities, it is women who have retained this knowledge and sought to pass it down to future generations. Within the UIP, the female par-ticipants from the Triana Group of Women and Men focused their participatory action research project upon identifying and doc-umenting the different plants and remedies which women in the community held. The idea is that the product of the investigation becomes a tool not only for the Triana community but to be shared with others in and beyond the UIP.

The Madhes movement produced new political leaders represent-ing diverse constituencies within Madhes, such as women, marginalised castes and deprived social groups. There was a strong belief amongst women activists that they were involved in the move-ment in order to secure a brighter future for their children. They recognised the structural inequalities and marginalisation that had disadvantaged their families, and therefore the Madhes movement was no longer a male-dominated phenomenon, unlike most gen-dered tasks, given the cultural traditions in Madhes. Even though women's freedom from patriarchy was a central gender-based agenda in the Maoist movement, the Madhes movement did not explicitly spell out women's suppressed social positions. Women joined the movement, like anyone else to struggle for their ethnic rights, freedoms and representation. As a result, female activists also emerged as political leaders as an outcome of the Madhes movement. Despite the largely disadvantaged position of women in Madhesi society, their role in the movement has been significant. During the 2015 uprising, women were at the forefront of the movement to oppose the constitutional provision that children of Madhesi women who are married to Indian citizens would be deprived of citizen rights, and to demand a legislative remedy.

BUILDING THE FUTURE IN THE PRESENT: PREFIGURATIVE POLITICS AND SOCIAL MOVEMENTS

A component of the shifting subjectivities within social movements observed in this research is a strong commitment to prefigurative politics. This is understood as a commitment to living in the present as you would like to live in the future. Yates (2015: 1) defines this as 'the attempted construction of alternative or utopic social relations in the present, either in parallel with, or in the course of, adversarial social movement protest'. This contrasts with a critique of traditional social movements, which were assessed to be too focused on future objectives and failed to model their utopian aspirations in the present. Examples such as the lack of internal and open democracy within traditional movements and lack of diversity have been contrasted with a contemporary push by many movements to mirror their aspirations in their own practices and conduct in the here and now.

In *Emergent Strategy*, Adrienne Maree Brown (2017: 57) argues that 'we have to create more futures' in the midst of all the limitations and destructions visited on our bodies and souls by the multiple sources of power under contemporary global capitalism. According to her, this can be done through us creatively 'applying lessons from our past to our future' and 'imagining an end that seems to be impossible as it has not yet been conceived' (2017: 198). Engaging in prefiguring a new future in the present, she argues, is the only alternative way to unleash our human creativity and turn those moments of impossibility into possibilities of hope. Thus, whilst prefigurative politics focuses on 'here' and 'now', it is fundamentally linked to the future as its prime focus is to bring about what Cooper calls 'everyday utopias' (Cooper, 2014). Eduardo Galeano describes this process as 'Walking towards the horizon' (quoted in Notes from Nowhere, 2003: 499). Ana Dinerstein has characterised prefigurative organising as 'a process of learning hope' (2014: 76). Our research supports this characterisation of prefiguration as a learning process. Indeed, based on our case studies, we argue that prefigurative organising should be understood as an essentially learning-based social movement praxis, through which activists come together to collectively work out solutions and develop a praxis which is congruent with the future utopia for which they strive. The cases of the HDK and NOMADESC/the UIP demonstrate the emancipatory potential of intercultural prefigurative organising. In both cases, activists described profound learning and counter-hegemonic knowledge production processes as a result of their participation in such an intercultural, prefigurative space.

For the HDK, the movement aims to create an alternative egalitarian, democratic and peaceful Turkey emerging from the 'cracks' produced by neoliberal capitalism, authoritarian nationalism and the patriarchal system, precisely through operating in that manner in the here and now, and thus modelling that behaviour. Their radical prefigurative politics fundamentally involved a new way of thinking (theory) and doing (practice). At the centre of HDK's prefigurative politics lies a strong commitment to constituting new subjects, norms and values in line with that desired future in the present. The prefigurative experiment of the HDK rests on its desire to foster alternative radical democratic practices both within the movement and in the wider society, and aimed at reconstituting new subjects and social relations in ways that can contribute to a new mode of alternative power, whilst simultaneously critiquing and challenging dominant social structures associated with neoliberal capitalism, nationalisms and patriarchy.

With these embodied new ways of 'thinking' and 'doing', the HDK seeks to challenge and critique the existing hegemonic construction of identities (gender, class, religion, ethnicity, sexuality, etc.), sense of belonging and relationship of one to another whilst at the same time creating a new way of being, sociability, solidarity necessary in constituting a new Turkey. This prefigurative politics has enabled the HDK to capture the imagination of a range of political organisations, groupings, trade unions, feminist women organisations and individuals to join them under its common roof.

Explicit in the HDK's prefigurative politics is the experimental nature of their social action as they carry on their struggle. Examples such as quotas for minoritised groups, co-chairs for all positions with equal gender representation, conscious recognition of the diversity of opinion, identity and priorities; decision-making through consensus; and 'safe spaces' for minoritised subjects to operate in, all mirror a fairer, more plural and open future society.

These important characteristics of the HDK's prefigurative politics stand in opposition to a linear, homogenising and universal understanding of social change in which change is expected to come about after taking power (such as by a revolution), and instead focuses on creating plural and diverse everyday futures in the present as a mechanism to project them into the future. Our research demonstrates that being part of this prefigurative organising praxis proved to be a transformative experience for HDK activists, generating counter-hegemonic knowledge and learning processes which served to deepen and consolidate this alternative model.

These prefigurative policies are particularly significant for those subjects whose agency is often regarded as secondary, such as women and minority groups such as LGBT communities. By implementing those prefigurative politics and practices they both vindicate and integrate these different subjects into the HDK and strengthen its power. All of the above policies, practices and mechanisms are the backbone of the HDK prefigurative politics and serve to challenge capitalist modernity and build an alternative counter-hegemonic power.

As our analysis shows, the HDK imagined utopia is far from being a singular homogenising and universalising utopia, but rather plural utopias that can co-exist alongside each other in a different Turkey. As mentioned by many activists, despite all the tensions and challenges the fact that the HDK still upholds its values within the membership is down to what the HDK 'means' and 'what it continues to offer' for their future:

> ... if there are still so many people here at the HDK, it means the HDK still promises something for people ... Nobody wants to continue in this struggle if the HDK was not offering something different ... Perhaps this the reason why we keep going under these extremely difficult conditions. For this reason, I think, the HDK still remains a projector for our future and a future hope that we hold onto ... But this hope is not such a romantic foolishness, even in these dark times. It is rather a radical hope that gives an emergence to a radical bottom-up movement. It is this radical hope that gives a new direction to these new bottom-up movements ... the kind of hope that I am referring to here is not just something that is related to optimism or about being optimistic in every situation. But this hope refers to a particular mindset that makes us think that there is always another way no matter what and asks us to act upon this thinking despite all fear and repression. Thus, this hope is not just a matter of courage, but rather a life potency (power), a political drive that acts as a driving force and leverage for organisations and mobilisation. I think, HDK still signifies this hope and that is why it is still a home for many of us standing here under these conditions.
>
> (Individual Interview T3, cited in Kutan and Çelik, 2021: 214–215)

This 'radical hope' that embodies a possibility of change for a better future becomes more crucial, especially at the present time when activists and their institutions have been subjected to increased violence and repression. The importance of this radical hope is therefore fundamentally linked to the future, knowing that what we do now has an important effect on our future. Thus, activists' determination to keep going is not that they think the collective struggle in the HDK spaces is challenge and conflict-free, but rather a continuous refusal to allow anyone to shape their future, even though it is hard to determine what that future holds. Talking about the significant value of this hope at a time of extreme difficulties, one activist notes:

> Now you will ask, what is the equivalent of this (hope) in society? It seems like there is not a direct equivalent at this particular moment. But this hope can only be turned into a potency that opens up new channels for our future struggle when it is kept alive at the core of our struggle that seems to be weakened and narrowed at this particular time. It only then becomes instrumental for the emergence of new possibilities, new exits and new beginnings. It is not my intention to say that this will inevitably happen or establish a direct causation. But what I am rather trying to say is that it will open new possibilities and new channels for us and that what we do now at times when we are less powerful, when we are at survival mode has an important dimension for our future.
>
> (Individual Interview T3, cited in Kutan and Çelik, 2021: 215)

To this extent, the diverse and rich repertoires of the HDK in (re) focusing on the histories, stories, memories, knowledges and experiences of each of its communities can be seen as challenging the homogeneous national hegemonic historiography, which has excluded and marginalised other histories and knowledges, in order to rebuild a bottom-up alternative historiography through vindicating each of these diverse past histories, stories and knowledges and uniting them under common collective memories without reducing one to another. By reconnecting the past with the present and future, the HDK not only shows that all that collective pain and suffering did not happen for nothing, but also uses all of the suffering and pain as bricks in the creation of a better future social life in the present struggle.

For NOMADESC and the UIP, the pedagogical programme that underpins the Intercultural University of the Peoples is itself a prefigurative political process. By drawing together Colombia's marginalised communities (Afro-Colombian, indigenous, women, trade unionists and students), they are envisaging a new intercultural reality. Similarly, central to the pedagogy is a vindication of the wisdom of the diverse groups, the 'ancestral' but also 'subaltern' knowledges, and a strong recognition that an 'ecology of knowledges' necessarily underpins an alternative future in Colombia. Part of the UIP process is for the participants to develop 'planes de vida' (life plans), which fits well with the logic of prefigurative politics that communities need to build their futures from the present, through analysis and social action. Concepts such as 'paz territorial' (territorial peace) similarly indicate that the future is constructed in the present through reclaiming space through social struggle. Whilst this future is utopian and aspirational, there is also a strong non-deterministic perspective, best captured in the phrase 'walking we learn'.

Whilst the prefigurative nature of the Housing Assembly and NEMAF is less pronounced, signs are emerging in both of new democratic mechanisms and an increased focus on ensuring diversity, particularly gender representation.

CHAPTER CONCLUSIONS

This chapter has shown that social movements are navigating uncharted waters in new and imaginative ways, and these counter-hegemonic processes of learning and knowledge-making are transforming movement activities. New framings, conceptualisations and ideas are emerging out of social movement praxis, which rather than mirror 'Western' models and solutions, are reframing problems and offering radical solutions and alternatives that grow out of the complex histories within which they are situated. These ideas are not binary, but often hybrid fusions of radical theory and endogenous knowledges, and their attraction is often much broader and more embedded, with the potential to be more sustainable than imported ideas. Central to this, is the recognition and activation of diversity as resource, both in terms of expanding the power of the movement, but also its knowledge resources. Building these inter-cultural, inter-generational, inter-gender relationships also creates the conditions under which new, more open, subjectivities emerge alongside those identities, pointing towards new prefigurative collectivities. We argue that these new modes of praxis are propitious for deeply transformative learning processes, which support the generation of new subjectivities and drive changes in movement cultures. Linked to this struggle, is the rise of prefigurative politics that refuses to wait until the revolution for real changes to come, and forces an internal movement politics of democracy, recognition of diversity, and radical hope.

At the heart of all these processes of innovative practice, are new ideas and ways of thinking that emerge out of praxis, emerge out of the tensions and frictions between what social movements aspire to do and the temporal, economic, social, political and cultural context which shapes the limits of the possible. Out of this process emerges new ways of thinking and being, of conceptualising problems and solutions, of testing out alternatives and modifying strategy. The movement becomes both a school for learning new things, new skills, new ideas, and a laboratory where strategies are tested and new ways of framing and shaping ideas emerge. In the next chapter, we will explore some of the effects that these processes of learning and knowledge-making have had on the movements, the activists and the societies within which they operate.

5

The effects of these learning and knowledge-making processes on peace with social justice

INTRODUCTION

Causality in social movement research is a very difficult thing to evidence, and extrapolating the particular role of an individual social movement institution from the broader contemporary and historical movement is even more complex. Furthermore, honing in on learning and knowledge-making, as separate components of a social movement institution's broader practices and contributions, is an equally difficult task – particularly as we have revealed already, that education and knowledge-making occur across all of those practices and are embedded within them, often implicitly. Similarly, the question itself poses a number of challenges for our work. What do we mean by effects? Do we judge effects by the objectives of the movement, which often aspire to the radical restructuring of society? How do we measure these effects, and how can we attribute these to specific social movement organisations? Do we see the effect as on the individual, on the movement, on the society – or all of the above? And can you separate them out? Do we rest at concrete material changes? Or do we also explore the discursive? Or both?

In response to this, we argue for both an exploratory and a pragmatic solution, which stays faithful to this work's central premise, of allowing the movements, their activists and leaders to guide our reflections to caveat assumptions with contextual insights, and to openly subject the findings to critical interrogation so that readers can judge for themselves the robustness of our assertions. Most importantly, we refuse to engage in a binary of success and failure when exploring these issues, but understand them as interrelated in complex ways. They are processes of learning, rich with insights that help build the future. More importantly, our focus is on how participants of the movement have expanded their knowledge base in methodologies of movement organising, and their collective capabilities to generate ripple effects and, most importantly, to adapt their struggle to new challenges and threats posed by hegemonic forces, including the oppressive actions of the state.

One reflection that we have constantly returned to in this project is that of the tumultuous years around 1968, which saw the emergence of civil rights protest movements around the world. In so many ways, and depending on where, and who you are representing, it was both a victory and a defeat for the left. In purely economic and political terms, the 1968 global uprisings failed to bring the revolutionary transformations that many of their participants aspired to. Yet, the cultural effects of 1968 remain with us today. The obsession with which the new right in the US and Europe over the last decade has denounced 'cultural Marxism' is a testament to the success of those 'cultural' changes in many parts of the world – student rights, women's rights, gay rights, racial equality, human rights, civil rights. All are a powerful legacy of the 'failure' of 1968, and evidence of its lasting effects. Drawing on this spirit, in the rest of this chapter, we will explore 'effects' thematically, and weave together the 'individual', 'institutional', and 'societal' effects of the learning and knowledge-making processes, and the inter-relationships between them.

FROM INDIVIDUAL VICTIMS TO COLLECTIVE SUBJECTS OF STRUGGLE

In the general literature on social movements there is a strong recognition of the personal transformative effect that engaging in social movements can have on both self-confidence and interpersonal relationships, and this is seen in our own research. In this section we try to illustrate some of the findings that have emerged out of this work.

One striking thing that emerged out of both the NOMADESC and Housing Assembly cases is the transformation of individuals from passive and often isolated individuals to active political subjects, and the role of education and knowledge-making in that transformation. For NOMADESC and the UIP, there is a strong emphasis on this process in relation to victims of human rights violations. As a human rights organisation that not only engages in popular education processes but also in the legal and advocacy dimensions of human rights violations, NOMADESC engages directly with victims of state repression, both individual and collective – from relatives of people who have been killed to communities forcibly displaced, the NOMADESC HQ is often a political refuge for these victims, where they gain moral and emotional support and legal and political advice. Many of these victims are inducted into a process of education, whether through the Diploma or the UIP, or the general process of claiming justice for their loved ones or themselves. In this process, they are made aware, some for the first time, of the broader picture and history of human rights violations; how their personal case fits into the broader economic, political, and social history of human rights violations in the country, and more importantly how people historically have fought against these violations.

That pain and personal experience often becomes a resource in the learning process, and for many a source of strength. It is also often a bond that ties activists together. In the domain of political activism in Colombia, few have been left untouched by this dark history of repression. As a result, in recent years movements have sprung up that have sought to turn victimhood into an active subjectivity and to campaign for justice, truth and reparations.* Having lived through, 'survived' and witnessed the reality of state-led political violence, these 'victims' are often the most committed and serve as beacons of the movement. Transforming what is often a highly passive subject into an active and transformative one is a powerful

---

* See for example the National Movement of Victims of State Crimes in Colombia, Website: https://movimientodevictimas.org/en/. Last accessed 3 April 2023.

example of the effect that social movements can have on the individual and in sum on the strengthening of the broader movement.

Below an activist of the National Movement of Victims of State Crimes describes her meeting with a NOMADESC human rights defender on the day her father was murdered:

> You appeared the night my dad was killed … you came to tell me a lot of things that I didn't understand before and if you hadn't then I would not be here [as an activist] today, 12 years later … if you had not arrived that night and had done all those things, little by little I was able to process and understand what had happened, and gradually to speak about it … but hang on, all these things are connected as that is connected with the other, it was so important and every time I have the opportunity to thank him, I do … because you did a great job of accompaniment to me and my family and that was fundamental and key at that painful and tragic time … we did not even understand what was happening, we did not know why the army had come to kill our father … it is essential, for the family and the victims that accompaniment is vital in all aspects, in the political, in the human, in the social.
>
> (Participant, territorial workshop, Cali, 2018, cited in Kane and NOMADESC, 2021: 182)

Similarly, but in a very different political context, the case study of the Housing Assembly is a story of the empowerment of some of the most marginalised and vulnerable people. Participants in the Housing Assembly recount how their engagement with ILRIG initially allowed them to work out that their personal and desperate situation was not due to their individual failure – as mother/father/son/daughter – but the structural injustice of the post-apartheid state and a highly unequal neoliberal economy that worked against them. The post-apartheid peace settlement had not brought positive peace to many historically marginalised communities, and the violence of the state and its militarised police units was an extension and enforcement of that unequal settlement.

Placing their personal situation in both the socio-economic and political context allowed them to see it as a collective situation requiring a collective solution. This powerful transformation, first experienced by the founding members, was then cascaded on through the Housing Assembly's organising and education strategies to turn homeless and precarious and vulnerable individuals, neighbourhood by neighbourhood, into a collective resistance movement, which began to extend geographically, numerically and thematically across Cape Town, and nationally.

The biggest impact that the Housing Assembly has achieved has been in building the confidence of those living in poverty. This confidence has been as a direct result of the production and learning of knowledge that has happened in the movement. Everyone interviewed for the research project said their confidence had grown because they now knew their rights, because of what they had learnt about capitalism, and that their living in poverty was not their fault. This helped to fill members of the Housing Assembly with pride and dignity, which the state has tried to strip away with the narrative that the reason for their living in poverty was because they didn't work hard enough or because they were lazy. 'What I have learnt from being part of the Housing Assembly is that I can stand for myself. I can walk in the city and say what I want to say because I know my rights. For me, it is a decent house for our children' (Individual Interview, 24 May 2019, Member of the Housing Assembly, cited in Benjamin, 2021: 96).

By producing knowledge and opening up learning spaces to explain the systemic and structural nature of the oppression of community members, the Housing Assembly has undone generations of state-sanctioned denial of education, knowledge and information for black people. The Housing Assembly was able to see and value their community members and thereby has created a cadre of housing activists that are strong and confident, and powerful agents of change.

As a woman, as a youth, I never thought there was something with my condition. I thought things are the way it should be. I never knew what housing meant ... What I am grateful for is that the comrades in the Housing Assembly are people who learn from us and they share experiences with us as well. I have a voice and I am not standing alone. That is what I learned for the past year when I had nowhere to go.

(Respondent, Commission 1, Witzenburg, 16 June 2019, cited in Benjamin, 2021: 96)

The two key organising tenets of the Housing Assembly reflect their commitment to mass participation and education and shared leadership: 'Everyone an Organiser' and the Big Fish/Little Fish image. This was a powerful learning tool that has not only created a movement but also given every individual a sense of ownership which has translated into a collective ownership of the movement. This was far more effective than the slogan, 'Everyone a Leader' used by other social movements, because it shifted from the individual leader and an individual pursuit to the collective building of a movement. When members were asked what they did with knowledge they had gained from the Housing Assembly, every single one of them said that they went back to their communities, to their families and passed on that information. They said they did this because they felt empowered after what they had learnt and they felt that this power needed to be passed on. This passing on of learning has developed a powerful knowledge base at the grassroots level that has translated into people being organised into the movement.

We can also see these processes manifesting themselves in similar but distinct ways in the HDK and the Madhes case studies. For the Madhes, we can see the transformation of the Madhes activist from a victim of humiliation to an agent of liberation. That identity that had been historically marginalised and ridiculed, through processes of education and popular resistance was being transformed into a positive one, not as a second/third class Nepali citizen but as a subject with a history, a culture, a language, an identity. They were given a sense that the injustices perpetrated against them were not legitimate or pre-determined, but illegitimate, and that there were structural and geopolitical reasons that underpinned this process.

NEMAF, in that sense, provided the intellectual tools and evidence through which shame became transformed into pride, and ritualistic humiliation was transformed into a sense of indignation and injustice. As in the case of NOMADESC/UIP and the Housing Assembly, victims emerged as political subjects.

The range of shared discriminatory experiences and critical reflections on the history and sociopolitical processes brought fellow Madhesis together to identify with a strong idea of ethnic struggle. This was essentially the awareness of generative mechanisms that were manifested through the lived experiences of symbolic and structural violence, exposing the absence or unequal representation of Madhesi voices within the state.

> When I personally encountered verbal abuse from a Pahadi individual on my way to Birgunj, I started reflecting on similar incidents which I had witnessed in my own town. Around 1996, one day, I went to the cinema in Birgunj. The cinema hall was crowded, so there was a long queue to buy the cinema tickets. While waiting in the queue, a Madhesi young man broke the queue. The Pahadi bouncer in the cinema hall started beating him up with his belt. The youth started vomiting blood. No one in the crowd defended the man. I had observed that cruelty myself. On another incident, in 1998, I remember an elderly Madhesi being beaten up by a local Pahadi thug in front of the police station. The police did not intervene despite witnessing the physical abuse. No one defended the old Madhesi. This made me feel that even the police administration was indifferent towards injustices against Madhesis.
>
> (Madhesi Leader 8, Birgunj, cited in
> Pherali and NEMAF, 2021: 135)

In the case of HDK in Turkey, in the bringing together of historically marginalised groups, we get a sense of the power of collective identity and the vindication and legitimation that resulted. The longstanding and powerful struggle of the Kurds for cultural and territorial recognition, through civil disobedience and armed struggle, had forged a space for other misrecognised and oppressed groups to build their confidence, reveal their history, their persecution by the state, and the rich and beautiful cultures that they represented. In the case of the HDK, the individual transformations of people's sense of self or identity cannot be confined just to members and activists, as their powerful movement was the driver of the vindication of minority rights across the country. Nationally endorsed antipathy towards all minorities was transformed into a powerful narrative of cultural heritage and rightful indignation that their histories and their rights had been suppressed in the name of an exclusionary patriarchal, hetero-normative, one nation, one religion state.

An activist member of the Peoples and Beliefs Commission shares his experience:

> What HDK is doing is a different reading. They did something we have never witnessed before. For instance, the moment I say I am feminist, or I am leftist, it would mean a denial of all other identities which it was. I am not trying to redraft what I've said in the past nor doing opportunism, but what HDK did was really something different. By giving a very large space to all identities, HDK gave all silenced identities a chance to speak up and continues to do so … Therefore, HDK did this, HDK said, let the Yezidi talk and made them do the right thing. As for Alevis, HDK noticed that candles didn't go out, and saw that Yezidis didn't worship the devil. HDK allowed us to see that Armenians were not greedy nor money-minded, and it allowed us to have different relationships with Jews. Therefore, intercultural communication was established on a very solid and reliable ground. HDK allowed us to see through the eyes and words of the people coming from that community and culture. That's a whole new reading. HDK did a kind of reverse-dialectic.
>
> (Individual Interview T34, cited in Kutan and Çelik, 2021: 273)

A woman activist who had long been active within HDK's Peoples and Beliefs Commission describes the experiences the Congress provided her as follows:

HDK made me notice my own worth. I say 'my own worth' because the society where I come from, although it seems to be an egalitarian society for women, in practice it is the local prototype of the system. For many years I have been part of the executive committees of Alevi organisations. The committee had seven members and as a woman I was myself part of these committees, I struggled for many years as being the only woman among six men. It was the same when we had the confederation. There was an executive committee of 21, and again I found myself struggling being the only woman among those 20 others. HDK had partly crowned that process of mine. It legitimised and revealed even more my Alevi woman identity. I think this had been a role model … HDK made me notice my own worth. A stronger woman came out of this process. And most importantly I gained this, I mean, I had already for my family, I mean for my society, all my interests, my love, my worries; I say this as a comment, HDK gave me all these identities. I feel myself as an Armenian, a Syriac or a Circassian or a Pomak; in other words, HDK gave me a lot. You have one Hatice in front of you talking to you, but in fact this Hatice that you are talking to here, contains in herself all the existing and extinct identities of this society, on this land. HDK created out of me a multi-identity, multilingual, multi-cultural woman.

(Individual Interview T22, cited in Kutan and Çelik, 2021: 275)

One of the activists of the *Call for a New World* magazine, one of the HDK components, explains the positive effects of the emergence of various marginalised groups within HDK in line with their demands:

Syriacs, for example, are at least as important as the Armenians. We call it all Armenians, but the Assyrians also suffered genocide as much as the Armenians. In other words, they are a society that suffered in 1915. For example, they started to express themselves on this ground for the first time [HDK]. So, it was a very important thing. They appeared and we started to get to know the Assyrians more closely for the first time and they started to explain themselves more intensely. Also, the Romanis, we all used to use this traditional definition and called them Gypsies. But for the first time, the Romanis emerged on the grounds of HDK and started to defend themselves and started to express themselves; I mean, I know, many people that we have not heard of or who have not even known the name until today have emerged. So, it was an extremely exciting situation. It's with HDK that I began to see and hear much more intensively of such colourful social structures in Turkey. This was an important thing ... In other words, there is something that these social segments are increasingly connected to internationally. There is an origin and a country. So, this gradually carried your studies to an international basis. Let me say that. For example, there were the Rums. What do we say to the Rums? It was the first time that the Rums who lived here came out and spoke on the grounds of HDK; they were talking about themselves, how much these discriminatory policies and marginalising approaches affected them ... Maybe we didn't know until then; but because they are Rum for the first time, after all, they are the people of these lands, they lived here and they remained as a very important minority and still persist here. To learn about their problems and troubles; it was an important experience, an important excitement, to get to know them and therefore to include them into the political discourse.

(Individual Interview T18, cited in Kutan and Çelik, 2021: 298)

In all of the cases, to paraphrase Judith Butler, we can see the complex relationship between 'vulnerability and resistance', that power and agency can reside in the oppressed and subjugated. Talking about vulnerability as an integral part of resistance, Judith Butler (2016) argued that: *'To say that any of us are vulnerable beings'* ultimately *'is to mark our radical dependency not only on others, but on a sustaining and sustainable world'* (Butler, 2016). A similar point is also made by bell hooks (1991: 149–150, emphasis added):

Marginality [is] much more than a site of deprivation ... It is also the site of radical possibility ... for the production of a counter-hegemonic discourse that is not just found in words but in habits of being and the way one lives ... It offers ... the possibility of radical perspective from which to see and create, to imagine alternatives, new worlds.

There is also something profoundly democratic about all of the processes, both in terms of attempting to make the nation-state more democratic, inclusive and reflective of the different 'nations' that exist within the state and also in a move away from vanguard-ism to modes of mass participation movements where processes of 'concientización' (Freirean awareness raising) cannot be just focused on an enlightened cadre but must extend to broad swathes of the oppressed. This fits in with broader global trends in oppo-sitional movements that have moved away from tightly structured hierarchical modes of organisation to more horizontal and mass par-ticipation modes. That is not to say that smaller, highly disciplined movements, whether armed or unarmed, are no longer present – or necessary – but it is to say that on their own, they are insuffi-cient or unequal to the task of radical social transformation. This, we argue, leads us back to an earlier discussion of Gramsci's notion of hegemony, whereby he reflected upon the need not only to take state power, but also to engage in the terrain of civil society, where hearts and minds could be won over. Importantly, for us, when you move towards a recognition of the need for mass participation and engagement, then education becomes a key strategy. For Gramsci, hegemony was itself an educational project and therefore required a pedagogical strategy.

THE EPISTEMIC STRUGGLE: COUNTER-NARRATIVES IN THE CONSTRUCTION OF ALTERNATIVES

Across the four case study movements we see in action a process that Boaventura de Sousa Santos has called a 'sociology of absences' or Michel Foucault has called the 'insurrection of subjugated knowledges'. Each of the movements, in different ways and to different degrees is playing a powerful role in rewriting the history of the nation, and telling often silenced/hidden/subjugated histories. In this sense, all of the movements are engaged in a process of epistemic struggle, which sits alongside the political and social struggle, reinforcing the idea that there can be 'no global justice, without global epistemic justice'. The struggle on the streets, through protest and mobilisation, runs in parallel with a struggle in the text, in the media, in the minds of the people, reshaping 'common sense' into 'good sense', in Gramsci's words.

For NOMADESC/UIP, the role of reconstructing historical memory is a central feature of the pedagogical process. The Diploma/UIP seeks to rewrite the orthodox narrative of the Colombian state and recover the stories and agency of its many victims: a story of colonisation, slavery, and oppression that began with Spanish conquest but extends to US and neo-imperial actions, and also a story of resistance, by multiple actors throughout this history. Whilst this broad historical sweep is narrated through popular education sessions, it is in recent history that there is a much more collective and visual process of narration. Through 'Galleries of Memory', the storytelling, the ritual processes of chanting the names of victims, they bring both participants and the general public into the realm of seeing this very different history of Colombia. These movement activities recover the history of state-sanctioned violence, impunity, forced displacement, collusion between state and paramilitary forces, selective assassinations, and the reneging of the state on its protective role and responsibility to its citizens. They also recover the struggles, processes, protest movements and actions that have challenged the multiple injustices that the Colombian people have faced. In turn, these activists communicate narratives of struggle that seep out of the education, the legal cases, and the protest movements to much broader publics.

This process reframes and reorders the state narrative that the leftist guerrillas in the mountains and the urban and rural opposition, in social movements, trade unions, Afro-Colombian and Indigenous movements are all 'terrorists' or 'terrorist sympathisers' or the 'useful idiots' of terrorists. This reframing instead evidences the terrorism of the state, the collusion between the state and para-state, and the links between other powerful nations and powerful corporations. This framing is brought together by a series of examples of state-sponsored massacres, assassinations, arbitrary detention and imprisonment, forced displacement and exile of oppositional movements and activists and poor communities. It is also the counter-narrative of the history of the country in all its diversity. A history of genocide against the indigenous community, a history of slavery of the Afro-Colombian communities, of patriarchy, of imperialism, and a history of working-class, peasant, indigenous, black, and women's struggles. Again, capturing both the pain of oppression but also the joy, wisdom and dignity of resistance.

This framing of history then travels with the participants back to their respective movements and the 'ripple effects' begin to be seen. As Kane (2021) reflected in his ethnographic notes:

Another impact which could be identified at the individual level relates to how activists reported that their praxis of organising was altered as a result of their participation in the Diploma programme, for example, in increasing their focus upon historical collective memory within their own organisation or movement. This is an example of a mechanism through which the learning processes at individual level can go on to lead to a transformation in the praxis at the collective level (organisation, movement, community).

(Kane, ethnographic fieldnotes, 2018, cited in
Kane and NOMADESC, 2021: 188)

Similarly, for all of the other movements there is the production of a counter-narrative to the official version that moves from the individual, to the institutional to the societal with smaller or greater coverage depending on the effectiveness and reach of the movements.

The HDK, across its political programme sought, on the one hand, the recognition of difference and diversity of all the multiplicities of Turkey's population by defying narratives of national unity and assimilation based on genocide, pogroms, massacres and forced displacement. On the other hand, they also demanded justice and a confrontation with this past by opening up a space for those oppressed, excluded and ignored identities to appear in the public sphere: from the Armenian-Assyrian genocide of 1915 to the Pontus and Dersim genocides, from the Circassian genocide to the Alevi massacres in Maraş, Çorum and Sivas, to the all-out violence against the Kurds in the 1990s. In this process, the HDK organised activities in all areas, including conferences, activities exposing and evidencing the state's crimes.

This new counter-memory revolt emerged out of a critique of the Turkish-Sunni character of the nation-state, and led to the birth of a counter-memorial regime. Whilst the narrative of the national-unity-based regime was formulated around the glorious victories of the past and defined as being *'for Turkey'*; the counter-memory-based regime, with the Kurdish Freedom Movement as its driving force, created a narrative with the emphasis on *'because of Turkey'*. A memory based on the victims of the regime's narrative.

HDK supported the emergence into the public sphere of the memories of the vulnerable groups imprisoned in their private spaces and caused this 'insurrection of subjugated knowledges'. An activist close to Kaldıraç, one of the HDK components, stated that HDK was an important bulwark against mainstream nationalism:

> [HDK] attempted to gather all these dynamics of struggle in this land under one roof. It succeeded to a large extent. Let's not say it broke it but let us say it caused a serious crack in the shell of nationalism ... The development of a common struggle played a serious role in the curbing of nationalism here. The peoples who started to express themselves thanks to the struggle of the Kurdish People started to stand together more organised and next to each other. It also made serious contributions.
>
> (Individual Interview T15, cited in Kutan and Çelik,
> 2021: 294–295)

A Yezidi activist and member of the Peoples and Beliefs Commission actively engaged in HDP also draws attention to the social pedagogy created by HDK in the context of confronting the past:

> The reasons for HDP's success in politics today are the infrastructural studies carried out by HDK. In other words, the political analysis and studies … HDK was established in 2011 and immediately sent deputies to the parliament. Therefore, despite all the pressures, this establishment idea and philosophy of HDK contributes to HDP's success. Because I think they had an accurate analysis. Because there is sensitivity for everything; from family to intercultural communication, from relationship between Muslims and Christians and pressure on Yezidis in Sinjar. Therefore, that sensitivity already forms a social pedagogy. It then gets back to you as a form of behavior in social pedagogy. For example, the Commemoration of Medz Yeghern, Commemoration of Sinjar … and discussing the status of Yezidi women at Galatasaray Square via HDK are some of the events that are crucial here … In our country, this is huge! … It is such an important attitude to thematise … This is a very different pedagogical or sociological manifestation.
>
> (Individual Interview T34, cited in Kutan and Çelik, 2021: 296)

A Syriac activist says that the most fundamental impact this has on Turkey is the development of a new awareness in society:

> So now, when we look at it as a whole, we can say that HDK's practice is very successful because it had an impact on Turkey. I mean, it has intellectually impacted the whole Turkish community. Turkey learned that there are structures that have different understanding to the dominant understanding, that there are different peoples, learned that there are different religious structures. This is the success of HDK.
>
> (Individual Interview T40, cited in Kutan and Çelik, 2021: 297)

This new cognitive or epistemic understanding also had its influence on peoples' daily practices:

> The most important thing was this; before HDK, the powerful were celebrating their existence in the middle of the street, out in the public area, others were imprisoned inside their houses to celebrate their holidays in agony, but HDK did create a brotherhood of holidays. All holidays were siblings. So now there is the calendar of the peoples, the agenda of rights, and HDK built incredible bridges, paved roads, laid signs for the peoples to touch each other.
>
> (Individual Interview T34, cited in Kutan and Çelik, 2021: 297)

An Alevi-Kurdish activist, and member of HDK's Culture and Art Commission, explains that HDK did not only create symbolic empowerment with regard to the marginalised oppressed social groups, but also intervened when their rights were infringed. They give an example from an attack on Alevis in Malatya:

> There was an incident in Malatya. There was an attack on a family in a neighborhood. There had been an attack on an Alevi family. I saw how difficult it was for the members of that family to convey what they lived somehow, okay? I remember it well. Then HDK came into play. With the involvement of HDK this issue that happened in Malatya, began to be discussed intensively in the Turkish media. As an Alevi issue. I understood that: yes, this excited me so much. This is why we went to Malatya twice. In other words, social segments that were seen as problems were not alone. After HDK, even if a Romani's little finger was harmed, we were in Edirne, this is very important. If an Alevi's house was destroyed in Malatya, we were there.
>
> (Individual Interview T18, cited in Kutan and Çelik, 2021: 299)

An HDK activist emphasises that HDK has become the target of the state, because it has managed to become such a counter-hegemonic actor:

I think HDK has proven itself as a project. In its one hundred years, this was the first time in the Turkish Republic, in terms of the regime and all identities and in terms of faith, that oppressed classes had a threatening and organised restructuring against the state in such a way. Both revolutionaries and Leftists and democrats should know this. The state already knew this before us, understood and valued it more than I think. It has better analyzed its value and its future effects. Because this is a six-century, seven-century-old reflex for the state and the state has taken measures accordingly. We have slightly underestimated our success for ourselves. Otherwise, it is a success to be able to frighten so many state institutions, its parties, the representatives of capital, armed or unarmed officials, and make them take such serious measures. So that in itself is an indicator of success.

(Individual Interview T21, cited in Kutan and Çelik, 2021: 299)

HDK reframed the narrative of the nation-state both epistemically and practically in the streets. This counter-narrative resonated well beyond its core members, and posed an existential challenge to the monolithic narrative of the Turkish state, which while reifying the hetero-normative/Sunni/mono-lingual/Turk systematically undermined the numerous other people whose own stories had been hidden away behind closed doors through a century of cultural and political chauvinism. Through the collective power of the HDK as social movement, these hidden narratives, hidden histories arrived forcefully in the public domain. Once out there they resonated with broad swathes of the population who instinctively knew these hidden truths, these diverse stories and began to embrace a much more broader cultural and political frame than was hitherto offered to them. Once out of the lamp, that genie was hard to put back, and the state's violent repression against the HDK/HDP is in part a response to that ideational challenge.

When the Housing Assembly activists knocked on the doors of community members' houses, they did not anticipate that this would transform their struggle from a single-issue struggle for decent housing to a broader struggle for the working class. This learning through practice that took place through the door-to-door and in the house itself, has shaped the movement into what it is today. And this has been a profound shift into an intersectional approach to struggle. On meeting people in their homes, they found different kinds of workers in various stages of precarity, and they found that the house was also a holding space for struggles around access to basic services, to education, to health services, transport issues, social issues – all of which have their roots deep in racial inequality. This realisation has helped to shape the Housing Assembly's struggle from one that was a working-class struggle for housing, to a working-class struggle for systemic change.

The tactic adopted by the Housing Assembly to engage in learning exchanges across the different housing types also transformed the strategy and political ideology of the movement, making it more intersectional with race and class. Organising across the different housing types using the door-to-door tactic, achieved two fundamental things: the first is that it showed the movement the vast inequalities that exist in accessing services across the different housing types and that this inequality also included race. And second, organising across housing types transcended the spatial inequalities that existed under apartheid but still persist today. This has gone a long way in cementing in members' minds that the problem they were facing was systemic and structural, and it also contributed to building unity within the diversity that the movement brings together.

We also saw that housing is not a Witzenburg issue, it's a provincial issue. It's a national issue. I think what is important to me is how different groups can come together and share information or share their experiences. Then Khayelitsha can see that they have the same issues as Wolseley and I think that also makes people stronger, because then people feel that they are not alone.

(Commission 1, Witzenburg, 16 June 2019,
cited in Benjamin, 2021: 98)

This building from the ground up, and building across geographical locations and housing types, has also opened up the space to talk through the racial disparities that still exist in housing and access to basic services. This has been a source of great tension within the movement and between communities, but the approach that the Housing Assembly has used – of learning exchanges between housing types – has gone a long way in building knowledge on racial discrimination. This has helped defuse racial tensions at the level of communities and build a collective struggle despite the Western Cape and City of Cape Town's attempts to cause racial divisions.

The effects of the how and what of learning and knowledge-making of the Housing Assembly are slower to see, but the groundwork has been established for real power shifts to happen that are driven by a grassroots movement. The Housing Assembly has turned the site of its struggle into a pedagogical tool and together with that, has grounded the pedagogy in the politics of systems of oppression as experienced through the house. It has taken an apartheid tactic for organising and turned it into a powerful tool to build a movement where its cornerstone is learning and knowledge-making. The house as the site of struggle has also enabled the movement to push through the barriers of former social movements and anti-apartheid movements to present the struggle as intersectional, as not a singular struggle by incorporating racial and class oppression (and more recently gender oppression). Perhaps one of the key effects of the knowledge-making and learning has been that in the bid to build a grassroots movement for systemic change, it has also defied the individualism perpetuated by capitalism, by creating a space – a common area almost – for community members and activists to feel like they belong, that they are part of a family, that there is a collective struggle and voice.

The Madhes movement, and NEMAF within it, has played an instrumental role in challenging the social and political exclusion of ethnic Madhesis. As the Madhes uprisings erupted in the aftermath of the Maoist rebellion and during the period when Nepal's major political forces were involved in the process of constitution-making, the movement had a significant impact on shaping the constitutional framework. Nepal's social struggles stem from the problem of a centralised political structure that has promoted a monolithic version of national identity and obscured cultural and ethnic diversity in Nepali society (Pherali et al., 2011). Hence, the federal political structure was imagined with the view of providing powers to the culturally diverse local communities, who are able to determine their own development agenda. It can be argued that federalism, the main agenda of the Madhes movement, is a political response to grievances of the marginalised populations who have been underrepresented in decision-making bodies. It is also a peace-building mechanism that is designed to decrease the monopoly of the Khas-Arya community on state power and improve the representation of historically marginalised communities in positions of decision-making.

The Madhes movement, through the force of its resistance, and as an effect of the learning and knowledge-making processes it was engaged in, has occupied a central position in national Nepali political debates in the last decade. It has secured the constitutional legitimacy of ethnic identities and their equitable contributions to shaping the nature of the Nepali state. Social hierarchies along ethnic, caste and gender lines have been ruptured, creating new spaces of contestations and convergences. In this process, Nepal has also seen some level of ethnic polarisation, but there are also convergences through the merger of political forces that claim to represent the most marginalised populations in the country. The struggle for social transformation continues, but Nepal has entered a new era of politics of social justice and equitable development, which has been enormously shaped by the Madhes movement and enriched by the learning processes that actors and activists have undertaken.

These political shifts have significant implications for peace and social transformation. Nepal's Madhes movement provides new avenues for analysis of peacebuilding in the sense that peace is not merely the cessation of violence but also a strategic goal that addresses various forms of structural inequalities (Galtung, 1976). The notion of 'peace with justice' could not be achieved through the model of liberal peacebuilding, which relies on liberal democracy and economic development under free market principles, thereby undermining deeply rooted social and cultural conditions of inequalities. Without the Madhes movement, recognition of cultural and ethnic identities, regional inequalities and oppressive ethnic hegemonies could not have been ruptured. What remains yet to be seen is how new political forces utilise the political capital gained by the Madhes movement to deliver tangible change in the Madhesi people's living conditions.

In all four social movements, we observed that hegemonic control by elitist power circles had been challenged through the reclamation of disempowered histories and narratives of the peoples. These new narratives spoke to the experiences of those who felt excluded from the so-called 'national' histories. It was also a revelation for many who had been trapped in a system of oppression that normalised their grievances and blamed the victims. All these ruptures were underpinned by transformative processes of collective learning, which go beyond classic notions of learning, and include strong Emotional Dimensions that serve to enrich and strengthen these collective identities various forms of resistance these movements had adopted over the years made not only the activists but also the peoples they represented realise that another history existed, and an alternative future was possible. Most importantly, these movements had created a strong base, a bottom-up power that celebrated diversity, local epistemologies and the importance of life with dignity despite ongoing state violence. This is where the hope for real peace resided – *peace with social justice*.

SHIFTING THE DISCOURSE

Social movements often change societies, but they also change people, from the activists that are engaged in the movement, the leaders, and the broader public. However, we rarely observe the micro-processes of those changes and their cumulative effect. Our research has thrown up examples that illustrate the process and provide glimpses of the way they operate.

We will start with the HDK in Turkey and then move to the other case studies. HDK is above all a movement that challenges the notion of *political Turkishness*, which was created around the top-down and monist ethos of Sunnite Turks and commonly referred to as 'one nation, one flag, one religion'. Unsurprisingly then, much of the change that we can see coming from members and activists, is linked to the experience of being involved in the making and remaking of new identities. The HDK, as an explicitly intercultural and diverse movement, has brought together people who had hitherto been apart. Within that process, activists often had a settled vocabulary for their own concerns, but were often less aware that the use of certain expressions could create discomfort in others. HDK fora then often became the spaces where these political discourses were shifted and challenged, where they lacked clarity, precision or were offensive:

One of the first things I have noticed when I joined HDK was how problematic our language was. The sentences we made. To give you an example, women used the word 'child bride' for many years and they were against it. Can there be a bride from a child? Those words make it look like something sympathetic and that's not the right approach. I also remember other previous debates on women like the women's shelter. I refuse to use that word; why a shelter? This is a word that tends to show women as powerless. But when we were debating with friends, I admitted it, yes, we take shelter; we take shelter to flee violence and abuse, let's make it clear. We had serious language problems. I used words and sentences that seemed to me quite normal in the daily flow of life that hurt LGBTI individuals, or whenever we said diabolic, our Yezidi friends pointed it out, and they disciplined us. They told us what that word meant ... I think we've been well disciplined in terms of language use. When we met there, at the Peoples and Beliefs Commission, we understood how important language was and we've been well disciplined in that sense.

(Individual Interview T12, cited in Kutan and Çelik, 2021: 276)

Beyond discourse reformulation, in the HDK we can see how engagement with different groups built a new-found respect. One such example relates to the interactions between the political left and the Kurds. One activist from the socialist magazine *Theory and Politics*, a component of HDK, recounts his encounter with the Kurdish Freedom Movement and its impacts:

> During that process, we have made a lot of friends from the Kurdish Freedom Movement. We have seen how individuals acquired a certain level of maturity thanks to the movement, how they managed to overcome their limitations stemming from their socio-cultural backgrounds. We have noticed that this was possible due to the existing dynamics within the movement and that was important for us. Those militants, I mean those who learned the hard way, had a maturity and this was a new horizon for us. Because in Turkey's Left Movement we are usually more doctrinarian, we were used to being surrounded by people who were trying to understand the world through books. That is why we were very reactive. But then there, we have seen something different. It was very instructive. Let me say it in other words; Kurdistan Freedom Movement is the main reason why we were in HDK and the reason why HDK has turned into a historical asset. As for us, if we are there with them with a peace of mind ... it is because of the militants of the Kurdish Freedom Movement. Those militants all have a great story to share. I know, for example, a militant whose big brother who was sentenced to aggravated life imprisonment and had been in prison for 15–16 years. He is also a militant like his brother and had been detained for months, as well as his wife and he has children. That's who they are and they continue their work confidently. This was eye-opening for us, very instructive. Individuals brought up by revolutionary history are very precious to us and those who are polluted by the failure of the revolution are dramatic. I say this with regard to Turkey's Left Movement. These are in fact bad lessons for us. Of course, we have learned a lot from this.
>
> (Individual Interview T44, cited in Kutan and Çelik, 2021: 270)

The above represents a good example of the way cultural exchange and respect were not just based on identity, but also on political culture: in this case, a recognition that the direct struggle history and experience of Kurdish militants brought rich assets to a movement that was often rooted in books and doctrine, but lacked direct revolutionary experience. Another activist from the Kurdish movement who found himself among the diversity of HDK noticed how the urgency and priority he gave to his identity as a Kurd might be different for other members:

> Our urgent needs and priorities are all based on identity, but having to work with many constituencies requires you to see that they have their own urgent needs and priorities too. Noticing it and tolerating it allowed me to mature. You become much more mature in HDK, and also more flexible.
>
> (Togetherness and Unity in Diversity, Workshop 2, cited in Kutan and Çelik, 2021: 271)

As the above highlights, the HDK became a context where different interests, priorities, objectives, would be worked out through debate, discussion and struggle. These engagements were often uncomfortable for the activists, and often exposed them to new experiences. For instance, a young HDK activist, also a member of the Democratic Islam Congress, tells of her first encounter with an LGBTI member from HDK:

> Once I attended a meeting, until then I had never seen an LGBTI individual in my life. I have seen there a person called K. Maybe you know him. I was pleasantly surprised (she laughs). We were at the same meeting. As a woman I was filled with admiration and I absolutely adored his speech. 'Well, they are just like us', I said to myself. In that sense HDK really transforms people, breaks down the prejudices.
>
> (Individual Interview T13, cited in Kutan and Çelik, 2021: 272)

Another activist noted:

> I had some hesitations as for working with diversity, creating together before joining HDK. HDK allowed me to overcome this.

Let me explain; I understood that all these are sources of richness, pluralism is a source of richness, that's what I learned there and that was important to me. Working with diversity and reaching common decisions were important. Another point is that during all the time I spent with HDK being closer to people and reaching common decisions on a local level were positive things.

(Writing the History of the HDK Together, Workshop 1, cited in Kutan and Çelik, 2021: 272)

An HDK activist who was from an Islamic tradition joined the Democratic Islam Congress and HDK's Peoples and Beliefs Commission. She tells about the impact the work on women had on her:

I met today at HDK with the Women's Council which continues to grow stronger and bring together all different woman structures within it. This is one of the examples that had an impact on me, both politically and socially. It is very local and small sized; in the past I had been in charge of projects where I was a founder and president of an association; but here it is really different; here you see women from so many different backgrounds under the same roof. Women's councils are authentic and autonomous, independent; the decisions that are taken here are not debatable, you see here women's self-confidence, power and freedom ... I went to such a meeting once, the Middle East Women's Conference, this was way before HDP. It was organised by Kurdish women. After that meeting when I got back to Istanbul I remember having discussed with my women friends, members of our women's movement in Istanbul, we said to each other 'we have always looked at and talked to women's movement in Europe and so, but we haven't even noticed that movement which was right under our noses'. This was really striking. There are so many steps that develop them and bring them to maturity.

(Individual Interview T41, cited in Kutan and Çelik, 2021: 274)

Another woman activist emphasises the dimension that made it meaningful for her to do politics that spares her from 'androcentric state policy':

From my point of view, I can say that HDK pulled me from dry and shallow politics and put me in a place where politics have a meaning, something deep. And I am not talking about political depth, it is more about human and consciousness depth. You can learn political depth from books, here and there. HDK allowed me to wipe myself clean of all this androcentric state policy and opt for a more social one.

(Women, Gender and Social Change, Focus Group 2,
cited in Kutan and Çelik, 2021: 274)

A significant number of activists in HDK indicate that they used to present themselves with identities such as 'leftist', 'socialist' or 'feminist', keeping their ethnic, religious and sexual orientation identities safely in the background. They say that they refrained from bringing their complex identity out until they joined HDK and note that they have seen important transformation since then. Activists reiterate that HDK encouraged them to own multiple identities all in one. HDK showed them it was possible to be Alevi and Kurdish and leftist or Circassian and leftist all at the same time. In that sense, we might say that in a Turkey where the left squeezed all ethnic and religious identities into a more 'universal' leftist identity, HDK stepped in to bring an end to this mainstream approach by creating an autonomous space where individuals could express themselves with the identity component they wanted to use. Many interviewees who had been continuing their struggle in the left movement, underline that HDK increased the value of multiple identities and encouraged them to express their other identity components in public.

A woman activist from HDK considers this opportunity of the multiplicity of identity as a new world promise:

HDK promises a world where a woman can live no matter what her identity is. That's the reason why I embraced HDK. It is a process where I can breathe. An umbrella where all my identities fit into. Because in the past, whenever I expressed my political identity, then my religious belonging would be left out or when I was able to show my religious identity, then my ethnic identity would be left out. What HDK offered is an inclusive space, embracing all; we were able to continue all the struggles all together. It is a precious space; HDK promises the world to women. HDK's demand for confrontation on what happened in Turkey's last hundred years of history seems also to have enabled the awakening of a counter-memory. HDK brings together minor memories that each individual with an identity has from his own community. Once side by side on HDK's ground these individuals start to know each other and communicate. Most importantly, each one of those memories that become public encourages other wounded memories that were silenced and trapped to speak up, to demand and call out their resistance. For instance, Circassian activists say that they started to build up political demands ranging from mother tongue education to the Circassian genocide recognition because they had the opportunity to witness the struggle that the Kurdish movement fought. Armenian and Syriac interviewers stress that testimonials on Dersim 38, Diyarbakir prisons or on state violence in the 1990s encouraged the memory of 1915 to talk in public space. In that sense, there is an important solidarity ground established to let the silenced identities speak up in the prefigurative space of HDK. Collective participation in various group commemorations, calls for confrontation with the past, important activities organised by the Peoples and Beliefs Commission, and sympathy towards a multiplicity of identities are proof of a symbolic, solid, solidarity inside HDK.

(Individual Interview T22, cited in Kutan and Çelik, 2021: 279)

An activist member of the Peoples and Beliefs Commission reflected on the fact that not only were different identities being vindicated, but it allowed a space for the recognition that we all hold multiple identities:

What HDK is doing is a different reading. They did something we have never witnessed before. For instance, the moment I say I am feminist or I am leftist, it would mean a denial of all other identities I have. I am not trying to redraft what I've said in the past nor doing opportunism but what HDK did was really something different. By giving a very large space to all identities HDK gave all silenced identities a chance to speak up and continues to do so ...

(Individual Interview T34, cited in Kutan and Çelik, 2021: 273)

One of the founders of HDK and one of the prominent revolutionaries of the 1968 generation, describes this experience:

[HDK] has proved that one never stops learning. First of all, you face the reality about Kurdistan, you see the life there and the truth, this is an amazing richness. Actually, seeing this opens your eyes to all. You start seeing the Armenian, the Rum and then it allows you to have a new look at the Turk. Your whole perspective on life is reinvented. I can't imagine any possibility of learning greater than this one.

(Individual Interview T45, cited in Kutan and Çelik, 2021:
282–283)

The HDK field research shows that the most effective learning and influence happens among people and components who are part of mobility-based activities. For example, the delegations that were created to organise the local level during HDK's establishment period and the work they carried out in different regions of Turkey are among the most impactful experiences. In this respect, activities such as rallies, travel, delegation work, training and seminars taking place in places other than those where the activists live, provide a very important learning dynamic. Mobility not only increases activists' interaction with different social facts, but also enhances their learning experiences on both an emotional and informative level. In particular, each visit of non-Kurdish activists within the HDK to Kurdistan affects and transforms them:

I mean [work done within HDK] has enriched me a lot. I got acquainted with the Kurdish movement and the struggle in Kurdistan, what it was really about, but also its place in the world's resistance history. In my opinion, HDK has made great contributions to the conceptualisation of Turkey's political life and society's transformation. That's huge. The turning point for me is the Semdinli Incident. There was a delegation going there, a big one, actually. Filmmakers, academics, people from the cultural sector, and literati. Many boxes of books were sent, and we went to that bookstore, there were still blood traces. We went to Van by plane. And then we took the bus from Van, friends from the bar joined us. We met local people in all the villages and settlements until Hakkari. We met with women, and what I will never ever forget in my life, the picture I can't take out of my mind is when they talked to us, those people whose husband, son, and daughter were killed, they came to us with the pictures of their lost ones, killed in unidentified murders, by the military or the police under the state pressure. They said: 'If women from the West knew what's going on here, I'm sure they'd be on our side, they'd understand us and we would find a solution together'. I've heard this everywhere and it hurts so much. Because I knew it, during my college years and my life after college, people don't want to know, don't want to see. The truth there is so devastating, it is so human, something we all need to stand up for, so when we know about it we need to do something, and this means something bad would happen. This is in the subconscious of people, even if it is not said out loud. This is valid for academics and other people too. Ordinary people didn't hear about what was happening there. Whereas those women there they say 'they'd react if they had heard about it'. During the reconciliation process, we have seen this clearly. I mean even the media wrote it. They went to Kurdish cities to write about the places Kurds lived. Reaching out to people, talking to them, sharing our repressed lives were very important. Indeed, those women were right; when people started to know more, they were more interested. That led to a socialisation of Kurdish issue reconciliation.

(Individual Interview T6, cited in Kutan and Çelik, 2021: 282)

Reflecting on the above, there is a sense of the power and efficacy of engaging with difference, which seems to support the idea of 'contact theory', which advocates engagement as a vehicle for breaking down barriers and lack of empathy between communities and building shared values and norms, assuming that creating a space for oppositional groups to interact, collaborate and understand each other can reduce conflicts between them (Allport, [1954] 1988). Criticisms of 'contact theory' have often been rooted in arguments around its avoidance of structural inequalities, focusing on the symptoms rather than causes of conflicts, for example, between Israelis and Palestinians. Importantly, unlike in the broader peace education literature, where historically divided communities in conflict are placed together, in this case, we have groups that are not in direct confrontation with each other, but are oppressed by the contemporary status quo and often unaware of other socially marginalised groups' sufferings. In this context, contact theory seems to have some explanatory value – a radical counter-hegemonic contact theory that is rooted in the commoning of ideas, resources, and solidarities.

Moving from HDK to NOMADESC, and extending from the individual to the collective effects, we can see very similar processes at work. It is clear from our research that the cumulative impact of the intercultural drive of NOMADESC's work to bring together different sectors and movements – particularly but not exclusively through the pedagogical process – has had a deep impact upon the praxis at the collective/institutional level. This has occurred in terms of increasing solidarity and collaboration between the different movements and organisations and their different struggles. Following their participation in the pedagogical initiative and their broader work with NOMADESC, many of the collective subjects come to be involved in broader social movement unity processes such as the National Movement of Victims of State Crimes (MOVICE) or the 'Congreso de los Pueblos' (Peoples' Congress) – both broad, national social movement processes.

Another important dimension has been the way that the process has made tangible the sense of a subaltern social movement, made up of movements struggling in different ways and different territories across the southwest region:

> I think that [the pedagogical process] contributed to the consolidation of the social movement in the region ... as well as the diplomas in the regions – Cali, Buenaventura etc., there were also spaces for reading and analysing the context at a regional level [the Tejiendo Resistencias annual events], that contributed to helping us understand the problems on a regional scale, and it has been a sustainable process because up until today we continue thinking in terms of the southwest region ... so in this sense there was an integration in our thinking in terms of the southwest, it is an important contribution which is sustained into the present.
>
> (Leading activist, Black Communities Process facilitator and ally throughout history of the pedagogical process, interview, 2018, cited in Kane and NOMADESC, 2021: 191)

Similar to the HDK case, the above reinforces the idea that these processes are not just about building understanding and respect between movements, between distinct identities – as important as that is – but also about forging new geographically expansive identities based upon those principles of respect and mutuality. Both the HDK and NOMADESC provide us with a glimpse of what a new society might be based on, and some of the democratic mechanisms that might support this – the Congress/Assembly model being one that is appealing in both contexts.

> The spaces of the intercultural university also serve as a mirror for the participants, who are involved in counter-hegemonic or alternative efforts but who may not have given themselves the opportunity to recognise themselves in this condition of marginalisation, as part of broader counter-hegemonic efforts and faced with the hegemonic forces ... it works as a mirror in the sense that they come to see themselves as counter-hegemonic or emancipa-

tory subjects involved in these struggles that are part of broader struggles ...

(Activist expert in participatory action research, UIP facilitator, interview, 2018, cited in Kane and NOMADESC, 2021: 111).

This is not just about broadening the activists' and movements' understandings of other linked social movements, other identities, but also about making links with the past, and past struggles: 'to have clarity of what we have and what our identity is to understand who our ancestors were, how they have struggled and built liberation processes in situations of slavery, feudalism, neoliberalism ...' (NOMADESC founding member and currently a leading member of the organisation, interview, 2018, cited in Kane and NOMADESC, 2021: 109).

Another respondent traces the evolution of the indigenous movement in relation to this:

the indigenous movements of today are not the same as the indigenous movements of a few years ago and nor are the peasant movements, nor is the black movement, or the urban movement the same today, so this interculturality is also a dialogue with time, with the historical identities but also with these new identities that are forming, it may sound cliché, but forming in the heat of the struggle, that is, those identities that are formed and inter-woven, and in the university this process has a very important class component, which makes it a common identity which exists based upon the cultural differences ... these differences are there and recognised, but also there is a common identity of class and territorial defence that gives the interculturality a common purpose, it doesn't separate them, which is the big theoretical discussion of interculturality, it is often used to end up separating peoples, but in this case, on the contrary, it ends by uniting them through dialogue.

(Movement intellectual allied to the process, interview, 2018, cited in Kane and NOMADESC, 2021: 110)

Whilst impacts are qualitative and often intangible, through our case study of the PCN in Buenaventura we identified 'learning ripple effects' in order to demonstrate the transformative impact which one social movement's participation had upon its praxis, and subsequently upon its struggle. Our case study demonstrated how the PCN's organising process was strengthened; how changes in the praxis of the PCN were generated through its participation in this pedagogical process; and how it played an important role in the conscientisation process of individuals who were already prominent activists, or who would later become leading activists.

PCN activists described how their participation created a shift in the collective consciousness of their movement in the way that they understood the structural causes of the violent context they were experiencing, as well as gaining practical tools to be able to respond to the human rights crisis:

The whole situation of violence began – all the massacres, displacements, assassinations ... and the human rights situation in Buenaventura became very complex ... we hadn't made an association in terms of what it meant and what was really going on, the link between violence and territory, or violence and capitalism – those relations of capital that were driving the violence, yes? In every meeting ... there was the issue of violence, but that it could be ... a war strategy based on trying to empty the territories, and then appropriate those territories, I came to hear that analysis on the NOMADESC Diploma ... because those of us who did the Diploma were the core of our PCN activists, very qualified activists with a lot of experience ... it had a very big impact ... especially the sections when the teacher talked about the whole topic of capital and development, but in the context of what Buenaventura meant for the world economy at that time as a key international port, when he explains all that and then explains that the violence that is happening in Buenaventura is not a coincidence but actually part of a strategy, we were all stunned ... and he told us to get ready ... I do feel that the Diploma served to help us to locate ourselves and give us a different perspective on what was happening in Buenaventura, and that analysis is just as relevant today.

(PCN activist, a former student of the Diploma
programme during the early years, current facilitator
for UIP, cited in Kane and NOMADESC, 2021: 192–193)

The citation above helps us to understand how the participation of the PCN in the Diploma course had an impact at the organisational level, in terms of how the movement came to understand the violence which was so affecting the communities in Buenaventura. They state that as a result of this participation, the PCN as an organisation began to understand that the violence that was being experienced was simply a strategy for the appropriation of the territory. In other words, PCN was able to see the logic beyond the everyday violence inflicted upon them and to realise that their struggle needed to be sustained as a permanent resistance rather than just a temporary defence to the current state violence. It is important to note that in the view of the interviewee, this change was not something temporary: it was something more profound than a change in the way of viewing the situation: it was a shift in collective consciousness which manifested in terms of the way the organisation collectively analysed the context and conjunctures. Participation in the Diploma course not only helped generate a deeper and more political analysis of the factors which were driving the violence, but also provided tools for the defence of human rights to respond to the immediate and urgent situation they were facing, and how these tools were implemented by the PCN:

I think that divided it into before and after in terms of the approach of the PCN, at least in Buenaventura, because we began to see a more political and organised approach to the violence, not just about picking up the dead bodies that were left in each massacre, but for example we started to make a more serious and accurate documentation and make our own reports because the state reports always underestimated and under-reported ... for me that Diploma marked the turning point for the PCN to begin to understanding and transcend what was happening with the violence and how it related to a much larger strategy linked to the megaprojects ...

(PCN activist, a former student of the Diploma programme during the early years, current facilitator for UIP, cited in Kane and NOMADESC, 2021: 194)

We can also see how for many individuals the Diploma/UIP process led them to rise through their movement in terms of leadership. As Kane and NOMADESC (2021: 188) note:

In NOMADESC/UIP, one indicator of the impact which the process has had at individual level are the examples of activists who have passed through the Diploma programme have gone on to take up leadership roles within their organisation, community or movement (Araujo, 2015). In most of the organisations participating in the process, we were able to identify key leaders who identified their participation in the NOMADESC pedagogical process as an important moment in their own political development as a leader, some of whom would later lead important social struggles in the southwestern region.

This gives a sense of the way the educational process built leadership qualities, intellectual capacities, social movement links and awareness.

At the collective level, an important dimension in which the impact of the pedagogical process can be identified is in the implementation of human rights knowledge and tools and in the praxis of the movements involved. As this book has shown, there was a strong sense from activists that the knowledge acquired had been applied to the struggles of their own organisations, particularly in cases relating to human rights violations or threats to territorial autonomy such as attempts by multinational corporations to gain licences to extract natural resources. The case of COPDICONC is one example of a rural community whose leaders argue that participating in the NOMADESC pedagogical process has increased the community's organisational ability to defend its territory: 'if you go now to our territory to try and do some kind of activity ... they [will] talk to you about the community's rights ... they stand up for themselves' (Rural Afro-Colombian community leader, ex-student of the Diploma from the early phase, interview, 2018, cited in Kane and NOMADESC, 2021: 189).

These shifts would lead to changes in organisational and political strategies as a result of the change in the organisation's way of understanding the context and the issues they faced. According to an interviewee, beginning to understand violence as a strategy to move communities aside spurred the development of a new urban organisational strategy by the PCN in defence of urban territories, under the same banner of the defence of territory which they used when organising in rural territories. Hence, the urban situation in Buenaventura began to be articulated as a struggle for the territory, and an organisational-pedagogical process was initiated in order to raise awareness of urban communities and organise them in defence of their territory.

One element which emerged in our research was how the NOMADESC educational process methodologically, philosophically and pedagogically influenced the pedagogical approach and activities of the participating organisations, generating new processes in some cases. The quotation below shows how the educational process of the PCN inspired new pedagogical processes in the PCN's sister organisations, replicating aspects of the methodology:

> [we set it up as] an initiative of our own, based on the experience we had already gained with NOMADESC, and from there the PCN began to run many diploma programmes with other organisations, and I think in turn this also served as an example or guide for others to begin their own processes.
>
> (ibid.)

Without arguing direct causality or ignoring the multiple factors and complexities involved in bringing about such large-scale social uprisings, our PCN case study gives a sense of a chain of influence of the pedagogical process, which we understand as a ripple-effect learning process which, through the participation of individual subjects representing the PCN, had a large impact at the collective level upon the political consciousness of one of southwest Colombia's most prominent social movements, and by extension upon PCN's sister organisations in Buenaventura. It demonstrates how it can be argued that the pedagogical process contributed to the Buenaventura Civic Strike in 2017, one of Latin America's most emblematic social struggles of the twenty-first century:

> ... the accumulation that led Buenaventura to the great strike didn't happen overnight because a leader appeared saying that it was a good idea to have a civic strike: it was an accumulation of organising and education in which these processes that we are talking about played an important role, we had an influence in Buenaventura, we worked with the leaders and they were part of this pedagogical process ... and gradually this started to have a cumulative effect ... I am not saying that it is the only factor or that somehow the civic strike is the direct heritage of this process, but it plays a part ... we are talking about an entire city that is fed up and angry, but why does it get fed up and angry? [the situation that caused the strike] ... did not appear here in the 21st century, that has been a historical issue, so why then? ... It was achieved by creating an understanding amongst the population that they are just as valid citizens as those in the capital, they are bearers of rights and above all that they stand on a treasure chest, when people in Buenaventura understand the importance of the city's port strategically not only for the country, but for the world economy ... that is part of the accumulated impact of the Diploma, of the UIP, of all the organising, working with the leaders all that travelling back and forth, taking international delegations to meet activists there ... it has been quite a process.
>
> (Interview with trade unionist organic intellectual who has been involved in the process since the early phase of the Diploma until present day, interview, 2018 cited in Kane and NOMADESC, 2021: 196)

It is important to highlight the timescale of this influence: it begins at the beginning of the 2000s with the start of the Diploma Programme in Buenaventura, and continues right through until the 2017 civic strike: the participation of the PCN in the pedagogical process has been permanent, and some UIP participants even played important roles during the civic strike. Throughout those two decades, the pedagogical process was only part of a broader NOMADESC strategy of strengthening social movements in Buenaventura in their struggles in the defence of human rights and to improve living conditions. It would be impossible to understand the learning process described above, without taking into account that it has gone hand in hand with close strategic collaboration between NOMADESC and PCN, and that NOMADESC has also played an active role in the struggle of social movements in Buenaventura, which has included mobilisations, research, publicly denouncing human rights violations, and developing legal strategies.

These impacts are facilitated by NOMADESC's long-term approach to working with social movements, in which the pedagogical process is often just part of a broader collaboration with the movements to support their struggles in defence of human rights and dignity. In our PCN case study, we argue these ripple learning effects can be traced from the beginning of the Diploma programme in the early 2000s through to the historic civic strike in Buenaventura in 2017.

In the case of the Madhes movement, NEMAF played a unique role in bringing together influential progressive intellectuals and oppressed Madhesi communities through their regional interaction programmes. The mass protests in 2007 and 2008 had sensitised people to the political cause of Madhesis that emanated from their longstanding experiences of humiliation and marginalisation, but the activists and Madhesi communities lacked a structured and evidence-based narrative that could lay the intellectual foundations of their struggle. The public intellectuals in Kathmandu had also suffered from historical amnesia due to the culture of epistemic domination that was ingrained in the hegemonic Khas-Arya political ideology. So, NEMAF's interaction programmes created opportunities for public intellectuals to familiarise themselves with the Madhesis' diverse but collective experiences of humiliation, and to inform the wider public through their writing and media appearances. For the Madhesi activists, these events were educational spaces to share their personal experiences; engage in critical dialogue with other activists and public intellectuals; and develop skills to articulate their ideas and justification for their resistance. Their participation provided them with a learning process in which they could draw on movement experiences to evidence their arguments. Similarly, the Madhes Studies Immersion course organised by NEMAF attracted youth from the Khas-Arya community who found unique educational experiences that were not available in any formal educational institutions. This enabled them to appreciate the wealth of knowledge, literature and cultural richness of Madhes but also to realise that this community had been persecuted in the process of nation-building. Out of all the four case studies, NEMAF's pedagogical approaches were also unique in contributing to the sensitisation of the learning community that was subconsciously integral to hegemonic epistemologies. That is to say, they focused on educating/re-educating national, cultural and political elites as well as the oppressed.

REPRESSION AND RESISTANCE: SURVIVING AND FLOURISHING IN TIMES OF AUTHORITARIANISM

In contexts of conflict, authoritarianism and repression, the dynamics of social movement organising are closely linked to these state–movement relationships. On occasions, repression can bring movements and actors together in adversity; at other times, it can fragment and destroy intra and inter-movement solidarity. Sometimes just surviving – to fight another day – is the best movements can hope for. All of the movements have felt these changing dynamics, as they have evolved, and faced greater or lesser degrees of repression.

Despite criminalisation, detention, displacement, exile, intimidation, etc., the HDK and its component parts have managed to stay loyal to its programme and principles. Whilst we noted earlier that there have been previous attempts by the Kurdish Freedom Movement to link its struggle with Turkey's socialist-revolutionary movement, this is the first time that this has managed to bring so many organisations together for such a period of time. This was emphasised many times by all the activists that we interviewed, and many linked this to the HDK's organisational structure and social vision. In an early stage of the research, at the peak of the repression going on in Turkey, one of our key partners from the HDK, a historic leader of the revolutionary left in Turkey, noted whilst reflecting on the theme of success in social movements that sometimes we should recognise that merely surviving as an organisation is itself a success at some points in history. This is particularly relevant to the case of both Turkey and Colombia, where periods of democratic opening and relative freedom to organise are often interrupted by periods of heavy repression, militarisation and violence where survival of both the individual and the movement are threatened.

Reflecting on the HDK case, Kutan and Çelik (2021: 258) comment that all the successes of the HDK/HDP project from 2010 to the time of writing led to an all-out offensive against them.

a state policy of total violence and oppression towards HDK and the social movement network that HDK was part of. We particularly need to address how this violence and oppression then influenced the impact that HDK generated and destroyed, at least partially, the achievements accumulated through struggle, and attacked the common memory and togetherness that had been reached. Society's most marginalised actors (LGBT movement, women's movement, ethnic and religious minorities) are under attack precisely because the idea of an alternative life and a pluralist solidarity generated fear and unrest from the status quo power – the AKP-led state. We believe that the main reason why there is such a disproportionate use of violence and power or the reduction of life to the dimension of what Giorgio Agamben calls 'naked life' (1998), or the reason why the government has created a 'state of exception' bringing up the issues of the wronged 'nation' and 'state' with the pretext of the 'indivisible integrity of a nation' is in fact linked with the impact created by this broad social movement of which HDK is part too.

A woman activist formerly active within HDK's Youth and Education Councils and now working in HDP's Education Commission as well as in the local organisation in Istanbul talks about the success of HDK in difficult times:

HDK actually did the impossible. For instance, today is the anniversary of the Ankara Massacre (10 October 2018). The country's Labor-Democracy Movements and Kurdish Freedom Movement went to Ankara Square, and 103 people died there and we were all walking there with these people. Five hundred people were injured. There are still 36–37 people with permanent injuries. We tried to collect prosthetic legs etc. These were the processes, and this was impossible. Nobody believed in it. People said, 'Leftists leave'. People said, 'Kurds will leave'. There was such insecurity among the movements. This has been greatly exceeded. Now, despite all the crises, massacres, and the end of the reconciliation process, HDK's ground, which is HDP's main foundation, has never shifted. That programme had been debated, of course … There had been a period during the establishment of HDK where we always won. We won in Rojava; we won in Gezi. I have never seen such a period. I don't know, maybe it just happens once in a person's lifetime. There had always been a time when we won and then afterwards, we always lost. In all of this, it was the common agenda that allowed us to continue healthily, our psychology or our policy; thanks to this programme, we kept saying our thoughts the same way we did. Because it is not easy to create a programme, you debate a lot, you argue a lot, people slamming on the table, leaving, and these are all great efforts, but everyone also learns to take a step back when necessary or give some space for another. This is all amazing. So, I said it after the Ankara Massacre too; You will get used to seeing Kurds and Socialists working together; you have to at this point. In fact, those massacres bring people together.

(Individual Interview T8, cited in Kutan and Çelik, 2021: 152)

In an interview in October 2018, a history teacher and activist who joined HDK as an independent member and worked actively in the Education Council noted that:

First of all, it is very precious for this wide spectrum to remain together for seven years without smashing each other's face in and overcoming many crisis moments. Even saying, 'We're together, and we stand by each other; we haven't broken' ... they are so afraid of Kurds, leftists, Alevis and the oppressed classes coming together in Turkey. The secret of the revolution. This state is fighting to prevent this from happening. In my opinion what they massacred in 1915 was the first ever authentic revolutionary movement of this land. I mean this is not Armenian nationalism. Taşnak. Our Armenian comrades were weaving this land's most authentic revolutionary movement. Both Taşnak and Hinçak. These two revolutionary comrades were both members of the International. The dream of teachers here and there in colleges in Elazig, Erzurum is HDK. Since 1915, the state's raison d'être is for these not to come together. HDK has shown them that this togetherness which had not been successful so far, was possible for a while with HDP-HDK. In that sense it is an undeniable success.

(Individual Interview T5, cited in Kutan and Çelik, 2021: 286)

A founding member of HDK and early left-wing leader, explained how the HDK has impacted society:

This experience is very instructive. There is a bridge constructed between philosophy and truth for the first time in Turkey. There is no experience more valuable than this. The pre-eighty experiences are very small and particular compared to this. There is a huge maturity here; there is prudence. You see, we criticise ourselves, but we should not overdo it. Everyone pushed their capacity to the end, their hopes, their ideas, and their maturity, and when people revealed everything, then too much material came out from very little material. Think about it, only six million people in Turkey are supporting us and assuming that all these six million are supporting this radical freedom project would be an exaggeration. Organising that much hope with so few materials, keeping it standing and saying, 'let me stand next to it' is not something that can be taken lightly at all. So, I can say that I see this journey to hope as proof that it can actually happen. We have come this far, and this is not something to be forsaken. Of course, Marx always says, 'Revolutions stop, they stop and look at themselves, and they mock the dwarfness of their situation'. Frankly, when we look back, we see that it can actually be thought of like this. I think we have already seen where the possibility of change in Turkey is. The state knows that we see it, and so it wants to blind our eyes and cut our fingers. However, this information is out.

(Individual Interview T45, cited in Kutan and Çelik, 2021: 303)

The Madhes movement in Nepal had to constantly deal with geopolitical dynamics, internal factionalism and opportunistic power-sharing agreements made by the movement's leaders. There were some tactical mistakes made by the movement when they failed to adapt to sensitive moments resulting in the loss of innocent lives. When police were killed at the Kailali uprising, the state took extreme measures to crack down on mass protests. Instead of halting the usual tactics and condemning the violence, the movement leaders proceeded with mass demonstrations in Rupandehi, where the police opened fire on the weekly market, killing six people. The Madhes movement over a period of time realised that overreliance on Indian patronage caused more harm in the long run. The movement leadership insufficiently appreciated that India's role would shift to suit their own strategic interests, which could be better fulfilled through alignment with the power centre in Kathmandu. In other words, India would utilise instability in Madhes as a negotiating position with Kathmandu but would barely risk its favourable diplomatic relations with the central political leadership in Nepal. As a journalist for a prominent national daily notes: 'I do not think the establishment in Delhi was sympathetic to Madhes at all. They had not imposed the blockade to support the Madhes struggle'. (Journalist 1, Kathmandu, cited in Pherali and NEMAF, 2021: 108). A Madhesi activist in Birgunj also mentioned, 'We [Madhesis] are charged for getting Indian support during the movement. If this could have been the fact [India's intention to split Madhes from Nepal], nobody could stop it' (FGD 1, Birgunj, cited in Pherali and NEMAF, 2021: 108). This statement indicates that Madhesi activists do see India as a decisive factor in Nepal's political movements but are also aware that Indian support for the Madhes movement was no different from the role they had played historically in asserting their role in Nepal's political processes. Another journalist who is based in Madhes and reports regularly on Madhes issues noted:

Delhi felt that the [blockade] could no longer be sustained. Various forces played up in this juncture. Delhi began to negotiate with Kathmandu that demanded the border to be opened and at the same time, some Madhesi leaders were involved in illegal trade and were weak in asserting their positions. This resulted in loss of people's enthusiasm to continue with the protest. When Delhi shifted its position and withdrew their support for the movement, the six-month-long blockade ended without securing its key demands.

(Journalist 2, Birgunj, cited in Pherali and NEMAF, 2021: 108)

A prominent Madhesi leader provides much deeper insights into the role of India in the Madhes movement. He notes:

The reality is that Beijing and New Delhi deal with Kathmandu. I can claim this not just from my knowledge but the experience I have had as a government minister. I have observed the reality from very close. If India had not supported the political movement in 1990, Panchayat system would not have been defeated. Why would India choose to play with the issues of

Madhes? If it did so, it would distance itself from the mainstream political establishment in Nepal. All the leaders here ultimately do business with the Indian establishment. They have nothing to do with the ideology. It is really nonsense to say that India wants to add Madhes in its territory.

(Madhesi Leader 1, cited in Pherali and NEMAF, 2021: 108)

The above perspective is particularly interesting in the sense that Nepali nationalist rhetoric plays on the fear that India supports Madhesi leaders in order for Madhes to secede from Nepal. Ethno-nationalist leaders in Nepal continue to spread this fear in their political campaigns, and ordinary Nepalis in the hills are broadly convinced by this narrative. Meanwhile, another Madhesi youth activist in Kathmandu also agrees that the idea that India is loyal to the Madhesi cause is a misunderstanding. He lamented:

Madhesi people believe that India supports them, and it can be seen during the time of blockade also. Though India has its own hidden interest behind the blockade, the common Madhesis believed that the bigger power India was with them. Because of this belief, they kept hope and stayed motivated in the protest. But I feel India had nothing to do with the Madhesi cause nor has any kinds of sympathy with Madhes. It only uses Madhes as a bargaining chip. Though we have grievances with our own state, we, Madhesis have never seen [merger with] India as an option for us.

(Activist 1, Kathmandu, cited in Pherali and NEMAF, 2021: 109)

Hence, the Madhes movement had to navigate the geopolitical interests of Nepal's powerful neighbours and activists in Madhes began to realise that their struggle did not only need to challenge Nepali state practices, but also needed to resist political manipulation from the outside as well, particularly by India.

Authoritarianism and repression can clearly have contradictory effects on social movements. On the one hand, they can atomise opposition, scare supporters away, and break down trust, but the opposite can also be true. The repression can push people together, build new relationships of trust and solidarity and strengthen bonds of loyalty.

In the Colombia Case Study, several participants pointed out that the repression served to spark processes of unity between different sectors in order to develop joint solutions to counteract violence:

> ... [ex-President] Uribe Vélez, when he arrived to the presidency, said all human rights defenders are guerrillas and so he made everyone a target, and from there that was a message that in that sentence, there are a number of readings that came from the social movement in that moment, his period was just beginning, and people said 'ah ok, is that right, we are all the same? Ah well let's get together because that's how they see us ...' I think that is the first great lesson [from that period], the stigma that is imposed on the different sectors, the different forms of mobilisation and of resistance, where all of us were categorised as being insurgents, and it got the social movement thinking well we had better unite then because they are coming for all of us, it's logical, we have to unite to defend ourselves, let's agree on a minimum common agenda, a process ... and we can continue to maintain our differences.
>
> (Trade unionist and organic intellectual who has been involved in the process since the early phase of the Diploma until present day, interview, 2018, cited in Kane and NOMADESC, 2021: 174)

Yet the success also brought with it attention:

> that period, although it was a fruitful period, it also marked us out and meant we had many people sent to do intelligence on us, it is impossible to know what consequences that had or what information they took, but we know that we had many infiltrators in the movements, and including in our educational processes, and that allowed the state and paramilitaries and intelligence agencies to gather a lot of information ... the state uses all the instruments it can to infiltrate social movements and we were no exception.

(Trade unionist and organic movement intellectual involved during the early years of the pedagogical process, interview, 2018, cited in Kane and NOMADESC, 2021: 172)

As a result, NOMADESC and the UIP, whilst progressing in their political and strategic objectives, have also paid a heavy price for that:

... modesty apart we say that very rarely organisations like ours have undertaken the work of investigating and testing the evidence point by point, to find out exactly what was going on, right? And obviously the result of that is that we carried out a very good investigation, but we also have eight assassination attempts, three bombings, two kidnappings, an attempted kidnapping of my colleague's son, five temporary exiles from the country, etc. etc.

(Trade unionist, lawyer and investigator, founding member of NOMADESC, interview, 2017, cited in Kane and NOMADESC, 2021: 171)

In such a context, social movements are often required to be creative and strategic in their actions:

There were several political and pedagogical legal tools that came together and a very important one was a creative initiative that we set up to protect life called the Forbidden to Forget Campaign ('prohibido olvidar'), which was around the raising awareness about leaders threatened, killed or forced into exile and the historical memory of what was happening, also with very strong components of international solidarity, and that component of international solidarity allowed a certain protective shield to the activity of the most threatened and most vulnerable activists, the campaign had several other components, there was the communication theme which produced materials, there were activities around diplomatic and political action, international delegations with visits by international organisations, but also activists travelled from here to other countries to denounce what was happening, and the campaign brought together workers from Colombia, England, Canada, Spain ...

(NOMADESC founding member and currently a leading member of the organisation, interview, 2018, cited in Kane and NOMADESC, 2021: 173)

The decision to stage the first Diploma course at the site of Cali's Universidad Libre, and for the course to be certified by the university, provided an element of security and the opportunity to securely gather activists from various sectors and parts of the region together:

... that was the way to be able to start to meet again because the armed conflict was so acute, the repression was so heavy that any more than two people gathered was seen as subversive and a meeting of three or four people could be attacked and threatened, even massacres were committed against this type of meetings of people who got together to think about what was happening in terms of the violence and talk about how it related to economics or politics, so the Diploma on the being coordinated with the public and private universities, allowed us some leeway and also allowed us to deepen our work, and be working on developing prevention mechanisms.

(NOMADESC founding member and currently a leading member of the organisation, interview, 2018, cited in Kane and NOMADESC, 2021: 173)

ORGANISATIONAL MODELS FOR NEW TIMES

Each of the distinct organisational models provided crucial learning moments for the movements that they engaged with. In this section, we explore some of the lessons learnt from those models and the effects that these experiments in organising had on the contexts that they were engaged in.

Although only founded in 2011, HDK contributed in a very short period of time to the formation of a new political culture in Turkey. This new political culture transformed Turkey's social struggle to take a more holistic approach with the ideal of a 'new life'. A central component in this success has been the adoption of an organisational model: the Congress, which has fostered a much more inclusive, participatory, responsive mode of politics, capturing the zeitgeist of a country and population tired of hierarchical models from both the state and the left, and hungry for a new more participatory structure.

HDK became the platform of a new bottom-up political movement organised via local councils and based on togetherness in diversity. A platform not only for the strengthening of organised sections of the society with its individual and component quotas but also aimed at strengthening of democratic participation for 'independent' individuals who don't see themselves as part of a particular organisation.

An HDK co-spokesperson explains how HDK became the standard for an optimum organisation:

> Well, when we look from an integral perspective like HDK does, then it becomes a standard. In other words, it becomes a standard for our own political movement. It allows you to see how narrow independent political movements are. I mean their organisational narrowness ... You have this power of standard. It's a fact. HDK can alleviate the obstacles set due to habits or dilemmas in the relations of components and political movements. I mean in terms of what HDK does in practice. HDK is also a structure that works with and benefits from a long-term perspective, organising the revolutionary transformation on a social basis as well as organising the possibilities in daily life.
>
> (Individual Interview T3, cited in Kutan and Çelik, 2021: 288)

An activist who had been active in the revolutionary struggle for more than 50 years and had important responsibilities in the pre-establishment preparations of HDK, explains from the perspective of that long experience how HDK had built a new political culture:

> Personally, my efforts over the past 12 years occupy a special place in my 50 years of experience. If truth to be told, if you look at

the outcome, an opposition that involves Turkey's revolutionary movement, Kurdish opposition and all segments that the Turkish state is not fond of, had gained 13 percent of the votes: this is an historic event. We used to party and celebrate when TIP won three per cent of votes and look what we have achieved now. Now if you ignore this and don't see it as a historic turning point then let me ask you, 'what are you doing in this class struggle?' This is really something very important not to be missed at all.

(Individual Interview T21, cited in Kutan and Çelik, 2021: 288)

A young woman activist tells how HDK became for her an optimum standard:

At the age of 21 I would consider becoming member of BDP but now, that's not enough for me. All the components would fall short of my expectations. At that point that's also valid for the components within HDP or HDK. I've seen an upgraded version therefore I wouldn't go anywhere else and be restricted. I haven't lost my mind yet. Because all of these were beyond imagination. That's why we have to protect this platform whatever the cost is.

(Individual Interview T8, cited in Kutan and Çelik, 2021: 288)

First and foremost, HDK has had a significant impact on the transformation of the political form of Turkey's revolutionary struggle. HDK was the main base of this transition from party form to congress form. Although HDP, which emerged from the Congress, made the political party-oriented traditional approach stronger, the 'Congress' form still has this quality of being the reference among activists, at least at the level of discourse and in the search for an organisational model for the future. From that point of view, it would not be an exaggeration to say that HDK's model has become a benchmark for social organisations in Turkey.

As a bottom-up form of organisation, HDK has led to the transformation of Councils and Commissions into the main benchmark of the organisation, inspiring new political forms, and new togetherness (see June movement). For example, as one of our interviewees stated, the idea of the Council has become the main organisational criterion:

> I think HDK made an important contribution to these lands, brought the idea of the councils back to the agenda and as I said, Gezi Forums and No Councils came about. For example, the idea of a council has now settled. If you are going to organise a people's organisation in this land, it will be named a council. When we say council, people think of an idea that started by people having their own participation and that they had a say in its formation. This idea gained ground. A line emerged from here. This is not something to be underestimated. I am not saying that there is no predecessor to it but the fact that it emerged stronger and that the two struggles are doing this on a common ground, that was the difference and also it emerged strongly. And now, there is nobody in this country who is discussing this. I mean, how do we organise? We will organise with the councils. This is very clear. Nobody thinks otherwise. This is not something to be underestimated, it is a step forward.
>
> (Individual Interview T15, cited in Kutan and Çelik, 2021: 293)

The class and national-based organisational perspective of revolutionary movements in Turkey has evolved into a holistic approach for the first time through the HDK's Congress programme, including peoples, individuals, beliefs, sexual orientations and new social movement vocabulary. The individual and component quota balance, the identities that the traditional left struggle has not always covered, have emerged in the public sphere, displaying their legitimate representations within HDK. The HDK has struggled with this new perspective, where identities are multiple and one is not silenced in favour of the other, yet this has become the prefigurative grammar for the future. By challenging the national narrative, HDK has demonstrated that different identities can form a line of struggle on the basis of equals under one umbrella and demonstrated this also in decision-making and participation mechanisms. It paved the way for the invisible, excluded, marginalised social groups to emerge in the public sphere with their own unique identity, which created a new awareness and knowing. This has been a steep learning curve for members and activists schooled in earlier ways of organising, and used to engaging in narrower modes of political organisation where this diversity is not felt and experienced in the same way.

This is expressed best by some of the activists of the HDK. First, one HDK activist addresses the issue of not setting up hierarchies of priorities, which is one of the highlights of this new understanding of political culture:

> Yes, by gathering on the basis of a congress, an ecologist does whatever s/he wants to do, respecting each other's ideas, and someone who wishes to do something for the proletarian class can implement their projects too. But this is considered as legitimate and acceptable for both sides. I think this is an important achievement.
>
> (Individual Interview T43, cited in Kutan and Çelik, 2021: 288)

Another HDK activist tells us that the left organisations have historically had a very rigid approach and individuals who left their organisations were excluded. But with the space opened by HDK through the 'independent member' individual quota, a new political culture has emerged:

> You know, the Left has a problem; it can be very brutal in itself. The Left is very cruel towards those who leave the movement. It's not just valid for the Left, but let's think that way. Consider it like AKP's attitude towards Fetullah today. Islamists are a little bit like this too. I don't know how this works in the West. I am sure it works the same. This is how it is in the Middle East. When one of them parts away, thinks differently, the conflict can be very harsh. This was our past experiences I mean the experiences of the Left. But there is a historical cross-section for the development of the HDK's ideology. There's no need for that harsh approach. What we are talking about is that we express in terms of moral values, or political values. We also need to be able to say that we can be with

people not like us. What we call by these individuals are the ones who have left Left organisations in the past or those who didn't agree on the problematics of the Left organisation. There are also those who do not leave the struggle, those who say I am part of this process. Those who do not dare to join another organisation are the ones we are talking about. HDK provided such a ground. HDK told them, 'you may not be in such a narrow organisational line, but you can add a lot as an individual'. This is not only about the form, but it is also related to the level of maturity reached by the organisations within HDK. We still have problems, but I think it's a maturity.

(Individual Interview T29, cited in Kutan and Çelik, 2021: 289)

Crucially, the HDK Congress model was able to open up, attract, and give representation to a broad swathe of oppositional political currents, gender and ethnic groups. Its model facilitated a process of knowledge exchange and knowledge-making that allowed these diverse groups to engage, co-construct new ideas, share histories and experiences and build solidarities. Crucially it allowed for the co-construction of a new identity, a 'new life' that embraced this diversity and sought to harness this in the pursuit of radical democratic transformation.

In contrast, NEMAF in Nepal had a very different institutional structure to HDK, a non-governmental organisation that worked as an independent intellectual and advocacy arm of the Madhes movement. Since its establishment in 2007, it has implemented a wide range of programmes to promote social harmony, peace, security and good governance in Madhes. At the core of its work is the goal of social justice through the empowerment of the Madhesi people. NEMAF aims to help secure social, economic and political rights for Madhesis within the Nepali state. NEMAF conceptualises the notion of empowerment as a process of gaining critical knowledge about Madhesi history, language and literature, geography, and social issues; and promotes these through activism at grassroots, national and international levels.

NEMAF primarily operates within two interrelated domains of activity: the first of which relates to activism which primarily supports and strengthens the gains of the Madhes movement and advocates for the protection of these gains – such as reservation for Madhesis in the civil service, legislature and security forces as well as promoting good governance and protection of human rights in Madhes. It publishes opinion pieces in national newspapers and digital media, organises public discussion fora and documents and archives knowledge about Madhes. The second domain is purely under the auspices of an NGO framework which operates with support from external funding to implement development projects in Madhes. It also carries out funded research to support programme implementation, advocacy and policy debate. All these activities are interconnected and mutually reinforcing to the Madhesi cause.

NEMAF's role in the Madhes movement was unique amongst the civil society actors that supported the Madhes cause. What was significant here was the process of building a knowledge system for the movement, reclaiming the intellectual void that provided the logic, evidence and resources for long-term struggle. NEMAF's work went beyond the immediate lobbying and alignment with the mass uprising but was also forward-thinking, agenda-based and sustainable so that new generations of Madhesis could draw on the knowledge to inform their activism. It also reminded activists of the importance of critical reflection rather than a purely emotional attachment to the movement, so that the movement itself was constantly learning from its praxis as well as working to transform social and political structures.

NEMAF assisted the Madhes movement in intellectually articulating and promoting those agendas in the wider political arena, through public intellectual debates and publication of relevant analysis, which would have been rare previously. NEMAF argues that its research and training programmes helped develop an intellectual and theoretical soul to the movement by offering research-based knowledge about the social realities in which the struggle was born. Its series of publications on 'Madhes Manthan' (Madhes Brainstorming) deal with a broad range of issues relating to the Madhes movement (NEMAF, 2020).

Reflecting on the current research during the systematisation process, NEMAF has learnt that the model of the social movement organisation as an NGO, operating under the regulatory framework of the state, struggles to connect with grassroots populations beyond the funding of projects. The NGO structures and programming tend to bureaucratise movement actions and are reliant on the availability of funding (Lewis, 2009). There is a strong realisation that the agenda of social transformation should be situated within the political struggle, rather than NGO-based campaigning. Hence, the movement organisation should carefully gauge the appropriate use of external funding. However, NEMAF's scholarly activities, such as Madhes-focused public seminars, journal publications and the media-based critical analysis of Madhes-related issues have given NEMAF a unique identity as an organisation for Madhes knowledge production, serving as a 'school' for promoting learning for struggle and promoting 'popular education' that challenges unequal political structures (Kane, 2012).

In the Housing Assembly, in Cape Town, South Africa, we have a grassroots organisation that was territorially rooted in the issues that it was dealing with. Emerging out of shack dwellers' struggles against land evictions, the movement expanded territorially through the segregated landscape of poor people's housing in its many forms. Its organisational ethos placed the home as the central focus, as it moved systematically to build the movement, shack to shack, house to house, through door-to-door activism, 'speak-outs' and political schools.

At its heart, it has been a learning movement, educating about rights, crossing housing divides, building commonalities and strategies and mobilising for change. It has reached across ethnic divides through building a common narrative rooted in the working class and linking itself to sections of the labour movement, but with a unique focus on the 'home' as the central focal point. It is from the vantage point of the 'home' that issues of public services and utilities are explored, and where discussions around inequalities of capitalism are addressed. With that in mind, the Housing Assembly has found a central role for women within the organisation and raised important issues around patriarchy, gender, and the division of labour both within and outside the home. It was also one of the first social movements in South Africa to elect a woman as the chair, and therefore leader, of the organisation.

Finally, for NOMADESC and the UIP in Colombia, it can be argued that it is at the forefront, maybe not of producing new organisational models for new times, but of trying to create new subjectivities for new times, as well as trying to create the conditions for new models to emerge by facilitating knowledge cross-pollination – intercultural dialogue which shares skills and knowledges between and across territories and movements. It has created a network of relationships that extend spatially and geographically across southwest Colombia and culturally between movements oriented around class, gender, and ethnicity. Its collective nodes of articulation intersect around popular education that builds a new united social movement through listening to and sharing between these different subjects. NOMADESC, as the organising hub that continually reaches out and supports the movements, shares their struggles amongst the movements and projects them outwards to the national and international stage. In the case study, we can sense the evolution of the movement as it embraces the ideas and wisdom of its collective parts, whilst carrying with it and sharing the important collective memory of the Colombian people's struggles against injustice. Finally, NOMADESC's creation of the Universidad Intercultural de los Pueblos (UIP) was also innovative in proclaiming that social movements could lay claim to the idea and role of the 'university', and that their processes of learning, education and knowledge-making were valid, legitimate and transformative.

CHAPTER CONCLUSIONS

In this chapter, we have seen the myriad effects that social movement learning and knowledge-making within the four case study movements has had on the societies, the activists, and the movements themselves as they have developed. We have seen the way new active subjectivities have been forged out of 'minoritised' and often victimised 'subjects'. We have evidenced the ideational transformation, from the epistemic to the discursive, of each of the movements and the powerful way in which social movements through praxis transform ideas through social action. We also explored the way social movements relate to repression and state persecution and its diverse and often contradictory effects on social movement organising. Finally, we reflected on the social movement institutions themselves and their particular organisational structures, geographies and activities. Across all of these dimensions, we can see the powerful effects that social movement learning and knowledge-making has on subject formation, social transformation, cognitive framing and their development. In the next chapter, we try to draw out some tentative conclusions from the rich findings explored in the previous chapters.

Conclusion

INTRODUCTION

This book aimed to be more than a synthesis of the four case studies, and instead to draw together key insights garnered during the different social movement studies and place them in dialogue. We hope that it has become more than the sum of its parts, and moves forward a broader discussion on learning and knowledge-making in social movements in the contemporary era, and has sparked ideas and new ways of thinking about social movement learning and knowledge-making. In these final reflections and conclusions we want to do two key things. First, to offer some evidence-based reflections on the findings around education and learning in social movements, conceptual and methodological issues, which will be useful for activists and movements alike. We then end the book with some broader and more holistic conclusions that can hopefully serve to stimulate ongoing debate and critique in this area, and move the discussion forward.

TWENTY KEY REFLECTIONS ACROSS EDUCATIONAL, CONCEPTUAL AND METHODOLOGICAL ISSUES

Educational

1. Our case studies point towards dynamic processes of learning and knowledge-making, happening inside social movements as people attempt to make their own history: processes of praxis through which new knowledges emerge. Whilst educational spaces, at their best, are spaces of dialogue where people share their own experiences and reflections, we should not see these as purely experiential. Activists and movements have their

backgrounds, literatures, political positions and histories, and in all of the social movement spaces we can see fusions of new and older ideas, and old ideas that are new to others. These rich processes of intercultural, inter-movement and inter-generational exchange produce new hybrid frameworks for action, firmly rooted in contextualised and conjunctural political challenges. As our research and the case studies evidence, these can be exciting new directions for movements that challenge both the state but also other social movement practices. The HDK has radically challenged the understandings of political action across Turkey and the radical democratic Congress model has become the new gold standard. In Colombia, the NOMADESC/UIP initiatives are having profound influences on concepts of unity and diversity, and movement strategy, and are producing a new conceptual grammar that is emerging across movements. In Nepal, the Madhes movement has revitalised the struggles of indigenous nationalities, Dalits and women for social justice well beyond the liberal directives and the federal constitution that was promulgated in 2015. This has brought tangible benefits not only to marginalised Madhesis but also to other oppressed groups who had been demanding cultural recognition and political representation.

2. Education is often perceived by activists as something that exists only in formal/non-formal contexts, yet the case studies evidence a rich process of education emanating from the range of 'spaces of learning' that social movements offer to members and activists. Activists learn new skills, build self-confidence and develop a greater understanding of the society they live in, its history and its power relations. Central to this process of learning in social movements is its often-experiential nature: activists learn from their peers, and from their elders, but they also learn from actively engaging in protests, meetings, activities and in the tasks involved in organising them. The effects of that learning process do not just improve their activism but often pervade all aspects of their lives, personal relationships, family, work life and opportunities. At the same time, increasingly movements

are recognising and seeking to harness different dimensions of learning and knowledge through their praxis, including emotional and embodied knowledge and learning.

3. In relation to the above, the research has made us reflect much more on what education means – its often-simplistic equation with 'schooling' – and the myriad ways in which people educate themselves through active political engagement. This is particularly important for people from historically marginalised socio-economic and cultural groups, where they have often been excluded from high-quality formal schooling. The process of social movement engagement, the intensive learning, can radically transform people's sense of self, sense of identity and sense of their future. This shows that learning through activism is transformational, as opposed to much formal education in state-centric educational institutions, which is often reproductive and conservative. We see this very clearly from the Housing Assembly case study, whereby activism opened up new horizons and possibilities for activists. But we also see it across the other case study contexts in Colombia, Turkey and Nepal.

4. Whilst learning takes place across social movement spaces, recognising the role and importance of education for members and activists and developing an education strategy has the potential to bring great benefits to movements. Thinking about member development opportunities, and developing non-formal education programming, can support movements in achieving strategic objectives. Consciously developing an education strategy, reflecting on curriculum and pedagogy, and critically evaluating the education process can be of great benefit and allow movements to project themselves forward. The case of the NOMADESC/UIP experience provides evidence of the powerful effect that a strategic approach to education can bring to movements. It also demonstrates that the process is as important as the learning content: the social movement non-formal classroom can be a space of interaction between different social subjects, building empathy and solidarity, sharing experience, trust and inter-group confidence; and leaders and movements

can also learn and develop during the process as they engage with activists, and in doing so build and rethink strategy. Treating education and learning as a holistic process that is intrinsic to political activism then becomes an organisational necessity. It also emphasises the fact that activism itself is a deeply learning-based activity in all its variety. This broad perspective demonstrates the need for an integrated education strategy that can support the movement's objectives.

5. Emanating from all the case studies, we find evidence of rich exchange between older activists and an emergent younger generation. This process of inter-generational learning can transmit teachings from previous struggles and ensure the passing on of historical memory. In HDK, we saw this in action through exchanges between young activists and the engagement of members from the 1968 generation and the 1980 generation (two previous periods of heightened social movement struggle). In the Housing Assembly, we see it in the processes of engagement between ILRIG, which emerged out of the anti-apartheid civic struggles, and the younger generation of housing activists. In NOMADESC/UIP, we see this process of inter-generational transfer occurring between tutors and leaders of the pedagogical process and the young generation of activists sent by the respective social movements, as well as older activists that participate in the process. These processes serve to link past struggles with the present, sharpen insights and help people learn from the past. This can also reinvigorate more senior activists' enthusiasm and commitment. Through building inter-generational connections beyond linking up the historical memory of political activity, the movements are also building cross-generational power that can strengthen their success in the struggles ahead.

6. Bringing a diversity of identity and thought into the social movement classroom – which in our conceptualisation of learning traverses all of the movement's activities – can facilitate rich engagement conducive to new thinking, new language and new ideas. This is evident across the movements under analysis, but to very different degrees. For the HDK, that diver-

sity represents all those constituencies left out of the 'one nation, one religion, one flag' mantra of the Turkish state. This has produced a rich dialogue between the left, the Kurds, women's movement, LGBTQ, Alevis and other faith-based identity and minoritised ethnic groups. It has also produced new framings, understandings, recognition of difference, new solidarities and a new more inclusive language and vocabulary. It also massively increased the mobilising and electoral power of the HDK/HDP. For NOMADESC/UIP, linking trade unions, left-wing activists, black, indigenous, peasant, student and women's movements has similarly transformed the classic aspirations and practices of the revolutionary left traditions that initiated the intervention. Breaking down barriers, building mutual respect, and building commonalities has opened up new possibilities, and strengthened the efficacy, of cross-movement alliances such as the national Colombian 'Congress of the Peoples' (Congreso de los Pueblos), and the 'pacto historico' which won the general election in 2022. For the Housing Assembly, whilst they organised around the unity of the working class, the constituencies they mobilised in operated across ethnic differences and divides. Whilst the organising focus was often articulated in terms of housing types and housing challenges, these issues often reflected the geographical boundaries of racial apartheid housing policy, and hence provided a platform to build common positions, or attempt to. Dialogues across these sectors helped develop a language that was inclusive of local difference, whilst framing the housing challenge within an anti-capitalist and anti-imperialist position. For NEMAF and the Madhesi, the challenge was to build commonality and a new language to encompass the diversity of the Tarai region, which incorporated different caste groups and cross-class identities. Engaging with diverse regional groups, excavating common histories, and constructing a coherent narrative of the 'Madhes' as a people, helped to forge the unity through which mobilisations were developed. For all the movements, building relationships between different 'minoritised' groups has been a way of 'majoritising' their opposition, and in doing so creating new subjectivities that regroup identities together in new and exciting ways.

7. Social movements and their activists often learn most intensely during periods of high-level struggle. From the fightbacks against daily evictions in Cape Town, South Africa; the Buenaventura Civic Strike, Colombia; the Madhes uprisings, Nepal; Gezi Park, Turkey, and the effects of uprisings in Rojava, Syria – big protest events and revolts can often be highly informative, inspirational and educational processes. This is the case not only during the events, but also afterwards as activists reflect on what happened, and try to make sense of successes and weaknesses in their actions. Those 'events' often trigger both personal and institutional transformation. Many social movements, and all of the four case studies here, often tell their movement's respective history through those milestone events. These learnings are then harnessed as part of the social movement's collective memory as they build the future in the present from that past.

8. The generalised desire for more horizontal and participatory movement strategies creates more favourable conditions for deeper and more expansive processes of learning and knowledge-making. Where more and diverse voices can be heard, new insights and learnings can be garnered. Crucially, this is not just an issue of cultural justice and recognition (though this in itself is important), but also that diversity of participation can create a vibrant context for the development of new ideas, which can support movement innovation and transformation. For Gramsci, the construction of hegemony/counter-hegemony was fundamentally an educational process, and building links and alliances between diverse resisting political subjects is central to the construction of that counter-hegemony.

9. Social movement development is centrally concerned with the production of identity, and that is necessarily an educational issue. Across all the movements, we can see the active pedagogical construction of common identities, which underpin allegiances, solidarity and collective power. The nature of this process is diverse across all of the movements, but there is

evidence of some commonalities. One key thing is the nature of the revolutionary subject and its rethinking/re-working/ adapting. Amongst the political left, this has historically been the working class and/or the peasantry, depending on geography and ideological persuasion. What we are seeing across movements is nuances and divergences opening up. In the politically violent context of Colombia, we documented the emergence of the 'victim' as a political subject, which links past experience of state and state-linked crimes to a collective analysis of Colombia's socio-economic history, in a context where state terrorism has been pervasive. We also saw a renewed role and respect for indigenous and Afro-Colombian movements as spearheads of the movement. In Turkey, we see an elevated role for 'women' as a new autonomous revolutionary subject, inspired by the innovative thinking in the Kurdish Liberation Movement. This has both strengthened the participation and role of women in the HDK and its leadership, and united diverse women's groups. We also saw the reawakening of a wide range of minoritised groups, inspired and supported by the example of the Kurds. In the Housing Assembly, we see the production of a working-class identity not rooted in the means of production/ exploitation but linked to the site of reproduction – the home: a working-class subject that is precarious, under- or unemployed and part of the informal sector. Commonality and identity are forged in relation to housing conditions, struggles over public services – and often struggles against the police and the state. For the Madhes movement, and for NEMAF, the struggle for identity has been constructed through the production of a community long marginalised, politically, economically, culturally and socially, from the Pahadi elites and their capital, Kathmandu. The solidification and evolution of these identities is developed through processes of engagement, research and knowledge-making, where challenges are raised, debates occur and modifications or transformations take place. Beyond the revindication of the sovereign subject of the minoritised group, in both the Colombian and Turkish cases, we can also see the tentative emergence of a new more unified post-national political subject that brings together all those minoritised groups to start the process of building an alternative majority. This has resonance with what Mamdani (2020) calls the 'post-national' political subject. Building unity between minoritised groups contains within it the hope of producing a new inclusive majoritised political subject that seeks to include this diversity in its political solutions.

10. State/social movement relationships can alter the conditions under which social movement education takes place. This is evident in both the Colombian and Turkish case studies. The peace negotiations period legitimated the HDK political project, expanded membership and provided the conditions under which public events could take place, diverse and often vulnerable communities could engage in dialogue and new knowledges and understanding develop. The post-coup period led to massive repression against progressive social movements and HDK activities became much more constrained. Open fora were more difficult to create, fear and anxiety reduced participation, and the politics of survival necessarily replaced some of the radical prefigurative work and debates. The openness of the political struggle during the peace process meant that many activists had become visible to the state and thus vulnerable to targeting, demonstrating that open, horizontal and public organising can prove to be a risky undertaking in authoritarian contexts. In Colombia, NOMADESC's popular education work began in the early 2000s in a period of intense repression and violence against social movements. Whilst fear of infiltration and repression are not conducive to engaging in large and open intercultural and inter-movement discussions, this atmosphere did build new bonds of trusts and solidarity between repressed activists and movements, under a broad and critical human rights banner. As the peace process has developed in Colombia, despite its many setbacks, the conditions for open engagement have increased and movement education can currently take place with more confidence. This openness, however, does seem

to be closing down, with increased numbers of activists being killed in recent years.

What is clear from this is that open, intercultural, inter-movement dialogue has the potential to be a fruitful and dynamic mode of engagement and effective in mobilising population groups, but it benefits from an open political environment where new activists and movements can come together and build trust. This of course can be a risky strategy if widespread state repression returns. However, as we saw in the case of Colombia, that same state repression and intimidation was a catalyst to push diverse groups together – under the banner of the defence for human rights – which later led to the formation of new, renewed and long-term solidarities. Clearly, different types of education and dialogue might need to be deployed in more politically restrictive environments and alternative ways need to be sought for inter-movement dialogue and strategy development to take place. This reflection might also be extended to different modes of social movement and political party structure, whereby more decentralised and horizontal structures suit more open political processes, and more tightly controlled structures might be necessary for movement survival during periods of intense repression.

Conceptual

11. There is a strong sense that diversity of identity and demands cannot be located in hierarchies and prioritisations. For both NOMADESC/UIP and HDK we can see a clear shift in left discourse from the unitary primacy of class identity – with other identities existing in the background and with less urgency – to a recognition that gender, race, cultural, and faith injustices need to be heard and redressed in parallel. This is not to diminish the importance of the working class as a political subject, but to recognise that class relations are inter-woven with other identities that themselves have a complex relationship with the evolution of capitalism, patriarchy and imperialism and need to be

taken seriously. Race, gender, sexuality, and faith-based oppression cannot wait until after the revolution to be resolved, and require intersectional solidarity in the present. This can itself then produce new meanings and understandings and cognitive framings and strengthen solidarities between different groups.

This is a marked shift, but it can also be seen as a way of unleashing the agency and power of diverse groups, who finally feel that they can express themselves as they are and as they see themselves. However, the realisation of the need for a plurality of priorities is not without its challenges. As the case of the Madhes shows us, whilst the Maoist revolution in Nepal was the catalyst to the revival of the Madhes movement, Madhesi interests were sacrificed in the peace negotiations that ensued. In Turkey, the HDK was slow to engage fully with the Gezi uprising, due to the priorities of the Kurdish Liberation Movement, which at that time was in a delicate stage in peace negotiations. This led to recriminations and accusations of missing the revolutionary opportunity, and produced deep disquiet, particularly amongst leftist and environmental affiliates. Parity of participation does not necessarily lead to parity in decision-making, and this remains a challenge for all movements to address. Perhaps what we are seeing here is a time lag between 'intellectual awakening' being transformed into 'political awakening', which is a longer process.

12. In contrast to this, there is also a challenge for identity-based movements not to succumb to a 'leaning in' form of politics, whereby they prioritise their own integration into the system, rather than the liberation and transformation of the system as a whole. In the Madhes, we see evidence of how some Madhesi politicians that emerged through, and on the back of the protests, entered parliament and pursued policies and politics based on individual or narrow interests. In post-apartheid South Africa, whilst a transition has occurred, it seems to have privileged the emergence of a black elite, without transforming broader inequalities. In both of those cases, it is the right to be equally unequal, rather than the pursuit of equality, that

prevailed. This is where debates between the revolutionary left and the identity-based movements can be most propitious for working out common platforms and positions that redress all forms of inequalities and processes of misrecognition and build transformational processes.

13. Linked to the broader embrace of diversity, are also notable ruptures and shifts in often long-held commitments towards 'modern' versus 'indigenous' knowledge, industrialisation, and environmental issues. Evidence from several of the case studies note a shift from not seeing indigenous and cultural minorities as fully sovereign, thinking subjects, towards recognising the wisdom and knowledge that these communities often hold, their relationship to the environment and their worldviews. We can find evidence of shifting attitudes towards the Kurds in Turkey, the indigenous and Afro-Colombian communities in Colombia, and the Madhes in Nepal. We can also see growing confidence in endogenous knowledge coming from the Housing Assembly, from movements inside UIP and HDK and from Madhes communities. Central to this reawakening were genuine processes of engagement and interaction between diverse constituencies, where ideas were exchanged, perspectives shared and new understandings constructed – all of which produced this new form of politics.

14. There is also evidence of a shift away from an 'ends justify the means' approach to social movement organising. There seems to be a stronger emphasis instead on a more prefigurative political stance: 'living in the present as we would like to in the future'. This is seen in moves towards more internal democracy and debate inside movements, more reflexivity on issues of diversity within movements, and less certainty as to the final destination, best encapsulated by the phrase 'we make our road by walking'. A less teleological, more deliberative approach. We argue that prefigurative approaches to social movement praxis can be understood as essentially learning-based modes of organising.

15. In tandem with new modes of organising, there is a similar shift in thinking about the state. Whilst a complex debate, there are

two dimensions we wish to emphasise here. Firstly, the objective of movements to take state power has increasingly shifted to different forms of territorial power. For the HDK, and the Kurdish Liberation Movement more generally, there has been a strong shift towards 'Democratic Confederalism', which demands not the taking of state power, but more autonomy and democracy that allows for a bypassing of the state. Rojava, Syria, has been the laboratory for this, but also the Kurdish regions of Turkey prior to the collapse of peace negotiations. In NOMADESC/ UIP in Colombia, 'territorial peace', projects of autonomy, and self-defence – e.g. 'indigenous guards' – are similar attempts to project and defend decentralised modes of community autonomy outside the logics, and often in confrontation with, the nation-state. For the Housing Assembly, there is a complex relationship with the state. For some, the Housing Assembly, rather than making claims of the state, is actually making claims on the market directly – by taking land, challenging private provision of public goods etc. For NEMAF, the objective is increased autonomy for the Madhes, whilst continuing to make representational claims on the nation-state in terms of quotas for Madhes in the civil service, military, etc. For all of the social movements, this inside and outside of the state position is not binary but hybrid, and can change as social movement struggle develops. The clearest example of this has been the brutal crushing of Kurdish autonomy from July 2015 onwards. Second, beyond a shift in the objective of taking state power, a strong critique has been emerging on the desirability of the nation-state as a destination. For many in Turkey, Colombia and Nepal, the relationship between nation and state is the problem. Rather than taking state power and replacing it with a different 'nation', or through separation and independence, there is a stronger push for breaking the link between nation and state. South Africa's shift to the 'rainbow nation' is for some a partial example of this (Mamdani, 2020). However, for the HDK in Turkey, the aspiration is to replace the state with a confederalist system of radical, democratic, self-governed entities.

16. In our initial research planning and thinking, we expected to evidence a lot of learning and knowledge-making content related to international solidarity processes. The reality has been somewhat different, with little evidence of impactful international solidarity processes. Where international solidarity was revealed, it was often more regional. The most important dimensions of solidarity were seen as the intercultural/inter-movement processes. This perhaps reflects increased national and regional confidence and less dependence on international solidarity, and/or also a decline in international solidarity processes in tandem with the decline of the global justice movement of the late 1990s, early 2000s and the decline of Western trade unionism over the last two decades.

Methodological

17. Social movement institutions, by their very nature, are often dynamic and in continual reactive mode. As we have learnt from this study, activists are often incredibly busy, and often have little time, either as individuals or as collectives, to fully reflect on their own movement's evolution, challenges and strategies; and even less to sit down and write about them. The research process, in that sense, was grasped by the respective movements as an opportunity to take stock and to reflect on their internal education processes and strategies, and seen as a useful and valued process. This both secured the respective institutions' engagement and also facilitated rich debate and discussion, with participants valuing the opportunity for open debate and critical reflection. Importantly, the final research products were useful both for the movements and participants and for academic publication and broader distribution. We have also seen examples of the movements learning from each other during the research process, with HDK now developing an education strategy inspired by the Colombian case.

18. The 'systematisation' methodology adopted during this research process was well suited to our overall approach and recogni-

tion that rich knowledge exists inside social movements, and that the task is to bring out that knowledge through research and dialogical spaces that facilitate this. It rests on the premise that those directly engaged in social movements have the best tools to provide an analysis of its evolution, strengths and challenges. However, we underestimated the crucial and specific role that the researchers themselves would play in categorising information, synthesising this, and processing and analysing it for the writing process. Acting as Boaventura de Sousa Santos's 'researcher as translator' is a time-consuming and skilled task, requiring a lot from the researcher, both in terms of intellectual skills, but also in mediation/diplomacy and the softer skills of interpersonal relations. The research and writing process is no less complex and difficult when adopting this posture towards intellectual inquiry. This is not in any way to elevate the role of the researcher in this process, but to recognise that distinct types of labour produce and develop different skill sets.

19. Language access and communication across the four projects has been challenging throughout the research, but efforts in this domain have produced strong results. Exchange trips to the different contexts often required translation into several languages: English/Turkish/Nepali/Spanish. Reports were similarly produced in multiple languages, which required extra financial and human resources. But this effort ensures access to knowledge from diverse contexts and enables dissemination processes accessible to communities. Part of the challenge of overcoming epistemicide is finding ways to overcome the dominance of the English language as the delivery device for the process. We can't claim to have overcome these challenges, but we feel vindicated that a diverse, multicultural, plurilingual research team was an asset to the project and helped to bridge some of those immense barriers.

20. Partnership between social movement institutions and researchers can be complicated. Social movements are often suspicious of researchers' motivations, and cautious about both sharing information and engaging in processes with funders

from 'imperialist' powers. This has been all the more evident in those contexts where violent repression and conflict are ever-present. Trust, respect and solidarity have proved crucial in overcoming some of these challenges, but this remains a process. Relationships with the movements preceded the project, with longstanding ties between different researchers and their respective movement partners. For some researchers, these relationships would be seen as undermining the objectivity of the research and weakening its veracity. We don't buy into these framings, and see our sharing of a strong normative commitment to the movements as a positive dimension, facilitating privileged access to information and open engagement. At no point, across the research, were we asked to censor or modify our work.

FINAL REFLECTIONS

Back in 1989, Alberto Melucci, in his pathbreaking work on social movements, *Nomads of the Present*, argued that social movements were cultural 'laboratories of experience' within which 'new problems and questions are posed. New answers are invented and tested, and reality is perceived and named in different ways' (Melucci, 1989: 207). Our research has drawn inspiration from this insight, and extended this to explore the ways that social movements are themselves 'laboratories of learning'. The central premise of these final reflections is that social movements have the potential, if we listen hard enough, to point the way forward to new modes of analysis, new ways of acting and resisting and new strategic directions to aim for and aspire to. Second, we also hope that we have made a case for the need to fundamentally rethink our understanding of what constitutes education and learning and expand our horizons beyond formal and non-formal education to a more holistic, temporal and relational understanding of the multiple learning spaces that social movements offer. Third, to those social movements, we also make the case that the laboratories' effectiveness can be enhanced by strategic efforts to engage with education processes, recognise the holistic nature of education and learning in movements, target diverse audiences, capture learning and knowledge, and process innovations. Fourth, we make a case for the centrality of education in the production of post-national subjectivities, new identities that emerge out of intercultural, inter-movement collaboration and struggle, that build majoritarian alliances and powerful new social forces. Fifth, we argue that bringing diversity into social movements is not just an ethical issue, but one with the potential for refreshing foundational thinking and building new and powerful cognitive frames. Sixth, we argue that there is no magic bullet for radical social change, but that we can learn a great deal from the contextually rooted praxis of social movements working things out from the ground up. Seventh, the narratives of these social actors are extremely important in building a new 'ecology of knowledges'. Finally, we make the case for academics and researchers to continue to work with social movements as partners in the struggle for peace with social justice, a process that is rich in both ethical and intellectual possibilities.

Let us begin first with some context. This is a difficult and complex time for progressive politics. We live in a period of reaction, where 'zombie' neoliberalism – brain dead and bereft of ideas – is still walking the world (Peck, 2010); where post-9/11 imperialism has once again become more aggressive, interventionist and brutal, both around the world and against its own internal others; where democracy is retreating in the face of rising authoritarianism and weakening its historical links to capitalism (Streeck, 2016); where the planet is in an existential crisis (Klein, 2020); where a New Cold War is emerging that threatens nuclear armageddon; and where previous leftist advances are in retreat, and only small pockets of hope are visible. These crises were exacerbated when a global pandemic hit us in 2019, crushed any hopes of economic upturns and killed millions of people. The virus, despite initially being hailed as class, colour, gender and geography blind, has both directly and indirectly impacted the most vulnerable, exacerbated already huge social and economic inequalities and amplified global debt. Like the last economic crisis of 2008, powerful elites are now attempting to take advantage of the post-pandemic period to push through reforms, and restructure finances, firms and societies in their favour. Now more than ever, we need strong social movements to stem this tide, yet in many parts of the world our movements are struggling rather than thriving. So where do we look for inspiration and guidance?

First, a way forward for Boaventura de Sousa Santos was to listen to the South, as both a site of resistance and of new knowledges, and as a metaphor for all those left out of our current global system. So having listened to these four movements, what are we hearing? In listening, we can bear witness to rich processes of struggle, where social movements are engaging with the crucial issues of the day: the revolutionary subject; class versus identity politics; gender and patriarchy; unity and diversity; prefigurative politics of living inside and outside of capitalism; state theory and state power; solidarity and its challenges – not in some abstract and distant academic way but through analysis, experimentation and adaptation. In doing so they are testing out the limits of the possible in contextually grounded situations and building sophisticated, nuanced analyses of the complexity of social action and social struggle. None of this is easy, nor necessarily successful, but it is rich with theoretical and practical possibilities – a vibrant learning process that is producing a new vocabulary and grammar of social movement resistance.

Second, emerging out of this research is a much stronger recognition of the need to return to definitional struggles over what constitutes education, learning and knowledge in social movements, and its challenges. One insightful challenge, noted by Tarlau (2014: 369) when reflecting on the weakness of the popular education/critical pedagogy literature on the one hand and social movement learning literature on the other, was that 'Critical pedagogues need more organisational thinking and social movement scholars need a more pedagogical focus'. At the heart of this challenge, we believe, is that much critical pedagogy literature focuses on the practices of radical learning and in doing so prioritises the non-formal learning space, rather than fully embracing the broader Freirean idea that the social movement itself – as a totality – is the school, and that the 'struggles and actions, their forms of organisation, their "culture", in the broadest sense, constitute the starting point of popular education and its on-going field of enquiry' (Kane, 2001: 13). Our research has clearly evidenced that whilst we can learn a great deal from exploring the processes of non-formal education – and the NOMADESC/UIP process is a rich example of that – we need to link it together with a broader exploration of the way activists, and the social movements themselves, learn and develop knowledge across the span of their activities – and delve deeper into those diverse 'spaces of learning'. These broader 'spaces of learning' should also be part of the pedagogy discussion, but this requires a broadening out of the concept of pedagogy to link these spaces together. Pedagogy usually refers to sets of practices of upbringing and education, methods and processes of transmission and acquisition that seek to develop knowledges, skills and moral order. Dominant pedagogies are often studied with the aim of understanding how communication systems might produce individual and collective subjectivities, ways of understanding and interpreting the world. Pedagogical modalities are realisations of symbolic control and therefore centrally implicated in cultural production and reproduction. As Bernstein noted: 'Symbolic control through pedagogy seeks to shape and distribute forms of consciousness, identity and desire' (Bernstein and Solomon, 1999: 269).

In this research, we have linked pedagogy to the particular oppositional social forces that are struggling over the production of new subjectivities. This has lead us to the task of inquiring into the different forms of 'socialisation, education and work that promote rebellious or, on the contrary, conformist subjectivities' (Santos, 1999a: 41). What does an alternative pedagogy of producing rebellious subjectivities look like? And what is its social base? Within this understanding of pedagogy related to particular social forces with particular goals and objectives we can begin to explore what a critical pedagogy of our movements might look like, the nature of the social forces that have given it life, and what the particular pedagogical modalities are that are being deployed in the construction of counter-hegemony. Whether declared or undeclared, explicit or implicit, each of our social movements has a 'strategic pedagogy' that transcends the movement's activities. It conditions and frames interactions, and it is these diverse social movement pedagogies that represent sites of learning and contestation.

Third, and in relation to this, our research has evidenced the potential value for social movements of taking a much more conscious strategic pedagogical approach to social movement learning and knowledge-making. A holistic approach that transposes the 'different spaces of learning' and develops a clear strategy to maximise opportunities for learning and knowledge-making, analysis and reflection. This might begin with a serious non-formal programme of education emerging from a solid diagnosis of movement learning needs, but which must open up to recognise the vibrant spaces and debates that can be stimulated to take place across the movement's activities. An approach that identifies the different learning needs of leaders, members, activists, interested and general publics, and builds a coherent strategy. This organic approach can enhance the potential of social movements to build 'hegemony', strengthen 'good sense' and build 'really useful knowledge'.

Fourth, we make the case for the centrality of education in the production of post-national subjectivities. Across our case studies, we have evidenced the struggle over the production of new subjectivities, revolutionary in aspiration, and rooted in the concrete realities and inequalities of the particular contexts analysed. We believe that these address, in different ways, a central contemporary challenge around the world. We live in societies shaped by very particular nation-state relationships, often rooted in colonialism, where dominant ethnic groups shape the nature of entry into citizenship regimes, with many unequally included, and others excluded. These exclusions are rooted in various combinations and degrees of racial, religious, gender, and class hierarchies, and the task of many contemporary social movements is to attempt to construct alliances between different resisting subjects to challenge that hegemony. This touches on a central challenge voiced by Mahmoud Mamdani (2020) in his recent book *Neither Settler nor Native: The Making and*

Unmaking of Permanent Minorities, where he calls for a break in the relationship between nation and state.

This is important for us, because we believe that this research provides some glimpses into that process, which is both prefigurative in aspiration and intention and extremely challenging in practice. Our research with the HDK evidences what it means to project a post-national vision in a highly aggressive and nationalistic state. It goes beyond the slogan of unity in diversity to showing what it really means to bring together divergent oppressed groups. In part, it has been about recognition and respect, but it is also about recognising historical injustices, unequal capacities and the need for space for historically marginalised communities to work out their positions and stances. It also means ensuring that different oppressed groups feel included in decision-making, do not get re-hierarchised and feel a collective stake in the political project. It is also about the construction of a collective vision that is inclusive of difference, but also projects forward bonds of unity and common purpose. For HDK, the post-national political project also requires the production of a post-national political subject that can hold these divergences together. The centrality of gender in this process is crucial as a unifying revolutionary subject, as is the recognition of the sovereignty of minoritised political subjects, long marginalised through state policy.

In Colombia, we can similarly see in the NOMADESC/UIP project the struggle over the production of new inclusive political subjectivities: one of which is the 'victim'. In that process, 'victims' of state crimes and human rights violations are reconceptualised as actors with agency, historical memory, dignity and purpose. The concept of 'victim' cuts across gender and ethnic lines and provides a collective and unifying framing for many Colombians that have suffered from state repression. For NEMAF and the Madhesh, a great deal of work has been done in building a unified Madhes political subject out of a history of maltreatment and humiliation. At this stage in their political struggle, rather than reaching out to other oppressed groups, they are working on building the confidence in their own collective political identity. This appears similar to the South African revolutionary Steve Biko's approach to 'black consciousness' and the need for self-organisation. Moving finally to South Africa, we can see in the Housing Assembly intensive work in building unity amongst Cape Town's precariously housed communities. Central to this has been the construction of the home as a site of organising and resistance, with strong gender dimensions. All of these processes of subject formation are highly educational processes requiring reframing, dialogue, and negotiation, but where successful they can unleash powerful social forces.

Fifth, whilst the struggle for diversity, inclusion and representation in social movements is an ethical position aimed at redressing historical processes of marginalisation, it is so much more than that. The process of bringing diverse groups together starts the process of redressing the epistemicide that has dominated social theory and social movements. Working towards an 'ecology of knowledges' is radically transforming some of the movements, changing both the means and the ends of their struggles. The ideas emerging from historically marginalised communities, like the indigenous, the black movements, women's movements, the Kurds, and the Alevis, are forcing social movements to rethink their relationship to industrialisation, modernity, the environment, the state, patriarchy and producing new 'cosmologies' that have the potential to construct very different futures.

Sixth, we argue that there is no magic bullet for radical social change, but that we can learn a great deal from the contextually rooted praxis of social movements working things out on the ground. Central to this argument is that doing research is not about the pursuit of the discovery of perfect formulas for radical struggle. Rather, it is about understanding that opportunities, decisions, and movement processes are taken in particular times and places, have unintended and intended outcomes and these dynamics change over time. As is clear from the HDK case, the highly successful, open dialogical form of organising during the peace process did not fit well with a period of massive state repression and made activists extremely visible and vulnerable. Rather than recipes, we should perhaps talk of repertoires of action amidst divergent contexts.

Seventh, the stories of these social actors, working in extremely difficult conditions, and often paying a very high price for their activism (emotional, social, political and economic), shine a light on the beauty of the culture, wisdom, knowledge and courage of people that have often been long marginalised, silenced, felt 'unwanted' and 'undesired', simply because of who they are and what they represent. Thus, studies like this are extremely important to make these spaces, these people and their knowledges and histories visible so that we can all be better informed and collectively build a just 'ecology of knowledges'. We have much to learn.

Eighth, we make the case for more collaboration between academics and social movements to break the impasse we find ourselves in. Working with and for social movements is firstly an ethical position. It is centred on the idea of breaking down the distinction between researchers and researched and also putting into practice the idea of 'nothing about us without us', which is a central pushback to an increasingly commercialised research industry. This is a messy and challenging process but can bring rich rewards both in terms of strengthening the effects of research for movements and in sharpening and strengthening research insights and findings.

Working through radical theory and ideas with social movements through praxis has the potential to bridge divides, enrich both social movement action and university campuses and support the development of both better theory and better practice. Our work as 'translators' can help to bridge not only theory and practice, but also diverse movement spaces, sharing experiences, strategies and knowledges. Recognising the rich ecologies of knowledge that exist between social movements and universities, building and strengthening links, provides a productive route forward for both social theory and societal renewal – a form of intellectual commoning that can help build the future in the present. A prefigurative future rooted in dialogue, dignity, joy, reciprocity, equality and solidarity – values that are needed now more than ever.

Finally, we wish to end this book with a brief return to the life and work of Aziz Choudry, a pioneer in researching social movement learning and knowledge-making, a member of our advisory group and a great support throughout this project. Aziz gave the keynote speech at the workshop that gave birth to this research in 2016 and we owe him a huge debt of gratitude. Aziz passed away on 26 May 2021, just a few weeks after he had moved to South Africa to take up a new position at the University of Johannesburg. His enthusiasm and belief in the veracity and power of social movements, their unique capacity to help us not only to understand this world, but also to radically transform it, and his commitment to raising up, amplifying and projecting the voices of the oppressed all around the world – and actively supporting their struggles – was exemplary. This work is dedicated to you Aziz, rest in peace brother.

References

Akkaya, A. H. and Jongerden, J. P. (2012). 'Reassembling the Political: The PKK and the Project of Radical Democracy'. *European Journal of Turkish Studies*, 14. http://journals.openedition.org/ejts/4615

Akkaya, A. H. and Jongerden, J. P. (2013). 'Democratic Confederalism as a Kurdish Spring: The PKK and the Quest for Radical Democracy'. In: Ahmet M. M. A. and Gunter, M. M. (eds), *The Kurdish Spring: Geopolitical Changes and the Kurds* (pp. 163–185). New York: Bibliotheca Iranica, Kurdish Studies Series, No. 12.

Allport, G. W. ([1954] 1988). *The Nature of Prejudice*. Reading, MA: Addison-Wesley.

Az, C., Philip, K., Zwick-Maitreyi, M., Hooper Lewis, P., Bouterse, S. and Sengupta, A. (2020). 'Centering Knowledge from the Margins: Our Embodied Practices of Epistemic Resistance and Revolution', *International Feminist Journal of Politics*, 22(1): 6–25.

Araujo, O. (2015). 'Una decada de encuentros y memoria': Sistematización de la propuesta educativa en derechos humanos para la region del suroccidente' 2001–2011 (unpublished).

bell hooks (1991). 'Marginality as a Site of Resistance'. In: Ferguson, R., Gever, M., Minh-ha, T. and West, C. (eds), *Out There: Marginalization and Contemporary Cultures* (pp. 341–343). New York: MIT Press.

Benjamin, S. (2021). 'Social Movement Learning and Knowledge Production in the Struggle for Peace with Social Justice: The Housing Assembly, South Africa'. ESRC Grant No: ES/R00403X/1. Final Project Report South Africa Case Study. Brighton: University of Sussex. Available at https://knowledge4struggle.org/

Benson, K. and Meyer, F. (2015). 'Reluctantly Loud: Interventions in the History of a Land Occupation', https://chimurengachronic.co.za/reluctantly-loud/

Bernstein, B. and Solomon, J. (1999). 'Pedagogy, Identity and the Construction of a Theory of Symbolic Control: Basil Bernstein Questioned by Joseph Solomon', *British Journal of Sociology of Education*, 20(2), 265–279, doi: 10.1080/01425699995443

Bevington, D., and Dixon, C. (2005). 'Movement-Relevant Theory: Rethinking Social Movement Scholarship and Activism'. *Social Movement Studies*, 4(3): 185–208.

Bhaskar, R. A (2008). *Realist Theory of Science*. Abingdon: Routledge.

Bookchin, M. (1995). *Philosophy of Social Ecology* (2nd edition). Black Rose Books.

Bookchin, M. (1996). *Toward an Ecological Society*. Black Rose Books.

Bookchin, M. (2005). *The Ecology of Freedom: The Emergence and Dissolution of Hierarchy*. AK Press.

Brown, A. M. (2017). *Emergent Strategy: Shaping Change, Changing Worlds*. Lopndon: AK Press.

Buechler, S. M. (2013). *New Social Movements and New Social Movement Theory*. London: The Wiley-Blackwell Encyclopedia of Social and Political Movements.

Burghart, R. (1994). 'The Political Culture of Panchayat Democracy'. In: Hutt, M. (ed.), *Nepal in the Nineties: Versions of the Past and Visions of the Future* (pp. 1–13). Delhi: Delhi Oxford University Press.

Butler, J. (2016). 'Rethinking Vulnerability and Resistance'. In: Butler, J., Gambetti, Z. and Sabsay, L. (eds.), *Vulnerability in Resistance*. Durham: Duke University Press.

Casas-Cortes, M. I., Osterweil, M. and Powell, D. E. (2008). 'Blurring Boundaries: Recognizing Knowledge-Practices in the Study of Social Movements', *Anthropological Quarterly*, 81(1): 17–58.

Cemgil, C. and Hoffmann, C. (2016). 'The "Rojava Revolution" in Syrian Kurdistan: A Model of Development for the Middle East?' *IDS Bulletin*, 47(3): 53–76.

Chesters, G. (2012). 'Social Movements and the Ethics of Knowledge Production', *Social Movement Studies* 11(2): 145–160.

Choudry, A. (2015). *Learning Activism: The Intellectual Life of Contemporary Social Movements*. Toronto: University of Toronto Press.

Choudry, A., and Vally, S. (eds) (2018). *History's Schools: Past Struggles and Present Realities*. Pietermaritzburg: University of KwaZulu-Natal Press.

Cooper, D. (2014). *Everyday Utopias: The Conceptual Life of Promising Spaces*, Durham and London: Duke University Press.

Cox, L. (2015). 'Scholarship and Activism: A Social Movements Perspective', *Studies in Social Justice*, 9(1): 34–53.

Cox, L. (2018). *Why Social Movements Matter: An Introduction*. London: Rowman and Littlefield International.

Cox, L. and Flesher Fominaya, C. M. (eds) (2009). 'Movement Knowledge: What Do We Know, How Do We Create Knowledge and What Do We Do With It?' *Interface: A Journal For and About Social Movements*, 1(1): 1–20. http://interfacejournal.nuim.ie/wordpress/wp-content/uploads/2010/11/interface-issue-1-1-pp1-20-Editorial.pdf

Cox, L. and Nilsen, A. (2014). *We Make Our Own History: Marxism and Social Movements in the Twilight of Neoliberalism*. London: Pluto Press.

Cramer, C. (2005). 'Inequality and Conflict: A Review of an Age-Old Concern'. Identities, Conflict and Cohesion Programme Paper Number 11. Geneva: United Nations Research Institute for Social Development.

de Angelis, M. (2007). *The Beginning of History: Value Struggles and Global Capital*. London: Pluto Press.

Deleuze, G. and Guattari, F. (2012). *A Thousand Plateaus: Capitalism and Schizophrenia*. London: Continuum.

Della Porta, D. and Pavan, E. (2017). 'Repertoires of Knowledge Practices: Social Movements in Times of Crisis', *Qualitative Research in Organizations and Management*, 12(4): 297–314. doi: 10.1108/QROM-01-2017-1483

Dinerstein, A. (2014). *The Politics of Autonomy in Latin America: The Art of Organising Hope*. London: Springer.

Doerr, N. (2018). *Political Translation: How Social Movement Democracies Survive*. Cambridge: Cambridge University Press.

Douglass, F. (1857). Address at Canandaigua, New York, on West India Emancipation. Available at www.blackpast.org/african-american-history/1857-frederick-douglass-if-there-no-struggle-there-no-progress/

Earl, J. (2013). 'Repression and Social Movements', in *The Wiley-Blackwell Encyclopedia of Social and Political Movements*.

Escobar, A. (2004). 'Beyond the Third World: Imperial Globality, Global Coloniality and Anti-Globalisation Social Movements'. *Third World Quarterly*, 25(1): 207–230.

Escobar, A. (2018). *Designs for the Pluriverse: Radical Interdependence, Autonomy, and the Making of Worlds*. Durham, NC: Duke University Press.

Escobar, A. (2020). *Pluriversal Politics: The Real and the Possible*. Durham, NC: Duke University Press.

Eyerman, R. and Jamison, A. (1991). *Social Movements: A Cognitive Approach*. London: Polity Press.

Fals Borda, O. ([1970] 1987). *Ciencia propia y colonialismo intelectual: los nuevos rumbos*. Bogotá: Carlos Valencia Editores.

Fals Borda, O. (1979–1984). *Historia Doble de la Costa* (4 volumes). Bogotá: Carlos Valencia Editores.

Fals Borda, O. (1987). 'The Application of Participatory Action Research in Latin America', *International Sociology*, 2(4): 329–347.

Fals Borda, O. (2013). *Socialismo Raizal Y El Ordenamiento Territorial*. Bogotá: Ediciones Desde Abajo.

Federici, S. (2012). *Revolution at Point Zero: Housework, Reproduction, and Feminist Struggle*. Brooklyn/Oakland: Common Notions/PM Press.

Federici, S. (2020). *Beyond the Periphery of the Skin: Rethinking, Remaking, and Reclaiming the Body in Contemporary Capitalism*. PM Press/Spectre.

Flacks, R. (2004). 'Knowledge for What? Thoughts on the State of Social Movement Studies'. In: Goodwin, J. and Jasper, J. (eds), *Rethinking Social Movements: Structure, Culture, and Emotion* (pp. 135–153). Lanham, MD: Rowman & Littlefield.

Foley, G. (1999). *Learning in Social Action*. London: Zed Books.

Fraser, N. (2022). *Cannibal Capitalism: How Our System Is Devouring Democracy, Care and the Planet – and What We Can Do about It.* London: Verso.

Fraser, N. (2013). *Fortunes of Feminism: From State-Managed Capitalism to Neoliberal Crisis*. New York: Verso.

Freire, P. (2000). *Pedagogy of the Oppressed*. New York: Continuum.

Galtung, J. (1976). 'Three Approaches to Peace: Peacekeeping, Peacemaking and Peacebuilding'. In: J. Galtung (ed.) *Peace, War and Defence: Essays in Peace Research* (Vol. 2) (pp. 282–304). Copenhagen: Ejlers.

Giugni, M., Tilly, C. and McAdam, D. (eds) (1999). *How Social Movements Matter*. Minneapolis: University of Minnesota Press.

Goodhand, J. (2006). 'Working "In" and "on" War'. In: Yanacopulos, H. and Hanlon, J. (eds), *Civil War, Civil Peace*. Open University in association with James Currey. Oxford: Ohio University Press.

Gramsci, A. (1971). *Selections from the Prison Notebooks*. Hoare, Q. and Nowell Smith, G. (eds). New York: International Publishers.

Gramsci, A. (1977). Hoare, Q. and Matthews, J. (eds) *Antonio Gramsci, Selections from Political Writings (1910–1920)*. New York: International Publishers.

Gramsci, A. (1986). *Selections from Prison Notebooks*. London: Lawrence & Wishart.

Güneş, C. (2015). 'Radikal demokrasiyle gelen yeni yaşam: Biz'ler HDP'. *Birikim*, 313: 24–28.

Güneş, C. (2017). 'Altmışlı Yıllarda Kürt Siyasal Aktizmi'. In: Kaynar, M. K. (ed.), *Türkiye'nin 1960'li Yillari* (pp. 701–725). Istanbul: Iletisim Yayinlari.

Gupta, N. (2017). 'Gender Inequality in the Work Environment: A Study of Private Research Organisations in India', *Equality, Diversity and Inclusion*, 36(3): 255–276.

Hall, B. (2004). 'Towards transformative environmental adult education: Lessons from global social movement contexts'. In: Lover, D. (ed.), *Global Perspectives in Environmental Adult Education* (pp. 169–192). New York: Peter Lang.

Halvorsen, S. (2019). 'Decolonising Territory: Dialogues With Latin American Knowledges and Grassroots Strategies', *Progress in Human Geography*, 43(5): 790–814. doi: 10.1177/0309132518777623

Hammond, J. L. (2014). 'Mística, Meaning and Popular Education in the Brazilian Landless Workers Movement', *Interface: a Journal for and About Social Movements,* 6(1): 372–391.

HDK (2012). *Foundation Bulletin.* Kongre: Nisan.

Hye-Su, K. and Tarlau, R. (2020). 'The Confluence of Popular Education and Social Movement Studies Into Social Movement Learning: A Systematic Literature Review', *International Journal of Lifelong Education,* 39(5–6): 591–604, doi: 10.1080/02601370.2020.1845833

Jara, O. (1989). *Aprender desde la practica : Reflexiones y Experiencias de la Educacion Popular en Centroamerica.* San José, Costa Rica: Alforja.

Jara, O. (2006). 'Theoretical and Practical Orientations for Systematisation of Experiences', Electronic Library about Experiences Systematisation. http://educacionglobalresearch.net/wp-content/uploads/02B-Jara-Ingl%C3%A9s2.pdf

Jara, O. (2010). *Trayectos y búsquedas de la sistematizción de experiencias en América Latina: 1959–2010.* San José, Costa Rica: Centro de Estudios y Publicaciones Alforja.

Jara, O. (2018). *La sistematización de experiencias:práctica y teoría para otros mundos posibles.* Bogotá: Centro Internacional de Educación y Desarrollo Humano – CINDE, 2018, p. 258. Primera edición, Colombia. Available at https://repository.cinde.org.co/bitstream/handle/20.500.11907/2121/Libro%20sistematizacio%CC%81n%20Cinde-Web.pdf?sequence=1&isAllowed=y

Jarvis, P. (2001). *Universities and Corporate Universities: The Higher Learning Industry in Global Society.* London: Kogan Page.

Jasper, J. (2015). 'Activism and Scholarship'. Paper to Politics and Protest Workshop, CUNY Graduate Center.

Johnson, R. (1979). 'Really Useful Knowledge: Radical Education And Working Class Culture, 1790–1848'. In: Clarke, J., Critcher, C. and Johnson, R. (eds), *Working Class Culture – Studies In History and Theory* (pp. 75–102). London: Hutchinson.

Kane, L. (2001). *Popular Education and Social Change in Latin America.* London: Latin American Bureau.

Kane, L. (2012). 'Forty Years of Popular Education in Latin America'. In: Hall, B. L. et al. (eds), *Learning and Education for a Better World: The Role of Social Movements.* London: Springer Science & Business Media.

Kane, P. and Celeita, B. (2018). 'No tenemos armas pero tenemos dignidad: Learning from the Civic Strike in Colombia'. In: Harley, A. and Scandrett, E. (eds.), *Environmental Justice, Popular Struggle and Community Development.* Bristol: Policy Press.

Kane, P. and NOMADESC (2021). 'Social Movement Learning and Knowledge Production in the Struggle for Peace with Social Justice:

NOMADESC & the Universidad Intercultural de los Pueblos, Colombia'.
ESRC Grant No: ES/R00403X/1. Colombia Case Study. Brighton:
University of Sussex. Available at https://knowledge4struggle.org/

Katz, C. (2001). 'Vagabond Capitalism and the Necessity of Social Reproduction', *Antipode*, 33(4): 709–728.

Kışanak, G. (2018). *Kürt Siyasetinin Mor Rengi*. Ankara: Dipnot.

Klein, N. (2020). *On Fire: The Burning Case for a Green New Deal*. London:
Penguin.

Kriesi, H., Della Porta, D., and Rucht, D. (eds) (2016). *Social Movements in
a Globalising World*. London: Springer.

Kutan, B. and Çelik, A. (2021). 'Social Movement Learning and Knowledge
Production in the Struggle for Peace with Social Justice: The Peoples
Democratic Congress (HDK), Turkey'. ESRC Grant No: ES/R00403X/1.
Turkey Case Study. Brighton: University of Sussex. Available at https://
knowledge4struggle.org/

Lal, C. K. (2012). *To be Nepalese ...* Kathmandu: Martin Chautari.

Levenson, Z. (2017). 'Social Movements Beyond Incorporation: The Case
of the Housing Assembly in Post-Apartheid Cape Town'. In: Paret, M.,
Runciman, C. and Sinwell, L. (eds), *Southern Resistance in Critical Perspective: The Politics of Protest in South Africa's Contentious Democracy*.
London: Routledge.

Lewis, D. (2009). 'Disciplines Activists, Unruly Brokers? Exploring the
Boundaries Between Non-Governmental Organisations (NGOs),
Donors, and the State in Bangladesh'. In: Gellner, D. (ed.), *Varieties of
Activist Experience: Civil society in South Asia*. New Delhi: Sage.

Mamdani, M. (2020). *Neither Settler nor Native*. Cambridge, MA: Harvard
University Press.

McAdam, D. (1982). *Political Process and the Development of Black
Insurgency 1930–1970*. Chicago: University of Chicago Press.

McLeod, J. (2017). 'Marking Time, Making Methods: Temporality and
Untimely Dilemmas in The Sociology of Youth and Educational
Change'. *British Journal of Sociology of Education*, 38(1): 13–25. doi:
10.1080/01425692.2016.1254541

McNally, D. (2013). 'Unity of the Diverse: Working-Class Formations and
Popular Uprisings From Cochabamba to Cairo'. In: Barker, C., Cox. L. et
al. (eds), *Marxism and Social Movements*. Leiden: Brill.

Melucci, A. (1980). 'The New Social Movements: A Theoretical Approach',
Social Science Information, 19(2): 199–226.

Melucci, A. (1989). *Nomads of the Present: Social Movements and Individual
Needs in Contemporary Society*. New York: Vintage.

Negri, A., and Hardt, M. (2019). *Meclis (Assembly)* (Pilgir, A. E., Trans.).
Istanbul: Ayrıntı Yayınları.

NEMAF (2020). *Madhes Manthan*. Kathmandu: Nepal Madhes Foundation, Accessed on 29 July 2020 at: http://nemaf.org.np/madhesh-manthan/

Notes from Nowhere (2003). *We Are Everywhere: The Irresistible Rise of Global Anti-Capitalism*. London: Verso.

Novelli, M. (2002). 'Keeping Services Public: SINTRAEMCALI's Campaign in Colombia to Stop Privatisation, December 2001–January 2002'. Ferney-Voltaire: Public Services International.

Novelli, M. (2004). 'Globalisations, Social Movement Unionism and New Internationalisms: The role of Strategic Learning in the Transformation of the Municipal Workers Union of EMCALI', *Globalisation, Societies and Education*, 2(2): 147–160.

Novelli, M. (2006). 'Imagining Research as Solidarity and Grassroots Globalisation: A Response to Appadurai', *Globalisation, Societies and Education*, 4(2): 275–286.

Novelli, M. (2010). 'Learning to Win: Exploring Knowledge and Strategy Development in Anti-Privatisation Struggles in Colombia'. In: Choudry, A. and Kapoor, D. (eds), *Learning from the Ground Up: Global Perspectives on Social Movements and Knowledge-Making* (pp. 121–138). London: Palgrave MacMillan.

Novelli, M., and Ferus-Comelo, A. (2012). *Globalization, Knowledge and Labour*. London: Routledge.

Novelli, M. & Ferus-Comelo, A. (eds) (2010) Globalisation, Knowledge & Labour, London: Routledge.

Öcalan, A. (1999). *Declaration on the Democratic Solution of the Kurdish Question*. London: Mesopotamian Publishers.

Öcalan, A. (2011). *Democratic Confederalism*. Cologne: International Initiative.

Öcalan, A. (2013). *Liberating Life: Woman's Revolution*. Cologne: International Initiative Edition & Mesopotamian Publishers.

Öcalan, A. (2014). *War and Peace in Kurdistan*. London: Transmedia Publishing.

Öcalan A. (2017). *War and Peace in Kurdistan: Perspectives for a Political Solution of the Kurdish Question*. Available at http://www.ocalan-books.com/#/book/war-and-peace-in-kurdistan

Onta, P. (1996). 'Ambivalence Denied: The Making of Rastriya Ithihas in Panchayat Era Textbooks'. *Contributions to Nepalese Studies*, 23(1): 231–254.

Paris, R. (2004). *At War's End: Building Peace After Civil Conflict*. Cambridge: Cambridge University Press.

Peck J. (2010). 'Zombie Neoliberalism and the Ambidextrous State'. *Theoretical Criminology*, 14(1): 104–110.

Pherali, T. and NEMAF (2021). 'Social Movement Learning and Knowledge Production in the Struggle for Peace with Social Justice: NEMAF and the Madesh Movement, Nepal'. ESRC Grant No: ES/R00403X/1. Nepal Case Study. Brighton: University of Sussex. Available at https://knowledge4struggle.org/

Pherali, T., Smith, A. and Vaux, T. (2011). *A Political Economy Analysis of Education in Nepal*. EU: Kathmandu.

Piketty, T. (2014). *Capital in the Twenty-First Century*. Cambridge, MA: The Belknap Press of Harvard University Press.

Pillay, S., Russell, S. and Sendin, J. (2017). *I Used to Live There: A Call for Transitional Housing for Evictees in Cape Town*. Cape Town: Ndifuna Ukwazi.

Pizzolato, N. and Holst, J. D. (2017). 'Gramsci, Politics and Pedagogy: An Interpretative Framework'. In: Pizzolato, N. and Holst, J. D. (eds), *Gramsci: A Pedagogy to Change the World*. Dordrecht: Springer.

Prashad, V. (2017). *Red Star Over the Third World*. London: Pluto Press.

Pugh, M., Cooper, N. and Turner, M. (eds) (2016). *Whose peace? Critical Perspectives on the Political Economy of Peacebuilding*. London: Springer.

Ranson, S. (1994). *Towards the Learning Society*. London: Cassell.

Rappaport, J. (2020). *Cowards Don't Make History: Orlando Fals Borda and the Origins of Participatory Action Research*. New York: Duke University Press.

Rasit, H. and Kolokotronis, A. (2020). 'Decentralist Vanguards: Women's Autonomous Power and Left Convergence In Rojava', *Globalizations*, 17(5): 869–883, doi: 10.1080/14747731.2020.1722498

Richmond, O. P. (2016). *Peace Formation and Political Order in Conflict Affected Societies*. Oxford: Oxford University Press.

Richmond, O. P. and Mitchell, A. (2011). *Hybrid Forms of Peace: From Everyday Agency to Post-Liberalism*. London: Palgrave Macmillan.

Rogers, P. (2016). *Irregular War: ISIS and the New Threat from the Margins*. London: I.B. Tauris.

Routledge, P. (2017). *Space Invaders: Radical Geographies of Protest*. London: Pluto Press.

Santos, B. (1995). *Toward a New Common Sense: Law, Science and Politics in the Paradigmatic Transition*. London: Routledge.

Santos, B. (2001). 'Nuestra America: Reinventing a Subaltern Paradigm of Recognition and Redistribution', *Theory, Culture & Society*, 18 (2–3): 185–217.

Santos, B. (2006). *Another Production is Possible: Beyond the Capitalist Canon*. London: Verso.

Santos, B. (ed.) (2007). *Another Knowledge is Possible: Beyond Northern Epistemologies*. London: Verso.

Santos, B. (2014). *Epistemologies of the South: Justice against Epistemicide*. Boulder: Paradigm Publishers.

Santos, B. and Meneses, M. P. (eds) (2019). *Knowledges Born in the Struggle: Constructing the Epistemologies of the Global South*. London: Routledge.

SC, IDS and UNESCO (2016). *World Social Science Report 2016, Challenging Inequalities: Pathways to a Just World*. Paris: UNESCO Publishing.

Scahill, J. (2013). *Dirty Wars: The World is a Battlefield*. New York: Nation Books.

Scandrett, E. (2012). 'Social Learning in Environmental Justice Struggles: Political Ecology of Knowledge'. In: Hall, B. L. et al. (eds), *Learning and Education for a Better World: The Role of Social Movements*, vol 10. London: Springer Science & Business Media.

Shah, S. (1993). Theories of a Fledgling Nation, *Himal*, 6(2): 7–10.

Shukaitis, S. and Graeber, B. (2007). *Constituent Imagination: Militant Investigations // Collective Theorization*. Edinburgh: AK Press.

Sobe, N. W. (2018). 'Problematizing Comparison in a Post-Exploration Age: Big Data, Educational Knowledge, and the Art of Criss-Crossing', *Comparative Education Review*, 62(3) [Open Access].

Sriprakash, A., Tikly, L. and Walker, S. (2020). 'The Erasures of Racism in Education and International Development: Re-Reading The "Global Learning Crisis"', *Compare: A Journal of Comparative and International Education*, 50(5): 676–692, doi: 10.1080/03057925.2018.1559040

Stanchev, P. (2016). 'The Kurds, Bookchin and the Need to Reinvent Revolution', *New Politics*, 4(5): 77–82.

Streeck, W. (2016). *How Will Capitalism End?: Essays On a Failing System*. London, Verso.

Stewart, F. (2010). 'Horizontal Inequalities as a Cause of Conflict: A review of CRISE findings'. World Development Report 2011 Background Paper. Washington, DC: World Bank.

Stewart, F., Brown, G. and Mancini, L. (2005). 'Why Horizontal Inequalities Matter: Some Implications for Measurement'. CRISE Working Paper No. 19. Oxford: CRISE.

Streeck, W. (2014). *Buying Time: The Delayed Crisis of Democratic Capitalism*. London: Verso.

Tarlau, R. (2014). 'From a Language to a Theory of Resistance: Critical Pedagogy, the Limits of "Framing", and Social Change'. *Educational Theory* 64(4): 369–392.

Tarlau, R. (2019). *Occupying Schools, Occupying Land: How the Landless Workers Movement Transformed Brazilian Education*. Oxford: Oxford University Press.

Tarrow, S. (1999). *Power in Movement: Social Movements and Contentious Politics* (2nd edition). Cambridge: Cambridge University Press.

Taylor, V. (2013). 'Social Movement Participation in the Global Society: Identity, Networks and Emotions'. In: Van Stekelenburg, J., Roggeband, C. M. and Klandermans, B. (eds), *The Changing Dynamics of Contention*. Minneapolis: University of Minnesota Press.

Taylor, V. and Whittier, N. (1992). 'Collective Identity in Social Movement Communities: Lesbian Feminist Mobilization'. In: Morris, A. D. and Mueller, C. M. (eds), *Frontiers in Social Movement Theory* (pp. 104–129). New Haven, CT: Yale University Press.

Tilly, C. (1985). *Social Movements, Old and New*. Center for Studies of Social Change, New School for Social Research.

Torres Carrillo, A. (2010). 'Generating Knowledge in Popular Education: From Participatory Research to the Systematisation of Experiences', *International Journal of Action Research*, 6(2–3): 196–222.

Torres Carrillo, A. (1999). 'La sistematización de experiencias educativas: Reflexiones sobre una práctica reciente', *Pedagogía y saberes*, no. 13. Bogotá: Universidad Pedagógica Nacional.

Touraine, A. (1981). *The Voice and the Eye: An Analysis of Social Movements*. Cambridge: Cambridge University Press.

World Bank. (2007). *Building Knowledge Economies: Advanced Strategies for Development*. WBI Development Studies. Washington, DC: World Bank. https://openknowledge.worldbank.org/handle/10986/6853

Yates, L. (2015). 'Rethinking Prefiguration: Alternatives, Micropolitics and Goals in Social Movements', *Social Movement Studies*, 14(1): 1–21.

Zibechi, R. (2007). 'Autonomías y emancipaciones: América Latina en movimiento', Programa Democracia y Transformacion Global, Lima.

Index

The Pluto Press Newsletter

Hello friend of Pluto!

Want to stay on top of the best radical books
we publish?

Then sign up to be the first to hear about our
new books, as well as special events,
podcasts and videos.

You'll also get 50% off your first order with us
when you sign up.

Come and join us!

Go to bit.ly/PlutoNewsletter

Thanks to our Patreon subscriber:

Ciaran Kane

Who has shown generosity and
comradeship in support of our publishing.

Check out the other perks you get by subscribing
to our Patreon – visit patreon.com/plutopress.

Subscriptions start from £3 a month.